Deliberate Discretion?

The laws that legislatures adopt provide a crucial opportunity for elected politicians to define public policy. But the ways politicians use laws to shape policy vary considerably across polities. In some cases, legislatures adopt detailed and specific laws in an effort to micromanage policymaking processes. In others, they adopt general and vague laws that leave the executive and bureaucrats substantial discretion to fill in the policy details. What explains these differences across political systems, and how do they matter?

The authors address these issues by developing and testing a comparative theory of how laws shape bureaucratic autonomy. Drawing on a range of evidence from advanced parliamentary democracies and the U.S. states, they argue that particular institutional forms – such as the nature of electoral laws, the structure of the legal system, and the professionalism of the legislature – have a systematic and predictable effect on how politicians use laws to shape the policymaking process.

John D. Huber is Associate Professor of Political Science at Columbia University. He has published numerous articles on the comparative study of political institutions and is author of *Rationalizing Parliament: Legislative Institutions and Party Politics in France* (Cambridge University Press).

Charles R. Shipan is Associate Professor of Political Science at the University of Iowa. He has published numerous articles on political institutions and public policy and is the author of *Designing Judicial Review: Interest Groups, Congress, and Communications Policy*. Professors Huber and Shipan were both Robert Wood Johnson Scholars in Health Policy at the University of Michigan.

Cambridge Studies in Comparative Politics

Other Books in the Series

Stefano Bartolini, *The Political Mobilization of the European Left, 1860–1980: The Class Cleavage*
Mark Beissinger, *Nationalist Mobilization and the Collapse of the Soviet State*
Nancy Bermeo, ed., *Unemployment in the New Europe*
Carles Boix, *Political Parties, Growth and Equality: Conservative and Social Democratic Economic Strategies in the World Economy*
Catherine Boone, *Merchant Capital and the Roots of State Power in Senegal, 1930–1985*
Michael Bratton and Nicolas van de Walle, *Democratic Experiments in Africa: Regime Transitions in Comparative Perspective*
Valerie Bunce, *Leaving Socialism and Leaving the State: The End of Yugoslavia, the Soviet Union and Czechoslovakia*
Ruth Berins Collier, *Paths Toward Democracy: The Working Class and Elites in Western Europe and South America*
Donatella della Porta, *Social Movements, Political Violence, and the State*

List continues on page following the Index.

Deliberate Discretion?

THE INSTITUTIONAL FOUNDATIONS OF BUREAUCRATIC AUTONOMY

JOHN D. HUBER
Columbia University

CHARLES R. SHIPAN
University of Iowa

PUBLISHED BY THE PRESS SYNDICATE OF THE UNIVERSITY OF CAMBRIDGE
The Pitt Building, Trumpington Street, Cambridge, United Kingdom

CAMBRIDGE UNIVERSITY PRESS
The Edinburgh Building, Cambridge CB2 2RU, UK
40 West 20th Street, New York, NY 10011-4211, USA
477 Williamstown Road, Port Melbourne, VIC 3207, Australia
Ruiz de Alarcón 13, 28014 Madrid, Spain
Dock House, The Waterfront, Cape Town 8001, South Africa

http://www.cambridge.org

First published 2002

Printed in the United States of America

Typeface Janson Text 10/13 pt. *System* QuarkXPress [BTS]

A catalog record for this book is available from the British Library.

Library of Congress Cataloging in Publication Data

Huber, John D.

Deliberate discretion?: The Institutional foundations of bureaucratic autonomy
John D. Huber, Charles R. Shipan.

p. cm. – (Cambridge studies in comparative politics)

Includes bibliographical references and index.

ISBN 0-521-81744-7 (hardback) – ISBN 0-521-52070-3 (pbk.)

1. Separation of powers. 2. Political planning. 3. Bureaucracy. 4. Law and politics. 5. Comparative government. I. Shipan, Charles R., 1961– II. Title. III. Series.

JF229 .H833 2002
320′.6 – dc21

2002016560

ISBN 0 521 81744 7 hardback
ISBN 0 521 52070 3 paperback

For our mothers, Maryann Stewart and Betty Shipan

Contents

Tables

Figures

Preface

In his 1775 *Speech on the Conciliation of America*, British statesman Edmund Burke spoke of Britain's "wise and salutary neglect" of the American colonies. This neglect, he argued – this independence from "the constraint of watchful and suspicious government" – translated into a great deal of freedom from outside interference and allowed the colonies to flourish by adapting their laws to their own needs and priorities. While this development was cast in a positive light by Burke, the negative repercussions for Britain soon became clear, as the wise and salutary neglect led to successful revolt by the colonists. Instead of wisely serving British interests, neglect redounded to their detriment.

This book considers the potential for wise and salutary neglect, but in an entirely different domain. Rather than examining the relationship between nations and their colonies, we explore the relationship between legislatures and their bureaucracies in modern democratic systems. Just as Britain's neglect allowed the colonies to develop their own set of laws, legislatures can allow bureaucrats considerable discretion to draw on their experience and expertise to shape policy outcomes. At the same time, however, allowing bureaucrats considerable autonomy can come back to haunt legislators, much as neglect of the American colonies came back to haunt the British. The problem is that bureaucrats can take actions that run counter to the interests of the legislature.

Our goal is to understand the role of laws in shaping bureaucratic autonomy. At times, legislatures adopt extremely detailed laws in an effort to micromanage the policymaking processes. At other times, legislatures write astonishingly vague and general laws that cede substantial policymaking authority to the executive and to bureaucrats. We want to understand the choice between these two possibilities, and the circumstances under which the vague laws can be understood as wise and salutary neglect.

Our argument emphasizes the importance of political and institutional contexts. Politicians in different political systems, when faced with the same basic policy issue, often take different pathways with respect to the design of laws, with some writing much more detailed legislation than others. How do features of the political system itself affect this choice? To address this question, we develop a theoretical model of the design of legislative statutes. We also draw on a range of empirical approaches to understand the nature of laws across a large number of advanced parliamentary democracies and across the presidential systems found in the U.S. states. The empirical approaches include interviews with policymakers, case studies, quantitative and qualitative analyses of legislative statutes, and large-*n* empirical tests of our argument.

In researching and writing this book, we have benefited considerably from the advice and support of others. The end result is much better than we ever could have achieved on our own. Two organizations deserve special thanks. A grant from the National Science Foundation allowed us to hire a number of research assistants who were indispensable colleagues on this project. We are very grateful to Todd Austin, Andrew Bargen, Kevin Chlarson, Maureen Connolly, Dan Fletcher, Cecilia Martinez-Gallardo, Madelaine Pfahler, and Kasia Stanclik. The Robert Wood Johnson Foundation also provided financial support and, in many ways, was responsible for sparking our interest in this topic. Both of us were scholars in the Foundation's Scholars in Health Policy program at the University of Michigan, where we first got to know each other, became interested in and informed about health policy issues, and decided to work on this project. At Michigan, we especially would like to thank the director of the program, Catherine McLaughlin, as well as Rick Hall, Matt Gabel, and John Moran, for providing helpful feedback and encouragement.

Over the course of working on this project, we were able to present pieces of our work at various seminars and conferences, and we would like to thank the participants in these venues for their constructive reactions, which were invaluable in shaping the final version of the book. Two such interactions deserve special mention. First, Margaret Levi invited us to present the entire manuscript at the University of Washington, where we benefited from the clear and insightful comments of a number of terrific faculty members who took the time to give an earlier version of the manuscript a close, critical reading. Second, Jim Alt organized a mini-conference on our manuscript at Harvard's Center for Basic Research in the Social Sciences. In doing so, Jim assembled an author's "dream team" of the best young scholars from across the country who work in areas relevant to our research. They gave the manuscript an exceptionally thorough reading and allowed us to benefit from their thoughtful comments and suggestions. Together, the invaluable feedback from the Washington and Harvard experiences enabled us to write the very best book that we are capable of writing, and we would like to express our deep thanks to all the participants.

We are also grateful to Dan Carpenter, Miriam Golden, Lucy Goodhart, Simon Hix, Kevin Quinn, Mike Thies, and Craig Volden, who gave us detailed written comments on all or significant parts of the research. In addition, thanks go to Chris Achen, Tim Amato, Dave Clark, Mike Lewis-Beck, and Greg Wawro for sharing their methodological expertise with us. And we would like to thank Clive Thomas, Morris Fiorina, Paul Warwick, and Tom Woxland (at the International Labour Organization) for providing us with useful data.

At the University of Iowa, we would like to thank Denise Powers, Jerry Loewenberg, and Pev Squire for their help. Shipan would also like to acknowledge the research support provided by the Obermann Center for Advanced Studies at the University of Iowa, along with the university's Faculty Scholar program. At Columbia, we would like to thank the Institute for Social and Economic Research and Policy.

Finally, we would like to thank our families. Our children – Ben and Jane Huber and Jeffrey and Rebecca Shipan – have grown from babies and toddlers into school-age kids during the time we have worked together. Between their schoolwork, athletic activities, play dates, more athletic activities, and music lessons, they have helped us to maintain a healthy balance between work and family, and in that way have made a major contribution to this project. Our wives – Lucy Drotning and Kathy Malville-Shipan – provide each of us with a wonderful mixture of love, distraction from our work, and occasional encouragement to get back to it. Finally, we thank our mothers, Maryann Stewart and Betty Shipan, for their lifelong support.

1

Laws, Bureaucratic Autonomy, and the Comparative Study of Delegation

Representative democracy is often defended on the grounds that regular elections are the best way to align the incentives of policymakers with the desires of citizens. The normative argument is well rehearsed. Politicians make policy commitments, and electoral winners are given the chance to make good on these commitments through the laws they adopt. The laws, in turn, affect outcomes, and voters can react to these outcomes in the choices they make at election time. If policymakers fail to deliver on their promises, voters can use the ballot box to depose them. This power of voters over the policymakers, the story goes, keeps policymakers doing what the citizens want, which is a good thing.

Legislative statutes that politicians adopt provide the most important and definitive mechanism for determining policy on most issues. These laws define – or at least could in principle – the types of actions or behavior that may, must, or must not occur by particular groups or individuals in government and society. The language of these statutes therefore plays a fundamental role in the policymaking process.

The role of statutes in democratic processes, however, is somewhat amorphous. Ordinary citizens and attentive groups have only an indirect interest in the policies that statutes describe. Citizens, for example, rarely pay attention to policy details, and few citizens have ever read even a small part of an actual law. Instead, citizens care about the outcomes of policies. They do not care, for instance, about the precise language of a statute that establishes a national park for them to visit. Instead, they care that there is actually an attractive and accessible park available. Or they do not care about the precise language of legislation aimed at reducing sulfur dioxide emissions. Instead they may care that the lake nestled in the mountains has not been killed by acid rain or that the electricity they use is not exorbitantly expensive. Irrespective, then, of the nature of statutory details, citizens reward politicians for outcomes they like and punish them for outcomes they dislike. Attentive interest groups are the same. Unlike citizens, they often pay very careful attention to the actual language of statutes. But like citizens, they care about the details of legislation only insofar as these details are expected to affect policy outcomes.

Since politicians should expect to be judged according to the outcomes their policies produce, they care a great deal about how the language of statutes will influence these outcomes. But in writing this language, politicians face a well-known tension. On the one hand, politicians can benefit from using statutes to delegate policymaking authority to bureaucrats and other actors who have knowledge and expertise that politicians lack, and who have the ability to address problems that politicians, all else equal, may prefer not to delve into. On the other hand, the very expertise that bureaucrats and other actors enjoy, along with their structural role in policy processes, provides them with opportunities to work against the interests of politicians and their supporters. How this tension is resolved ultimately determines the extent to which the electoral connection between voters and policymakers is severed by the practical need for politicians to delegate.

This book is about how elected officials use statutes to establish policy details in efforts to achieve desired outcomes. We focus on two different pathways that politicians can take in designing statutes. One is to write long statutes with extremely detailed language in an effort to micromanage the policymaking process. The other is to write vague statutes that leave many details unspecified, thereby delegating policymaking authority to other actors, usually bureaucrats. Our main objective is to develop and test a theory of delegation that explains the choices between these two pathways.

While we are hardly the first to explore this question, our specific focus is quite different from that of previous studies. As we will discuss in the next chapter, the study of delegation has typically been pursued within the confines of single countries. Consequently, the broad institutional context in which politicians find themselves cannot play a part in theorizing or empirical testing because this context is fixed. In contrast, we study delegation comparatively. By examining the choice between vague and specific statutes across a wide range of political systems, we can come to understand how the institutional context affects delegation strategies.

Vague and Specific Statutes

The following examples illustrate the types of differences we wish to understand. First, consider two statutes from the Irish and German parliamentary systems that focus on the issue of sexual harassment. Whenever politicians create new laws, they must define the individuals and the behavior that are affected. In the case of equality of men and women in the workplace, sexual harassment is one dimension where such definitions are necessary, and legislation takes quite different tacks defining who can be considered a harasser and what constitutes an act of harassment. Figure 1.1 shows how Ireland's Employment Equality Act of 1998 deals with this issue. Article 23 is very detailed, comprising four subsections and approximately 400 words. It sets out an exact definition of who might be accused of sexual harassment and under what conditions. It also includes extensive examples of behavior that will be construed as harassment, including not only requests for sexual favors but also "spoken words, gestures or the production, display or circulation of written words, pictures or other material" that "is unwelcome" and that "could reasonably be regarded as sexually, or otherwise on the gender ground, offensive, humiliating or intimidating." Thus, the statute itself gives reasonably clear instructions to any state agent that is trying to determine whether to classify an act as sexual harassment.

The relatively narrow discretion and specific construction of the Irish statute become clear when we compare it to the German statute, which is shown in Figure 1.2. Compared with Ireland's definition of sexual harassment the German law is unmistakably more ambiguous. The definition in Germany is much shorter, less than one-third the length of the definition in Ireland (it has 128 words as opposed to the 400 in Ireland). It is less precise about defining who can be found guilty of sexual harassment, simply stating that "Employers and managers shall be required to protect employees against sexual harassment at the workplace" and thus leaving ambiguous, for example, the responsibilities of employers for the behavior of clients, customers, or other business contacts.

The German law is also vaguer about which acts constitute harassment. In Ireland, for example, "any act of physical intimacy" is harassment if that act is "unwanted" by the employee. From Section 2, we know that this definition holds regardless of whether the act occurs in the workplace itself and regardless of whether it occurs in the course of the employee's employment. In Germany, by contrast, the law states that harassment occurs if

23. Sexual harassment in the workplace etc.

(1) If, at a place where A is employed (in this section referred to as "the workplace"), or otherwise in the course of A's employment, B sexually harasses A and either:

(a) A and B are both employed at that place or by the same employer,

(b) B is A's employer, or

(c) B is a client, customer or other business contact of A's employer and the circumstances of the harassment are such that A's employer ought reasonably to have taken steps to prevent it, then, for the purposes of this Act, the sexual harassment constitutes discrimination by A's employer, on the gender ground, in relation to A's conditions of employment.

(2) Without prejudice to the generality of subsection (1) in its application in relation to the workplace and the course of A's employment, if, in a case where one of the conditions in paragraphs (a) to (c) of that subsection is fulfilled:

(a) B sexually harasses A, whether or not in the workplace or in the course of A's employment, and

(b) A is treated differently in the workplace or otherwise in the course of A's employment by reason of A's rejection or acceptance of the sexual harassment or it could reasonably be anticipated that A would be so treated, then, for the purposes of this Act, the sexual harassment constitutes discrimination by A's employer, on the gender ground, in relation to A's conditions of employment.

(3) For the purposes of this Act:

(a) any act of physical intimacy by B towards A,

(b) any request by B for sexual favours from A, or

(c) any other act or conduct of B (including, without prejudice to the generality, spoken words, gestures or the production, display or circulation of written words, pictures or other material), shall constitute sexual harassment of A by B if the act, request or conduct is unwelcome to A and could reasonably be regarded as sexually, or otherwise on the gender ground, offensive, humiliating or intimidating to A.

(4) According to the nature of the business of A's employer, the reference in subsection (1)(c) to a client, customer or other business contact includes a reference to any other person with whom A's employer might reasonably expect A to come into contact in the workplace or otherwise in the course of A's employment.

Figure 1.1 Ireland's Employment Equality Act of 1998

Section 2. Protection against sexual harassment. (1) Employers and managers shall be required to protect employees against sexual harassment at the workplace. This protection shall also include preventive measures.

(2) "Sexual harassment at the workplace" is any deliberate, sexually specific behaviour which offends the dignity of employees at the workplace. This shall include:

(i) sexual activity and behaviour which is punishable under the penal law; and (ii) other sexual activity or invitations in this respect, sexually specific touching of the body and remarks with a sexual content, together with showing and putting up in public pornographic pictures which are clearly objected to by the person affected.

(3) Sexual harassment at the workplace is a violation of obligations under the contract of employment or a breach of work discipline.

Note: Bundesgesetzblatt, 30 June 1994, No. 39, pp. 1406–1415.

Figure 1.2 Germany's Second Equality Act of 1994

there is "sexually specific behavior which offends the dignity of employees at the workplace." Rather than adopting the clear criterion of an "unwanted act," the German law does not define what it means for an act to "offend the dignity" of the employee. And its list of examples of behavior is less well developed than Ireland's. In Germany, if you circulate but do not publicly display offending pictures, must a state agent consider this harassment? Can written words be harassment? What about gestures? In Ireland such acts clearly have to be interpreted as harassment, whereas in Germany there is wiggle room. Finally, the German law leaves unanswered questions about where and when such acts have to be committed in order for the acts to be harassment. If one employee makes unwanted physical contact with another employee at a pub after work, is this harassment? By Subsection 2(b) it evidently seems so in Ireland. By contrast, there is much more room for interpretation by other actors in the German case.

We see this same sort of variation across the presidential systems used in the U.S. states. Each of the U.S. states implements the federal Medicaid program, which provides health care to a variety of disadvantaged groups. In implementing Medicaid programs, states have considerable autonomy in devising policy details, and in the early 1990s a number of states began to move Medicaid patients into managed care arrangements.[1] These Medicaid managed care (MMC) programs were adopted in large part to combat skyrocketing costs, and a sense of crisis, in the Medicaid program.

In reading the legislation that created these MMC programs, one is struck by the variation in the extent to which legislation spells out the actual details of policy. The states of Idaho and Texas provide a remarkable contrast. Idaho adopted a statute in 1993 that established a managed care system for Medicaid patients. The statute is about as vague as they come with respect to the level of policy details, saying little more than "establish a system of managed care." The section dealing with managed care reads, in its entirety, as follows:

SECTION 2. The Department of Health and Welfare is hereby directed to develop and implement, as soon as possible, a new health care delivery system for those clients on Medicaid, utilizing a managed care concept. (Idaho HB 421, 1993)[2]

While there were other sections in this statute, none dealt with the issue of managed care. Thus, the legislation initiates steps toward creating a managed care system but does nothing to determine the contours of MMC policy. On the contrary, the law simply instructs the Department of Health and Welfare to "develop and implement" such a system, leaving all policy details to the agency itself.

A 1997 Texas statute also gives an agency the authority to implement a managed care system. The Texas law, SB 1574, begins in much the same way as Idaho's, instructing the agency to

design the system in a manner that will enable this state and the local governmental entities . . . to control the costs associated with the state Medicaid program and that, to the extent possible, results in cost savings to this state and those local governmental entities through health care service delivery based on managed care. (Article 2, Section 2.01 (a) (2))

[1] We describe the Medicaid program and the policy issues it involves in more detail in Chapters 3 and 6. The main point at this stage is to note that the states are dealing with the same sets of policy issues, and they have autonomy with respect to the programs that they design.

[2] This was one of two bills that Idaho passed in the 1980s and 1990s about the transition to managed care for Medicaid clients. The other bill, passed in 1994, was equally broad in its delegation of power to the agency.

Although this very general instruction parallels the language in Idaho, the Texas statute then goes on to provide a number of particulars about how the managed care system for Medicaid clients should work. In several pages of text containing nearly 2,000 words, the Texas state legislature specifies numerous aspects of the managed care system.[3] Rather than simply leaving all of these sorts of decisions to the executive branch, or to the courts, the legislature mandates that the agency do the following:

- Design the system to emphasize prevention and promote continuity of care.
- Expand Medicaid eligibility, especially for children.
- Collect data, conduct comparative analyses of these data in order to assess the relative value of alternative health care delivery systems, and report this analysis to the Speaker of the House, as well as to the governor and lieutenant governor.
- Ensure that both private and public health care providers and managed care organizations are allowed an opportunity to participate in the program.
- Give extra consideration to providers who agree to ensure continuity of care for Medicaid clients for 12 months beyond the period of eligibility.
- Use, when possible, competing managed care systems.
- Establish pilot programs to deliver health care services to children with special health care needs.

The legislation also provides other instructions, telling the agency, for example, how it should determine which sorts of providers can participate in MMC. Without listing every detail of the Texas statute, it is clear that this legislation provides more specific instructions to the agency than does the Idaho statute. The Texas law does not spell out every detail about how the managed care system should work; but it does provide a large number of specifics, and in so doing, it constrains the decision-making authority of the health care agency.

These sorts of differences do not exist only when a program is first being set up. In 1996, for example, both Alaska and Florida addressed the question of how to deal with "mandatory enrollment" – in other words, whether Medicaid participants *must* enroll in a managed care program.

[3] Technically, this bill (SB 1574) was a revision of an earlier law. The provisions discussed later come from the portions of the law that were newly added by this bill.

The Alaska statute, HB 396, spells out briefly how mandatory enrollment should work:

The department, under this Act, may require that a recipient of medical assistance under AS 47.07 must participate in a managed care system in order to remain eligible for medical assistance under AS 47.07. This participation requirement may be based on geographical, financial, social, medical, and other factors that the department determines are relevant to the development and efficient management of the managed care system.

In other words, the legislation essentially tells the agency that it has the right to require Medicaid (i.e., medical assistance) clients to enroll in a managed care system.

The Florida legislature takes a different approach in its statute, SB 886. The legislature tells the agency that all Medicaid patients should be required to enroll in managed care programs, but then spells out who should be exempt from this rule: people in institutions; clients enrolled in the Medicaid Medically Needy Program; and people who are eligible for both Medicaid and Medicare. Unlike the Alaska legislature, which gives the agency the discretion to determine whether enrollment should be mandatory, and if so, for whom, the Florida legislature not only makes enrollment mandatory, it also spells out exceptions to this requirement.

The Florida law thus provides greater constraints on the agency's discretion than does the Alaska law. In fact, the Florida law goes into even further detail on this topic. After determining who should be exempt from the mandatory enrollment rule, it then specifies the conditions under which people who might be exempt still can be enrolled in managed care programs. For example, patients who meet the exemption conditions but voluntarily choose to enroll in managed care programs will be allowed to do so. Furthermore, the bill states that no clients shall be required to enroll in a managed care program unless the program meets certain criteria for care, also spelled out in the legislation. Finally, the bill stipulates that the clients should have a choice of private managed care programs or MediPass, the state-run program in Florida. In the end, the statute spends approximately 1,500 words spelling out who must enroll in managed care programs, who is exempt, what sorts of information clients should be provided about their options regarding managed care, and what their rights are. Clearly, all of these instructions function to constrain the actions of bureaucrats and others who are involved in setting MMC policy.

Our Argument

These examples illustrate the basic empirical puzzle that we explore. When faced with the same policy issue, politicians in different political systems make different choices regarding how to design legislation. Some politicians – such as those who wrote the statutes in Idaho, Alaska, and Germany previously described – adopt astonishingly vague laws. Others – such as those in Texas and Ireland – attempt to micromanage the policy-making process by inserting substantial policy details into the legislation itself. What explains these different choices, and why might they matter?

Understanding why politicians sometimes allow substantial discretion and at other times tell bureaucrats precisely what to do is important for a number of reasons and has held a central place in political science research agendas for many years. Often the issue of discretion arises with respect to fundamental concerns about political control of bureaucrats. Since vague laws give bureaucrats in the executive branch substantial discretion in formulating policy, such discretion is at times held to symbolize the wresting of policymaking control by bureaucrats from politicians. Thus, the idea that politicians give substantial discretion to bureaucrats often raises the specter of a vast, dominant, out-of-control bureaucracy.

As we will discuss in Chapter 2, recent studies challenge this alleged link between bureaucratic discretion and bureaucratic dominance. These studies correctly emphasize that such discretion is often *deliberate*. It is purposefully granted by politicians to bureaucrats because doing so is the best strategy for achieving desired policy goals. Of course, it is also possible that granting discretion is not a deliberate strategy for achieving policy goals, but rather is an unavoidable consequence of the political and institutional contexts. Legislative majorities may wish to limit discretion, but for a variety of reasons may be unable to do so. Thus, if one's goal is to link the study of discretion to the issue of political control of bureaucrats, it is important to understand when discretion is deliberate and when it is not.

Political control of bureaucrats, however, is hardly the only, or perhaps even the most important, reason to worry about discretion. The level of discretion also has important ramifications for the question of *which* politician is most able to influence policymaking. In March 2001, for example, President George W. Bush reversed course on a campaign promise to regulate the emissions of carbon dioxide. Bush had promised during the presidential campaign to establish mandatory reductions for carbon dioxide and three other gases that contribute to global warming, a promise that outstripped the calls by his challenger, Al Gore, for voluntary reductions. Yet for a variety of reasons, Bush decided, once in office, not to mandate such reductions. He was able to make this policy decision precisely because the Clean Air Act (CAA) did not preclude him from doing so. If the CAA *had* limited his discretion by mandating the reduction of carbon dioxide, perhaps by specifying target levels and a timetable, Bush could not have simply decided that the gas need not be regulated. This example, like others we describe in this book, indicates that discretion levels often influence not just the relative roles of bureaucrats and politicians, but also which political actors are most able to influence policy.

Strategic incentives involving discretion affect other salient aspects of politics as well. We will argue, for example, that our theory of how politicians design laws has important implications for transparency in policymaking. Our case study of Michigan (Chapter 5) provides an excellent example. In Michigan, a very vague, high-discretion statute moved the policymaking process behind the closed doors of the relevant agency, causing frustration among even politicians with their ability to know how decisions were being made. By contrast, a more specific, low-discretion statute one year later moved many decisions into the more open arena of the assembly and forced information to be revealed in the legislature during the policymaking process. We will also argue that studying discretion has implications for our understanding of compliance by bureaucrats with laws and for the ability of politicians to respond to the need for policy change.

Our simple purpose at this stage is not to develop these arguments, but rather to underscore the fact that understanding the level of discretion is important on a variety of levels. It contributes to our understanding of why legislators make the choices that they do in writing these statutes. It helps us to address traditional concerns about political control over bureaucrats. It provides insights into which politicians are able to influence policy. And it gives us a way to address other issues, such as transparency, compliance, and responsiveness.

Our central goal is therefore to develop an argument about the factors affecting the design of legislative statutes. The distinguishing feature of our argument is not only that it is applicable across a range of political systems, but, more importantly, it allows us to understand how differences in the institutional features across these systems influence delegation processes. Thus, we look to see how political and institutional differences among the U.S. states affect the design of statutes in these states and, similarly, how such differences across parliamentary democracies influence statutory design in a variety of countries.

It may seem strange to some readers that we combine the study of Idaho and Texas with that of Ireland and Germany. Yet since we want our theory to apply to both presidential and parliamentary systems, and since we want to examine important differences that exist within these broad constitutional categories, it makes good sense for us to combine the study of U.S. states with the study of parliamentary systems. The advanced parliamentary democracies vary considerably in their electoral laws, level of decentralization, and legal structures, to take a few examples. As noted previously, they take different approaches to legislating on similar topics and thus provide a clear opportunity to study how the broad institutional setting affects delegation processes. In the same way, the U.S. states are all presidential systems that must legislate on similar issues, but they also differ in their institutional arrangements, such as in the details of legislative–executive relations and the organization of the legislature. This combination of U.S. states with advanced parliamentary democracies thus provides a very rich opportunity for exploring the influence of the institutional setting on delegation.

Our argument draws attention to four general factors that affect politicians' incentives and ability to use legislation to micromanage policymaking. These are:

- the level of *policy conflict* between the politicians who adopt the statutes and the agents who implement them;
- the *capacity* of politicians to write detailed statutes;
- the *bargaining environment* (e.g., the existence of vetoes or bicameral conflict) in which statutes are adopted; and
- the expectations that politicians have about how *nonstatutory factors* – such as the role of courts or legislative oversight opportunities – influence policy implementation, independent of the language of statutes.

Our theory describes how these four factors affect the design of legislation. Policy conflict between politicians and bureaucrats, for example, creates incentives to use policy details in legislative statutes to constrain bureaucratic autonomy. But whether a particular level of conflict leads to the adoption of such policy details depends on other factors. Legislative majorities across and within different systems, for example, differ in their costs of writing detailed statutes. The level of conflict among the political actors who must agree on legislative details also varies across (and within) systems. The upper and lower houses in a bicameral system, for example, may disagree, influencing the ability of legislative majorities to write detailed statutes. The institutional arrangements that affect policymaking after statutes are adopted are also important. There are many nonstatutory factors that influence policy implementation. If factors related to oversight opportunities, judicial protections, or nonlegislative policymaking arenas (such as corporatism) are sufficiently reliable from the perspective of legislative majorities, incentives to use statutes to micromanage policymaking should diminish. Thus, each of these four factors is important, but they are important in conjunction with each other.

Chapter 4 lays out the details of the model on which our specific argument about these four factors is based. At this stage, we highlight three specific attributes of this argument to provide a better sense of its nature and scope. First, many arguments about bureaucratic autonomy focus on issue characteristics. Different policy areas raise different strategic considerations for politicians and require different delegation strategies. Although we do not for a moment imagine that issue characteristics are irrelevant to understanding the design of statutes, our argument is not about the design of legislation in particular policy areas. It is not, for example, an argument specifically about health policy or labor policy. Instead, our goal is to develop an argument that is helpful across a range of policies. Put differently, we want to demonstrate that after controlling for issue-specific effects, we can uncover systematic political and institutional factors that affect the design of legislation across polities.

Second, although our argument for understanding bureaucratic autonomy springs from a comparative institutional perspective, we do not intend our study to apply everywhere one finds politicians and bureaucrats. Instead, our study rests squarely on the assumption that bureaucrats are *Weberian* – that they have substantial policy expertise and the capacity to implement policies.[4] Though this assumption seems entirely innocuous among the modernized bureaucracies that we study, it is worth underlining that such bureaucracies are not the norm everywhere in the world. We therefore do not claim that our arguments generalize to systems where bureaucratic capacity is lacking.

[4] We define precisely what we mean in this regard in Chapter 4.

Finally, much existing literature on relations between politicians and bureaucrats focuses on the question of how well politicians control the behavior of bureaucrats. The central concern in this literature is that bureaucrats exercise undue influence over policymaking. For reasons we point out in Chapter 2, addressing this issue of political control is not our primary focus. We argue that efforts to make broad claims about the quality of political control over bureaucrats are fraught with conceptual and empirical difficulties. We also contend that the predominant focus on control has led scholars of bureaucratic relations with politicians to overlook other important normative issues that are raised by the study of delegation processes.

Rather than asking to what extent politicians control bureaucrats, we ground our study on the assumption that in any political context, there typically exists a politician who has greater opportunities than other political actors to influence bureaucratic behavior. This is often a cabinet minister in parliamentary democracies, for example, and the president or governor in presidential systems. Since these actors can exploit their privileged position during policy implementation, strategies for delegating policymaking authority to bureaucrats are often driven as much by asymmetries in political opportunities to influence bureaucrats as they are by the general need for all politicians to constrain bureaucrats who would otherwise run amuck. Legislative majorities in presidential systems, for example, want to delegate in ways that constrain the policy influence of chief executives (e.g., governors and presidents), and parliamentary majorities need to worry about the privileged opportunities of cabinet ministers during policy implementation. Our analysis therefore focuses on the design of legislation as an important element in the strategic bargaining *between* political actors.

Finally, though not our primary focus, our analysis does shed some light on the broad issue of political control of bureaucrats, albeit through a back door of sorts. Our argument is based on the assumption that a political actor exists who has a privileged position to influence bureaucratic behavior during policy implementation. If we are wrong in this assumption that particular actors have greater opportunities than others to influence bureaucratic behavior, then the predictions of our theory should not be confirmed in our empirical tests. Thus, to the extent that our theory based on this assumption is verified empirically, we gain confidence that our privileged actor in fact exercises a nontrivial influence on bureaucratic behavior. We return to this point in Chapter 8.

Plan of Attack

Our central objective, then, is to develop and test a comparative theory of delegation, one that looks specifically at how the institutional context in which politicians find themselves affects the extent to which politicians use the language of statutes to micromanage policymaking processes. To accomplish this objective, our approach blends qualitative, quantitative, and formal analyses. We begin in Chapter 2 by reviewing previous studies of the relationship between legislatures and bureaucrats. The chapter does not review all studies of this relationship, a task that would be all but impossible, given the enormous size of the literature. But we do focus on the specific claims that mark our point of departure.

Chapter 3 examines the main object of our study: the design of statutes. To some readers, the idea of comparing laws across a wide range of polities may seem farfetched, given that laws mean different things in different countries. For us, this is precisely the point – to understand and explain these differences and their impact on the democratic process. It is therefore important to describe in careful detail the actual nature of legislation across polities. What exactly do we find in statutes across political systems? What kind of language is used to limit discretion? What are the roles of executive decision-making procedures that are defined in statutes? How can we compare the amount of discretion that politicians place in statutes across polities? We address these questions in Chapter 3 through an extensive examination of the language of legislation across polities on similar issues. Across the U.S. states we examine Medicaid legislation, and in parliamentary systems we focus on legislation related to labor law in general and gender discrimination in particular.

Chapter 4 develops the main theoretical argument of the book. The theory, which presents in much more detail the argument we outlined earlier in this chapter, is based on a formal model of the legislative process and policy implementation. It describes the circumstances under which politicians adopt detailed statutes that limit the policy autonomy of bureaucrats, as opposed to more general statutes that leave substantial policymaking autonomy to bureaucrats or other political actors involved with policy implementation. This chapter carefully describes the elements of our model, the main theoretical results that we intend to test, and the intuitions underlying these results.

Our basic theoretical argument, though based on a specific set of formal assumptions, can be conveyed without reliance on the technical details. In

Chapter 4, therefore, we describe our theory in the most accessible way we can. This will make it possible for all readers to understand and digest the logic of our argument. For those who are interested, the technical details are contained in Appendix D.

Chapters 5 through 7 provide the main empirical analyses in the book. We begin in Chapter 5 with a brief qualitative excursus on Medicaid policymaking in the state of Michigan. Since our theory has a wide range of explanatory variables, a case study approach is hardly conducive to achieving the main objective of this study. It would take a huge number of such studies to give us the empirical leverage we would need. We feel one such study, however, can serve a useful role because it fleshes out the ways in which our theory helps to explain delegation. By looking at actual legislation and legislative proposals, and by seeing how these vary over time in response to political changes, we are able to demonstrate a connection between the assumptions in our model and the motivations of actual legislators, as well as gain some initial support for our theoretical arguments.

Chapters 6 and 7 provide the quantitative empirical tests of our argument and thus mark a significant departure from previous studies. Though there exist a host of competing claims about how delegation works across a wide range of democracies, systematic empirical tests are, with the exception of a handful of recent studies of U.S. politics, all but nonexistent, and none examine the impact of the institutional context on the design of legislation. Chapter 6 focuses on explaining variation in statutory design across the U.S. states, and Chapter 7 focuses on parliamentary systems.

The empirical tests in these chapters have two components. The first is to measure the level of policy detail in legislation while controlling for the effect of issue type. The second is to measure broad conceptual variables in our theory. What creates policy conflict between legislative majorities and bureaucrats in different types of political systems? What factors affect the capacity of politicians to write detailed statutes? What are relevant nonstatutory factors and how do they operate?

In addressing these questions, we highlight two general points. On the one hand, the specific factors that affect the level of policy conflict, the capacity to write policy details, and the reliability of nonstatutory mechanisms for influencing policy implementation clearly differ across political settings. In the presidential systems of the U.S. states, for example, the presence or absence of divided government affects incentives to write policy details, whereas in parliamentary systems we cannot consider divided government, but instead must examine the coalition status of the government. Similarly, across the presidential systems in the U.S. states, legislative professionalism affects legislative capacity, whereas in parliamentary systems, where most policymaking occurs in the cabinet, we must take into account factors like cabinet instability.

On the other hand, though operationalized with different measures, the abstract variables in our theory operate in a similar fashion across the different settings. Divided government in presidential systems and minority government in parliamentary systems both create policy conflict between the legislative majorities and bureaucrats, and, all else equal, both lead to stronger efforts to write detailed statutes. Low levels of legislative professionalism in the states and high levels of cabinet instability in parliamentary systems make it more difficult, all else equal, for legislative majorities to include policy details in legislation. And the need for legislative details declines as institutionalized legislative oversight opportunities improve in the U.S. states or as legal structures or corporatist bargaining arrangements protect legislative majorities in parliamentary systems. These examples from the results we present later illuminate our argument that broad systematic forces influence the design of legislation across political systems, although the way we conceptualize and measure such forces varies with the nature of the political system.

Chapter 8 concludes our study. The chapter reviews our main arguments and evidence about how the political and institutional settings affect incentives for legislative majorities to micromanage policymaking processes by writing detailed statutes. We then discuss the normative implications of our study. If our argument is correct, what are the implications for the distributive consequences of the policymaking process? That is, can the privileged actors during policy implementation use their position to shape policy outcomes or can legislative majorities limit this power through the careful design of legislation? Another issue is transparency in policymaking. How does the institutional context affect the propensity of politicians to make fundamental policy decisions in the relatively open legislative arena rather than in more closed, smoke-filled rooms outside the legislature? We also consider compliance. When will bureaucrats be most likely to comply with statutes and when will they be likely to ignore the dictates of statutes and pursue instead their own interests? And finally, we explore the ways in which the risks inherent in delegation affect the ability of politicians to respond to the need for policy change.

2

Rational Delegation or Helpless Abdication? The Relationship between Bureaucrats and Politicians

Political leaders in all forms of government must delegate policymaking authority to bureaucrats. Since this practical necessity can result in substantial authority by bureaucrats over society, concern about excessive influence by bureaucrats has a long history. Montesquieu's *The Spirit of the Laws*, his eighteenth-century defense of a decentralized aristocratic society, offered perhaps the first argument that political centralization leads to a bureaucratic state and that a bureaucratic state is a distinctive form of despotism. Tocqueville, in *Democracy in America*, shared a similar concern about centralization and bureaucratic despotism, though his observations of the United States convinced him that decentralized federal systems could be useful mechanisms for preventing the abuse of bureaucratic power.

Max Weber, however, set the modern agenda for research on bureaucracies. In arguing that particular forms of bureaucratic organization were most effective, he also pointed out that "democracy inevitably comes into conflict" with its own "bureaucratic tendencies" (1946, 222). But Weber did not say how this conflict is resolved. On the one hand, he argued that in any form of government

> the power position of the bureaucracy is always overtowering. The "political master" finds himself in the position of "dilettante" who stands opposite the "expert," facing the trained official who stands within the management of administration. (1946, 233)

On the other hand, Weber argued that bureaucracies are designed to serve the interests of the individuals at the top:

> The objective indispensability of the once-existing apparatus, with its peculiar, "impersonal character," means that the mechanism . . . is easily made to work for anybody who knows how to gain control over it. (1946, 229)

Weber recognized the effective exercise of political control over bureaucrats by Bismarck in Germany and throughout the course of French political history.

Understanding the tension so elegantly described by Weber between the valuable expertise of bureaucrats, on the one hand, and the need for politicians to control their behavior, on the other, has been the central focus of a vast political science literature on the relationship between bureaucrats and politicians. In this chapter, we describe how this literature has evolved and lay out our interpretation of what we have learned, both from U.S. and from comparative studies. In so doing, we describe what we believe to be inherent limitations and biases in these studies. We also describe how our own study will attempt to build on what other scholars have learned and how, in so doing, we move *away* from the predominant preoccupation with making claims about the specific level and quality of political control over bureaucrats in modern democracies.

Bureaucratic Autonomy and the Administrative State

An early and enduring theme in the literature on relations between politicians and bureaucrats concerns the inevitability of an *administrative state*. From this perspective there is a practical necessity for politicians to grant bureaucrats substantial autonomy in the policymaking process. In complex modern societies, this leads to the undemocratic result that bureaucrats hold all meaningful policymaking power, with elected officials having little opportunity to influence policy outcomes. This perspective of bureaucratic dominance is nicely summed up by Putnam (1975, 87), who writes:

> Can there really be much doubt who governs our complex modern societies? Public bureaucracies, staffed largely by permanent civil servants, are responsible for the vast majority of policy initiatives taken by governments. . . . In a literal sense, the modern political system is essentially "bureaucratic" – characterized by "the rule of officials."

Claims regarding the existence of an administrative state are extremely widespread and well known.[1] They exist in studies of Britain,[2] France,[3]

[1] See relevant discussions, for example, in Waldo (1948); Marx (1957); Eisenstadt (1965); Mosher (1968); Redford (1969); Dogan (1975); Wilson and Dwivedi (1982); Etzioni-Halevy (1983); Peters (1989); Page (1992); and Rothstein (1995).

[2] E.g., Thomas (1968); Roseveare (1969); Rose (1974); Benn (1990); Hall (1986); and, more humorously, Lynn and Jay (1984).

[3] E.g., Williams (1964); Debbasch (1969); and Suleiman (1974).

the United States,[4] Japan,[5] and virtually all other modern democratic states.

Scholars suggest several reasons for the dominance of bureaucrats in policymaking. Ironically, the central reason for granting policymaking autonomy to bureaucrats – their technical expertise – also creates the biggest problem, as bureaucrats can use their knowledge against politicians. Bureaucratic expertise is thus a double-edge sword, creating both the incentive for legislatures to give policymaking power to bureaucrats and the opportunity for these bureaucrats to act counter to legislative preferences (e.g., Peters 1981, 74; Rourke 1984).

For many scholars, the informational problems are compounded by "government overload."[6] With the growth of government and the increased complexity of society, it is no longer possible for politicians to possess the expertise necessary to make important policy decisions. Weir and Beetham (1999, 170), for example, argue that "[m]inisters who are likely to be taking up to 50 'decisions' a day are not in a position to query any but a few of the background briefings which accompany their civil servants' recommendations." Similarly, Kerwin (1999, 29) notes that the lack of "range and depth of expertise . . . among members of Congress or staff" necessitates delegation to bureaucracies.

Structural factors also contribute to the dominance by bureaucratic actors in the administrative state. Ultimately bureaucrats implement policy, and their privileged position in this process allows them to take actions that politicians would not want them to take. This observation is central to the moral hazard arguments in theorizing by Niskanen and other public choice scholars,[7] descriptive accounts of bureaucratic behavior,[8] and complete information formal models of delegation.[9]

Finally, sociological arguments provide several theoretical underpinnings to explain administrative dominance. Selznick's (1949) classic study of the Tennessee Valley Authority in the United States emphasized the importance of examining the internal wants and needs of organizations themselves in order to understand how these organizations respond to

[4] E.g., Yates (1982); Dodd and Schott (1986); and Gruber (1987).
[5] E.g., Kubota (1969); Okimoto (1989); and Johnson (1995).
[6] E.g., Crozier, Huntington, and Watanuk (1975) and King (1975).
[7] E.g., Niskanen (1971); Borcherding (1977); Orzechowski (1977). For critiques, see Bendor, Taylor, and van Gaalen (1987); Peters (1988); Bendor (1988, 1990); Dunleavy (1991).
[8] E.g., Suleiman (1974) and Weir and Beetham (1999, 167–171).
[9] See Ferejohn and Shipan (1990) and Hammond and Knott (1996).

unexpected external forces. Wilson (1980; see also 1989, ch. 5) builds on this framework and argues that in addition to internal preferences and structures, the behavior of bureaucrats is determined by the environment in which agencies and departments find themselves and by the structure of interest group conflict. Other scholars claim that since policy implementation occurs from the bottom up, individuals at the bottom rungs of organizations will not take any actions that are inconsistent with the values, norms, and routines of the organization, dooming any such policies to failure.[10] Still others argue that the growth of professionalism in the bureaucracy insulates it from political influence (cf. Knott and Miller 1987) and that the clash of professions within an agency largely determines policy choices (Katzmann 1980). And from a related but different sociological perspective, Crozier (1964) argues that to understand bureaucratic decision making in France, one must understand the French cultural proclivity to resist authority. In this regard, he turns on its head the common argument in French politics that French society is shaped by the powerful elites who are at the top of the administrative hierarchy.[11]

Though many scholars acknowledge the existence of an administrative state in modern democracies, there is less consensus about its consequences. Some see clear advantages to a prominent bureaucratic role in decision making. Mashaw (1985, 1997), for example, contends that in U.S. politics a case can be made in favor of broad delegation on the grounds that policymaking under such a system will minimize errors in policymaking and mistakes in implementation.[12] More historically, public administration scholars in the second half of the nineteenth century and the first half of the twentieth century lauded bureaucracy for its possibility of what Kaufman (1956) called "neutral competence," which is the idea that bureaucrats can bring their expertise to bear in ways that would yield an objectively best outcome. Woodrow Wilson (1887) was among the first to elaborate on this idea that administration could be kept separate from politics and to argue that such separation would make bureaucracy completely consistent with the ideals of democracy. This notion found additional support in the scientific management movement that swept both the

[10] See Lipsky (1980); Hanf and Hull (1982); Hanf and Toonen (1985); O'Toole (1986); Sabatier (1986); and Linder and Peters (1987).

[11] See Suleiman (1974, 1978, 1984) and Kessler (1978).

[12] See also Arnold (1990), who discusses the benefits of vague legislation and broad delegation.

United States and Europe during the early 1900s, a movement that held out the possibility of perfectly efficient bureaucratic organizations (e.g., Goodnow 1900; Taylor 1911). And public administration scholars in the United States, such as Luther Gulick during the New Deal era and Harold Seidman more recently, have argued that the idea of a politics–administration dichotomy represents the best normative model for bureaucratic involvement in policymaking (Gulick and Urwick 1937; Seidman and Gilmour 1986).[13]

Scholars in comparative politics likewise have pointed out the advantages of an administrative state. LaPalombara (1958), writing on the Fourth Republic in France, argues that if the French look not to parliament but rather to the "administrative arena as the place where the aggregation of group interests occurs . . . [then] French society may, in fact, derive important benefits" from the central role of bureaucrats in the policymaking process (138). Heclo (1974) and Sacks (1980) argue that bureaucracy is a key source of policy innovation, which benefits society. And Moe and Caldwell (1994), to take a final example, argue that granting broad authority to neutral, competent, and professionalized civil servants leads to more coherent policymaking.

Many others, however, view the consequences of administrative dominance quite dimly. The previous quote by Putnam points out that bureaucrats do not just serve political masters, but rather are responsible – often inappropriately so – for a vast amount of policymaking. Many other scholars have deplored the rise of the administrative state as elitist, undemocratic, and biased. Offe (1972) and O'Connor (1978) focus on the disconnect that administrative authority creates between voters and policymakers. Others worry that the administrative state entrenches the interests of the capitalist class (e.g., Miliband 1973; Poulantzas 1978; Wright 1978). Still others emphasize the fact that administrative dominance moves decision making into private rather than public arenas. Bertrand Russell (1967, 37) writes, for example, that "[t]he increased power of officials . . . has the drawback that it is apt to be irresponsible, behind-the-scenes power, like that of Emperors' eunuchs and Kings' mistresses in former times" (see also Strauss 1961; Debbasch 1969; Meynaud 1969). Hall argues that the

[13] Of course, as Knott and Miller have noted, "The politics/administration dichotomy has served as an umbrella for bureaucratic political influence under the guise of neutral expertise. . . . It is difficult to imagine an idealogy (sic) that could have done more to justify bureaucratic politicization than the idealogy (sic) of bureaucratic neutrality" (1987, 190).

dominance of the British civil service reduces the state's capacity to make innovative policies, produces great secrecy in the policymaking process, and concentrates power in the hands of a small number of experts (Hall 1986; see also Hall 1983). Debbasch (1969) goes so far as to argue that the next revolution will be not against the governments but against the bureaucrats.

We see similar complaints in the context of American politics. Dodd and Schott portray the existence of the administrative state in pejorative terms precisely because the bureaucracy does not simply implement policies that elected politicians have chosen:

> The administrative state is . . . in many respects a prodigal child. Although born of congressional intent, it has taken on a life of its own and has matured to a point where its muscle and brawn can be turned against its creator. Over the past several decades, the federal bureaucracy has come to rival the president and the Congress, challenging both for hegemony in the national political system. Protected by civil service tenure, armed with the power to issue orders and rules that have the force of law, supported by strong clientele and interest groups, and possessing a wealth of information, knowledge, and technical expertise, it goes forth to battle its institutional rivals on equal, and sometimes superior, terms. And, though occasionally defeated, it rarely returns home repentant. (1986, 2)

The historian Grant McConnell (1966) wrote persuasively of the negative consequences of overly broad delegation in his study of business, labor, and agricultural policy. Several years later, Lowi (1969, 1979), in a work that is often cited by political scientists, reprised many of McConnell's themes. Lowi's primary shot across the bow of delegation was that vague delegation leads inexorably to what he called *interest group liberalism*, a system in which interest groups dominate the government and the state is in a position of "permanent receivership," existing only to please these groups. Other scholars and critics of delegation have sounded similar themes. Aranson, Gellhorn, and Robinson (1982), for example, developed a positive theory of delegation to show why Congress writes vague statutes, but then used this theory to develop the normative claim that such delegation is welfare-reducing. These negative consequences are all brought about in the United States because Congress chooses to abdicate its rightful role as the primary policymaker in our political system. And empirical studies of Congress and the bureaucracy indicate that because Congress has little incentive to influence the actions of bureaucrats, it therefore rarely engages in systematic oversight (Scher 1963; Ogul 1976, 1981; but see Aberbach 1990).

Challenging Perceptions of the Administrative State

There are two striking features of the literature we have just described. The first is that the concept of the administrative state is typically invoked in the broadest terms and thus is conceptually muddled. How do we know when an administrative state exists? Or put differently, what specific benchmark constitutes effective political control of bureaucrats?

To answer these questions, one would need to address a variety of issues. Should the benchmark focus on the relationship between policy outcomes and politicians' preferences? If so, since many politicians are typically involved in policymaking, which politicians' preferences should we consider? And are we sure we care about policy outcomes? Bureaucrats may adopt exactly the policies that politicians ask them to, but the outcome may be poor for reasons having nothing to do with administrative dominance. Maybe we should focus instead on whether bureaucrats adopt the policies that politicians say that they want, without worrying about the outcomes of these policies. But then if politicians want to harness bureaucratic expertise, they may *want* to give bureaucrats autonomy by not describing these policies very precisely. Does this represent lack of political will or political control? This brief discussion illustrates that a variety of complicated issues must be addressed before the claims about the administrative state attain the conceptual clarity necessary for empirical evaluation.

The second notable feature of this literature is the lack of evidence. Claims about administrative dominance often are based on appeals to intuition and anecdotes rather than on rigorous empirical study. Given that the concept of an administrative state lacks clarity, this is not surprising. But even if these conceptual issues were to be sorted out, the obstacles associated with assessing administrative dominance are formidable. Accurately measuring the preferences of politicians and bureaucrats, the policies that bureaucrats are asked to implement, and the outcomes of their actions – all of these are difficult tasks. And even if we were to measure these things accurately, how do we interpret the results? It seems obvious that control, however conceptualized, will never be perfect. But how will we decide whether a particular departure from any particular benchmark represents good or bad control? Given the conceptual and empirical limitations in the arguments about the administrative state, one reasonable intellectual response would be to ask: "Can we sort out in what sense these claims are correct?" As we will show, this is *not* the approach we will take in this book. Others, however, have attempted to respond, particularly in the past two decades, to the issues just raised. Many scholars of developed democracies have attacked the notion of administrative dominance, arguing instead that the relative roles of bureaucrats and politicians have been widely misunderstood. These efforts have led to a fundamental reorientation in the way that scholars study relationships between politicians and bureaucrats.

According to some of these recent challenges, the central problem with arguments about administrative dominance is one of "observational equivalence," as Weingast and Moran (1983) first argued. Consider a world, for example, that would seem entirely consistent with the conventional wisdom about the administrative state. In this world, bureaucrats play the central role in creating policy. Legislation is very general and places minimal constraints on bureaucratic action. After legislation and regulations are adopted, there is minuscule effort at bureaucratic oversight by politicians.

The world just described is exactly the world described by scholars who decry the rise of the administrative state. And yet this same world could be observationally equivalent to one in which the bureaucracy is extremely responsive to politicians. This possibility of a responsive bureaucracy depends on the extent to which the political system allows politicians to trust the bureaucrats to make choices that the politicians would want them to make. If such trust is possible, the grant of seemingly vast powers to bureaucrats can represent rational delegation to trusted policy experts rather than helpless abdication under an all but authoritarian bureaucratic state.

The problem, of course, is precisely the aforementioned one of observational equivalence. Although one can interpret the world just described as being consistent with effective political control, it is also consistent with the pejorative view of an administrative state. So how does one adjudicate between the two conflicting interpretations?

The main approach in this regard has been to examine whether there exists a systematic relationship between the preferences of politicians and the nature of political outcomes. The simple idea is that if the perception of administrative dominance is correct, there should be no relationship between the preferences of politicians and agency actions. By contrast, if bureaucrats are responsive to the preferences of politicians, then changes in the preferences of politicians should lead to changes in agency actions.

A number of empirical studies have established the existence of a link between political preferences and policy outputs in the United States Indeed, the contemporaneous influence of elected politicians on bureaucratic actions and outcomes has been one of the most widely studied topics in American politics during the last two decades. Initially some of these studies focused almost exclusively on whether Congress (e.g., Weingast and Moran 1983; Weingast 1984) or the president (e.g., Moe 1982) dominates the bureaucracy.[14] This emphasis was soon replaced by a broader concern for whether elected politicians influence the actions of agencies (e.g., Moe 1985). While not all studies have found that bureaucrats are responsive to the preferences of elected politicians (see the discussion in Krause 1999), most have (e.g., Wood 1988, 1990; Ferejohn and Shipan 1989a, 1989b; Wood and Waterman 1991, 1994; Olson 1995, 1996; Canes-Wrone 2000; see also Ferejohn 1974; Arnold 1979). Indeed, Wood and Waterman declared that the "evidence for active political control is so strong that controversy should now end over *whether* political control occurs. . . . Future research should turn toward exploring the *determinants* of political control" (1991, 822).

In research on parliamentary systems, numerous studies examine how the preferences of politicians influence policymaking in general, though these studies are less clearly tied to the specific issue of delegation. The main thrust of this work has been to examine how the ideological preferences of parties in government affect policy outcomes. Bawn (1999), for example, demonstrates that spending levels across different ministries in Germany are influenced in expected ways by government composition. Tsebelis (1999, 2002) shows that the ideological heterogeneity of government coalitions affects the ability of these coalitions to adopt policy change. Budge, Hofferbert, and Klingemann (1994) examine the relationships between party promises and policy outcomes. And a huge amount of research has demonstrated that there often (though not always) exists a relationship between the preferences of parties in government and the nature of the welfare state[15] or the substance of economic policymaking.[16]

[14] For general discussions of congressional versus presidential influence, see Moe (1987); West and Cooper (1989/1990); and Fiorina (1981, 335), who contends that "Congress has the power but not the incentive for coordinated control of the bureaucracy, while the president has the incentive but not the power."

[15] E.g., Jackman (1980); Pampel and Williamson (1989); Hicks and Swank (1992); Janoski (1994); and O'Connell (1994).

[16] E.g., Hibbs (1977); Sachs and Roubini (1989); Garrett (1998); and Iversen (1999).

These studies in American and comparative politics are relevant to debates about the administrative state because the evidence they present of a link between the preferences of politicians and policy outcomes allows us to reject the notion of an independent bureaucracy setting policy without regard to what the politicians in power desire. We feel, however, that this research hardly puts a nail in the coffin of claims about the administrative state. Even if studies do show a consistent link between political preferences and policy outcomes, we still need to ascertain the degree of political control over bureaucrats. Using the metaphor of regression analysis, the effects could be statistically significant and in the correct direction, but unless our null hypothesis is the implausible "no effect of politics on policy," it is difficult to know to what *degree* political control exists, making it difficult to defend claims for or against administrative dominance. Almost certainly, the ability of politicians to control bureaucratic behavior will always lie somewhere in the gray area – neither perfect nor nonexistent, but rather somewhere in between.

Institutions for Political Control of Bureaucrats

Attacks on claims about the administrative state have not, however, focused exclusively on measuring relationships between political preferences and policy outcomes. Scholars have also developed causal arguments about how politicians design institutional arrangements that allow the politicians to grant bureaucrats discretion without fear that this will lead to unwanted outcomes. Such research has been enormously influential, and our study builds directly on this line of research.

The principal–agent framework from economics has played an extremely prominent and powerful role in this institutional approach to relations between politicians and bureaucrats.[17] The central thrust of this approach has involved developing maps from particular types of informational problems to the best possible institutional solutions. The informational problems central to this mode of theorizing are varied but well

[17] Sappington (1991) offers an excellent overview of principal–agent theory in economics. See also Dixit (1996, 1997); Milgrom and Roberts (1992); Tirole (1994); and Williamson (1996) for relevant discussions. For overviews of the applicability of principal–agent and transaction costs theories to legislators and agencies, see Moe (1984); Kiewiet and McCubbins (1988); Gill (1995); Horn (1995); Spence (1997); Bendor (1988, 1990); Bendor, Glazer, and Hammond (2000); Chang, de Figueiredo, and Weingast (2000); and Huber and Shipan (2000).

known. One category is general uncertainty about what events might happen tomorrow. A politician, for example, may want to devise pollution standards, but no one may know how technology will develop in this area. Private information is also important. A bureaucrat, for example, may know more than the politician about the state of pollution abatement technology or about the feasibility of setting particular standards. The bureaucrat might also have private information about his or her skills or objectives, which leads to the problem of *adverse selection*. A third type of informational problem is unobservable behavior. If bureaucratic behavior is difficult to observe, there will often be incentives for post-contractual opportunism, called *moral hazard*.

These different types of informational problems imply different types of institutional responses. If there exist, for example, difficulties with observing the actions of an agent, incentive schemes, such as linking pay to output, or instruments for monitoring should be put into place. If there is a problem with learning important characteristics of bureaucrats (such as their preferences or abilities), then signaling and screening devices are appropriate. More generally, the goal of this approach is to develop theories about how particular institutional forms can be used to increase the likelihood of compliant behavior by bureaucrats.

This approach to institutional choice underpins much recent work in political science that challenges claims about the administrative state. The general goal of these studies is to examine the role of institutional arrangements in addressing the types of principal–agent problems that exist between politicians and their bureaucratic agents. In this regard, although the modes of inquiry are related, studies of parliamentary and presidential systems have necessarily diverged somewhat. It is therefore useful to discuss these two literatures in turn.

Parliamentary Systems

Before examining claims about institutions for delegation in parliamentary systems, it is useful to be reminded of the broader institutional context in which problems of delegation occur.[18] To begin with, we must bear in mind

[18] For an interesting discussion of how principal–agent theory shapes our understanding of parliamentary democracies, see Strøm (2000) and the individual contributions in the special issue of *European Journal of Political Research*, "Parliamentary Democracy and the Chain of Delegation," edited by Torbjörn Bergman, Wolfgang Müller and Kaare Strøm (May 2000).

that parliamentary politics is typically party politics. That is, political parties are organized to act as reasonably cohesive and homogeneous wholes in their interactions with each other after elections. Party leaders have at their disposal a variety of punishment mechanisms that can be used to force individual representatives to "toe the party line" and follow the dictates of party leaders.[19] Representatives of the same party therefore act cohesively in parliaments and cabinets, resolving their intraparty differences out of public view.

Furthermore, "cabinet government" prevails in parliamentary systems. By definition, parliamentary systems have a fusion rather than a separation of executive and legislative power. Consequently, the arena of parliament typically plays a rather marginal role in the policymaking process. The marginalization of parliaments has some institutional foundations, which vary across countries but which typically include forms of agenda control, amendment rights, and other procedural prerogatives, such as confidence vote procedures, for the cabinet. And even when legislative institutions are most firmly tilted toward creating a strong role for parliament, most significant legislative action occurs in the cabinet because this is where the leaders of the parties in the governing majority are located. It is therefore very rare for scholars to assert that backbench members of parliaments play more than a secondary role in the legislative process.

Given that parliamentary politics involves cabinet government with cohesive parties, the issue of political control typically involves assessing the extent to which party leaders in the cabinet can exercise control over bureaucrats. To this end, a variety of institutional arrangements have been described. Central among these is appointment power. In many countries, cabinet ministers can make key personnel decisions at the top of their departments.[20] In some countries, including France and Belgium, formal institutions allow ministers to appoint political cabinets that function as a politicized inner civil service, able to monitor the bureaucracy and to warn the minister if senior career civil servants are causing trouble. But formal institutional arrangements are not necessary. Many scholars have noted the

[19] See a review in Laver and Schofield (1990). For an excellent argument about why members of parliaments consent to having their hands tied by parties, see Cox (1987). See also Epstein (1980) and Diermeier and Feddersen (1998), who argue that the logic of confidence relationships in parliamentary systems requires cohesive parties.

[20] E.g., essays in Laver and Shepsle (1994); as well as Derlien (1988); Dogan (1975); Mayntz and Derlien (1989); Moulin (1975); Peters (1997); Ramseyer and Rosenbluth (1993); Ridley (1983); Steiner (1972); Stevens (1985); and Van Hassel (1975).

politicization of bureaucracies across Western democracies, whereby the political preferences of civil servants become an important criterion for appointment and advancement, independent of the alleged neutrality of the civil service personnel structure.[21] This politicization of civil servants is now perceived as a common characteristic of modern parliamentary systems, even in the United Kingdom, which purportedly has one of the world's most professionalized and politically neutral civil services (e.g., Plowden 1994; Dowding 1995, ch. 6; Weir and Beetham 1999).

Another instrument used to control civil servants is the budget. If a department does not produce outcomes that the majority likes, then the majority can cut the department's budget. Dunleavy (1991) has done perhaps the most to develop this argument in the parliamentary context through his study of Britain. He points out that the effectiveness of budgetary controls depends on the type of department. Some departments, like those that deliver social security benefits, have very small discretionary budgets (i.e., budgets that give senior civil servants autonomy to make substantive decisions about spending). Others, like those charged with environmental regulation and enforcement, might have very large discretionary budgets. With the support of empirical data on budget cuts, Dunleavy argues that the budget can be used effectively to reward and sanction bureaucrats only in the second type of agency.

A third weapon that politicians use to control agencies in parliamentary systems is the reorganization of departments and jurisdictions. Such reorganizations are touted as a way to break up the insulation that departments have with respect to policymaking in particular policy areas. This, and the more general goal of administrative efficiency, was a motivating force behind British "Next Steps" reforms (e.g., Efficiency Unit 1988, 225; Dunleavy 1991; Carter and Greer 1993; Fry 1997; Hoggett 1996). And Edgar Pisani's successful reform of the agriculture bureaucracy in France in the early years of the Fifth Republic has been viewed as central to the reform of French agricultural policy (Suleiman 1974).

Finally, monitoring institutions have received some attention in the parliamentary politics literature. Bennett (1997), for example, identifies three monitoring instruments that have helped politicians and citizens hold bureaucrats accountable: ombudsman offices, freedom of information laws, and data protection laws. Similarly, Barzelay (1997) focuses on auditing procedures.

[21] See an excellent discussion in Mayntz and Derlien (1989) and Peters (1997).

Although the studies previously discussed often touch on themes that are central to principal–agent models, many of these works do not explicitly or rigorously invoke the principal–agent framework.[22] The best example of an explicit invocation of principal–agent ideas in the parliamentary studies of delegation to bureaucrats is Ramseyer and Rosenbluth's (1993) study of Japan. Their book aims to dismantle the conventional wisdom that Japanese civil servants use their enormous informational advantages in policymaking and their central role in drafting legislation to control policymaking in that country. Ramseyer and Rosenbluth do not view the role of Japanese bureaucrats in policymaking as evidence of the administrative state, but argue instead that the governing Liberal Democratic Party (LDP) rationally delegates this authority and that it benefits from such delegation.

In so arguing, they identify a wide range of institutions that help the LDP members to solve problems of control. With respect to adverse selection problems, for example, they argue that the LDP leaders identify and work primarily with moles in the bureaucracy who want to become LDP politicians. For such bureaucrats who want to enter politics, satisfying current elected members of the LDP becomes extremely valuable. The LDP also forces civil servants to "post a bond" – that is, to accept below-market wages while working in the government in order to gain access to highly lucrative job opportunities that are controlled by LDP sympathizers outside of government. Finally, Ramseyer and Rosenbluth describe how the LDP sets up competitions across multiple agencies to ensure responsiveness to LDP wishes.

Ramseyer and Rosenbluth's analysis is, as we already mentioned, more explicit about the mechanisms of delegation and control than most other comparative studies. In general, these comparative studies share two striking features. First, most of the research is highly interpretive or descriptive, with little actual development of testable hypotheses and even less systematic empirical investigation. Not surprisingly, then, the literature is awash in competing claims about the ability of cabinet ministers to influence policymaking. Consider the case of Britain. As noted earlier in this chapter, considerable work claims that civil servants are in control of

[22] An important exception, albeit not one focusing on a specific country, is Franchino's (2000a, 2000b) exploration of delegation to the European Commission. For an alternative rational choice approach to legislature–agency relations, see Golden's (2000) recent analysis of corruption in Italy.

policymaking in Britain. But coexisting with this work are claims challenging this notion. Dowding (1995, 123), for example, cites an advisor to Prime Minister Harold Wilson on the indeterminacy of when and where important policy decisions are made:

> In our seamless web of government, it is never easy to identify the moment and place at which crucial decisions are taken, let alone who takes them. . . . [And] when it is so difficult to be certain when and where crucial decisions are taken, it makes it even more difficult to decide whether ministers or civil servants have the more powerful voice. (From Kellner and Crowther-Hunt 1980, 210)

More generally, scholars writing about Britain contend that there is a declining influence of civil servants in policymaking. Barker and Wilson (1997) use surveys of senior civil servants in an attempt to gauge the extent to which these bureaucrats will follow orders with which they disagree. They find that when confronted with what is believed to be a very bad policy idea that will hurt the department or the country, most senior civil servants will either comply or try to dissuade the minister. Only a very small minority will actually disobey the minister by going around him or her (by contacting other departments). Others have also noted a strong ability of ministers to control civil servants (e.g., Hennessy 1989; King 1994). Furthermore, Moe and Caldwell (1994) describe Britain (and other parliamentary systems) as places where civil service departments are "granted lots of discretion, built to do their jobs well, and coordinated within a system of democratic control" (193). One can only conclude, then, that scholars who see administrative control of policymaking in Britain are well balanced by those who see control by leaders of the majority party in the cabinet. This indeterminacy is not limited to Britain, of course. As noted, Ramseyer and Rosenbluth attack the notion of bureaucratic dominance in the case of Japan, and others have attacked this orthodoxy in the French case (e.g., Thiébault 1994; Rouban 1995; Clark 1998) and in the case of monetary and fiscal policy in New Zealand (Horn 1995).

A second striking feature of this review of instruments of control in parliamentary systems is the almost complete absence of discussion of legislation as an instrument for controlling bureaucrats. As discussed in the previous chapter, legislation is potentially the most definitive set of instructions that can be given to bureaucrats with respect to the actions they must take during policy implementation. We also have noted considerable variation in the level of detail found in statutes that deal with the same issue in parliamentary systems. Moreover, as we discuss in detail later, legislation plays a central role in the literature on delegation in the United States.

Yet the role of legislation in the delegation process is missing from most studies of parliamentary systems. And to the extent that it is present, it is perceived as at most tangential to policymaking processes. As Peters (1992, 289) notes, for example, many scholars who work in a sociological tradition emphasize that "policy is what actually happens, rather than a nominal program written on a piece of paper. Implementation and the actions of even the lowest echelons of public organizations define the substance of policy." Di Palma (1977) argues that legislation in Italy is typically fragmented, disaggregated, and noncontroversial, so that specific groups are targeted for positive benefits and the imposition of costs on specific groups is avoided. The most careful argument about legislation in the delegation process is offered by Moe and Caldwell (1994), who contend that in Westminster systems there is no need to adopt complex legislation. In sum, we are aware of no research that develops systematic arguments about the role of legislation in influencing bureaucratic actions in parliamentary systems. Instead, if it is discussed at all, it is typically regarded as vague and unconstraining.

U.S. Politics

Turning to the literature on American politics, we find that many of the institutional arrangements described in the parliamentary context also play a prominent role in a separation of powers context.[23] But the issue of political control over bureaucrats is framed quite differently. Unlike the parliamentary context, where parliaments are marginalized and interbranch conflict is peripheral, in studies of U.S. politics Congress is often the central focus, and competition for control between Congress and the president is a recurring theme.

The literature on Congress saw a new generation of research in the 1980s that began to question claims about the pervasiveness of an administrative state. Unlike the parliamentary literature, however, a strong theme in studies of Congress concerned the role of legislative language in

[23] Weingast and Moran (1983), for example, explicitly discuss appointments and budgets as tools that Congress can use to control agencies. Moe (1987) counters by arguing that these are essentially presidential, and not legislative, powers. On Senate responses to executive nominations, see McCarty and Razaghian (1999).

general – and of administrative procedures in particular – in addressing the types of principal–agent problems discussed earlier.

Two observations frame much of this recent literature. The first is that, as many scholars have noted (e.g., Moe and Wilson 1994), the president enjoys substantial opportunities to influence policy implementation. The executive agencies are constitutionally enshrined under the president's purview. The president has substantial powers to appoint the senior leadership of the executive agencies (McCarty and Razaghian 1999). And presidents can issue executive orders to instruct agencies on how to implement policy. This presidential influence over bureaucrats creates incentives for Congress to use the language of legislation to constrain the types of actions that bureaucrats take.

The second observation is that Congress often lacks the knowledge it needs to obtain desired policy outcomes (e.g., Fiorina 1982; McCubbins 1985). A central problem is technical expertise. Moe (1989), for example, argues that technical complexity overwhelms even the groups that legislation is intended to benefit. His argument is worth quoting at length:

> It is perhaps natural that, since a dominant group can have anything it wants, it would proceed by figuring out what types of behaviors are called for by what types of people under what types of conditions and by writing legislation spelling all this out in the minutest detail. If an administrative agency were necessary to perform services, process applications, or inspect business operations, the jobs of bureaucrats could be specified with such precision that they would have little choice but to do the group's bidding. For simple policy goals – requiring, say, little more than transfer payments – these strategies would be attractive. But they are quite unsuited to policy problems of any complexity. . . . The world is subject to unpredictable changes over time, and some will call for specific policy adjustments if the group's interests are to be pursued effectively. The group could attempt to specify all future contingencies in the current legislation and, through continuous monitoring and intervention, update it over time. But the knowledge requirements of a halfway decent job would prove enormously costly, cumbersome, and time-consuming. (270–271)[24]

[24] In this passage, Moe is writing about interest groups, which, in his account, play a dominant role in the politics of structural control. Legislators, he contends, act almost as conduits for the desires of interest groups, "owing to their almost paranoid concern for reelection. . . . Legislators therefore have strong incentives to do what groups want [and] cannot satisfy interest groups with empty position taking" (1989, 277). Furthermore, for a variety of reasons, "legislators tend not to invest in general policy control. Instead, they value 'particularized' control: they want to be able to intervene quickly, inexpensively, and in ad hoc ways to protect or advance the interests of particular clients in particular matters" (1989, 278).

In response to these two problems – executive control of agencies and uncertainty about policy and agency actions – what should Congress do? One common answer is negative: Congress often cannot effectively control implementation by specifying policy details in statutes. Instead, legislators can influence bureaucrats more effectively by including in legislation appropriate *structure and process* provisions that guide agency decision making. McCubbins and Schwartz (1984), for example, argue that although it may be difficult for legislators themselves to discover unwanted bureaucratic behavior, they can place agency decision-making procedures in legislation to ensure that interest groups supporting Congress will stay informed about bureaucratic decision making. This allows affected groups to sound "fire alarms" to their representatives in Congress when bureaucrats are pursuing policies that the groups do not like.

In their seminal articles, McCubbins, Noll, and Weingast (1987, 1989) further develop this reasoning. Their research has led to a complete reexamination of how legislators use statutes to control agencies, and of the role administrative procedures play in this regard. In their view, Congress can fill legislation with procedural instructions, the goal of which is to increase the likelihood that agencies will make the sorts of decisions the enacting coalition of Congress and the president would approve of. To do this, Congress designs procedural provisions that favor the interest groups that support the majority in Congress, thereby increasing the likelihood that future agency actions will conform to the desires of the current legislature. These procedures that stack the deck in favor of certain constituents also put agencies on autopilot, which means that agencies will continue to favor these enfranchised interest groups even in the absence of direct legislative intervention and even when new, unforeseen issues arise. Through such provisions, then, Congress can increase the likelihood of favorable outcomes from the bureaucracy in the future, thus ensuring, as Kiewiet and McCubbins (1991) have stressed, that delegation does not imply abdication.

Moe (1989, 1990a, 1990b) was also one of the first to recognize the role of administrative procedures in the design of legislative statutes. He argues that in addition to policy uncertainty, political actors are motivated by *political uncertainty* (i.e., uncertainty over whether they and their legislative allies will have political power in the future).[25] Politicians and the groups that support them may possess political power now, but they do not know

[25] Horn and Shepsle (1989) and Horn (1995) refer to a similar concept as *legislative drift*.

who will control policymaking in the future. Politicians therefore have incentives to include in legislation procedural encumbrances that will make it very difficult for other groups to influence future agency behavior. Moe argues that the use of constraining procedures represents an effective tool for limiting the influence of other groups in the future because the fragmented nature of the American political system makes it difficult for future legislative majorities to undo past policies. Unlike scholars such as McCubbins, Kiewiet, Noll, and Weingast, however, he concludes that rather than ensuring that agencies will act on behalf of congressional majorities, legislative procedures result in generally ineffective and inefficient bureaucratic decision-making processes.

In making these arguments, scholars identify a wide variety of legislative procedures. Congress, for example, enfranchises favored constituents by requiring the agency to consult certain groups during rulemaking processes. This will make the agency more dependent on the information that comes from these favored constituencies. Similarly, Congress can require the use of reporting requirements, or notice and comment procedures, which force agencies to move more slowly, present interest groups and legislators with notification of the sorts of actions that agencies are planning to take, and give groups and legislators an opportunity to influence the agency while it is making policy.[26] Other procedures include sunset provisions (which terminate agency authority at a fixed moment in the future), exemptions of particular groups from agency control, or the creation of specific processes for appealing agency decisions. Depending on which study one reads, these types of legislative procedures, some of which are found in policy statutes and some of which are found in the Administrative Procedures Act, either enable legislative coalitions to maintain substantial control over policymaking or ensure that agency decision making is unresponsive and ineffective. From either perspective, however, scholars seem to agree that the use of procedural rather than policy details represents the most important way in which congressional majorities use legislation to influence bureaucratic autonomy.

These studies offered a fundamental reinterpretation of the role of agency procedures. Other scholars had, of course, realized that structures are not neutral, but rather have important policy consequences (e.g.,

[26] See also Lupia and McCubbins (1994, 1998), who argue that the use of administrative procedures can raise the cost for bureaucrats of changing policy and can increase the amount of information Congress receives about the agency's activities.

Polenberg 1966; Seidman and Gilmour 1986, 15). Yet it was the scholars discussed previously, along with others, such as Ferejohn (1987), Horn and Shepsle (1989), and Horn (1995), who challenged the prevailing view in administrative law, which held that such procedural provisions were important primarily because they enhanced normatively appealing values like fairness and due process. These interpretive studies presented procedural provisions in an entirely different light, and connected them squarely to issues of strategic delegation.

Like the studies in the parliamentary context, these early applications of principal–agent theory to the study of U.S. politics did not always have clear, testable implications. Some scholars argue that the McCubbins, Noll, and Weingast theory is too general and, as a result, too hard to test or refute (e.g., Robinson 1989). Others point out the need for clearer distinctions between structures and procedures (e.g., Macey 1992a). And still others contend that these interpretive studies need to do more to specify the conditions under which the structure and process hypothesis will operate (e.g., Arnold 1987; Hill and Brazier 1991; Mashaw 1997).[27] Thus, although this first generation of research on how legislative language is used by Congress to affect agencies provided a novel and insightful interpretation of why U.S. legislation takes the form that it does, it did not lend itself easily to empirical testing because it did not predict clear variation in the use of procedural instruments.

Not surprisingly, then, direct tests of these arguments have been difficult to operationalize and, at least until recently, relatively rare. Some of these empirical studies have not supported the interpretive studies (e.g., Hamilton and Schroeder 1994; Balla 1998; Spence 1999b), while others have provided only mixed support (e.g., Spence 1999a; Balla and Wright 2001).[28] While these empirical studies have been innovative, they

[27] More specifically, Hill and Brazier (1991) maintain that ex ante controls operate effectively only when (a) the enacting coalition provides the agency with clear guidance (i.e., specific legislative directives); (b) the procedural provisions maintain agreements reached by the coalition; and (c) courts are committed to preserving the designs chosen by the enacting coalition.

[28] Olson (1995) finds support for the procedural control hypothesis. Spence (1999b) provides an especially subtle and thoughtful analysis in which he finds evidence for the importance of structural controls and *specific* procedural controls – in effect, those that increase the costs of making particular decisions – but not for *general* procedural controls. Volden (2002b) finds support for a number of hypotheses that are consistent with the structural and procedural control arguments. Case studies also have supported aspects of the procedural control hypothesis (e.g., McCubbins, Noll, and Weingast 1989; Bawn 1995; Horn 1995; Shipan 1998).

encounter several difficulties right off the bat. First, as already mentioned, many of the interpretive studies are very difficult to pin down and do not have directly testable hypotheses. Thus, these empirical studies need to infer testable hypotheses from the theoretical studies. Second, the theories focus on whether or not control exists. This is an important question, of course, but the theories are usually posed starkly – control exists or it doesn't – whereas in reality, the answer to whether administrative procedures constrain bureaucrats is somewhere in the gray area. To test whether or not control exists, empirical studies need to make all sorts of potentially questionable assumptions about who procedures are supposed to benefit, when the benefits should occur, and so on.

But unlike the studies in the parliamentary context, this first generation of interpretive studies spurred further theoretical development concerning the relationship between legislators and agencies. In particular, it led to theories that identify the specific conditions under which legislatures will attempt to engage in various types of activities. The choice of institutions – of legislative procedures – thus becomes a function of the broader political context. Epstein and O'Halloran (1994, 1999), for example, develop rigorous formal models of Congress that suggest that statutes that constrain agencies will be most important during divided government, when conflict between Congress and the executive is heightened.[29]

Other studies have argued that the substantive topic of a statute influences delegation strategies, with different possibilities presenting themselves when policies must be made on issues that are technically complex (making it more difficult to write detailed statutes), on issues that are highly distributive (and thus encourage credit-claiming through detailed statutes), or on issues that are politically treacherous (and thus invite blame avoidance tactics that delegate to bureaucrats). Bawn (1995), for example, argues that the delegation strategy that a legislature pursues is a function of the issue's complexity. More specifically, the degree of an agency's independence on a particular policy issue reflects the legislature's willingness to trade uncertainty about policy consequences for uncertainty about agency behavior. Thus, efforts to use statutes to control agencies are, in part, a function of the technical complexity of the policy that the agency addresses. Similarly, Epstein and O'Halloran (1994) show that an agency

[29] See also McCubbins (1985); McCubbins and Page (1987); Lupia and McCubbins (1994, 1998); O'Halloran (1994); Bawn (1995); Martin (1997); and Volden (2002a).

will receive less discretion from a legislature when the amount of uncertainty surrounding a policy is low.

Scholars also have recognized the role played by other institutions in controlling agency policymaking. Whether a legislator prefers to implement statutory controls (i.e., ex ante controls) by writing policy or procedural details into legislation, or prefers instead to rely on traditional oversight (ex post controls), depends in part on the legislator's institutional position – namely, whether he or she is on the relevant oversight committee (Bawn 1997). In another vein, legislators have the ability to choose between writing specific statutes and delegating; but when delegating, they have the option to include a legislative veto as part of the statutory delegation (Martin 1997). At the state level, the line-item veto is a mechanism that governors can use to influence policy outcomes (de Figueiredo 1997). Finally, the courts can play a key role in making sure that agencies choose policies that are consonant with the preferences of legislators (Mashaw 1997; Shipan 1997, 2000; but see Hill and Brazier 1991; Macey 1992b).

The development of systematic theories has made possible systematic empirical tests regarding the types of strategies used for controlling bureaucrats. Bawn (1997), for example, shows that members of congressional committees prefer to use ex post oversight, while members of Congress who do not serve on congressional committees prefer to enact legislation with ex ante restrictions on the behavior of the agency (although Balla 2000 finds that committee membership has no effect on the use of one specific ex ante tool, congressional review). Drotning (1993) and Drotning and Rothenberg (1999) provide evidence that language in various sections of the 1990 Clean Air Act Amendments is affected by technical and political aspects of the specific policy issues at stake. And Volden (2002b) shows why legislatures delegate advisory and policymaking authority to Aid to Families with Dependent Children (AFDC) agencies.

The most impressive empirical account to date has been provided by Epstein and O'Halloran (1999) in their book *Delegating Powers* (see also Epstein and O'Halloran 1996). Drawing on *Congressional Quarterly* summaries of important congressional acts over the post–World War II period, they measure the amount of discretion that statutes give to agencies by coding, for each section of a bill, whether some form of delegation occurs, as well as the number of procedural constraints placed on agencies. They then demonstrate that, consistent with their theory, the amount of discretion varies systematically with the presence of divided government and the technical complexity of the issue.

Biases in Theories of Delegation

These studies of American politics differ from parliamentary studies in several key respects. First, the two literatures focus on different institutional arenas as the locus of efforts by politicians to constrain bureaucrats. In parliamentary systems, the executive arena is central. There is no separation of executive and legislative power, and parties are relatively disciplined, which implies little space for interbranch conflict. Thus, cabinet ministers are central to the exercise of political control because they draft legislation and regulations, and they head the departments that implement policy. In U.S. politics, the legislative arena is central. There is a clear separation of powers, and since the president has substantial influence on executive agencies, scholars have paid a great deal of attention to the strategies of Congress for controlling these agencies.

Second, the two literatures emphasize different instruments. In parliamentary systems, virtually no attention is given to the role of legislation. Most research focuses instead on appointment powers, with less attention given to budgets, monitoring, and departmental reorganizations. Recent studies of U.S. politics, by contrast, pay a great deal of attention to the role that statutes play in allowing Congress to control bureaucrats. Moreover, they focus on a specific aspect of statutes: the administrative procedures that are intended to govern agency decision processes.

Finally, studies of U.S. politics have achieved a higher level of theoretical and empirical rigor. It is difficult to pinpoint theoretical arguments with clear and testable implications in the parliamentary literature, and systematic empirical research is almost nonexistent. By contrast, the literature on the U.S. Congress has seen the development of clear and testable theories, as well as an impressive and growing array of empirical research. Given the greater degree of systematic analysis of Congress, our general understanding of how politicians attempt to influence bureaucratic behavior has been influenced considerably by studies of this specific political system.

Though the questions and answers posed in the literature on Congress are certainly helpful, when this literature is viewed from a broader comparative perspective, two important issues emerge. The first issue concerns the applicability of arguments in this literature to other settings. Perhaps the central theme in the literature on Congress, for example, is that divergence in the policy goals of Congress and the bureaucracy will cause Congress to write statutes that grant agencies less discretion. In the U.S. case, this policy divergence is much more likely to occur during divided government due to the president's influence on the policy goals and actions of bureaucrats. A simple empirical question that arises is whether this same relationship would be found in other presidential systems, such as the U.S. states. A conceptual question arises as well: How could policy divergence between politicians and bureaucrats be operationalized in parliamentary systems, where cabinet government is the rule? And do we find an empirical relationship between such divergence and the design of legislative statutes, which are virtually ignored in research on parliamentary systems?

The second issue, of greater concern to us, is the theoretical bias that can occur when we develop theories within a fixed institutional context, such as the U.S. Congress. Theories of delegation in the United States have focused primarily on factors that vary within the United States, and in particular on electoral outcomes and issue characteristics. Such explanations, however rich and compelling they might be, provide no insights into how the specific political system of the U.S. federal government affects delegation because this system is obviously set and unchanging. We cannot know, for example, how the existence of an executive veto affects the design of legislation because this veto is an institutional constant in the study of the U.S. Congress. There exists a bias, then, in our theories of delegation, one that emphasizes explanatory factors that vary within polities – and particularly within the U.S. Congress – at the expense of explanatory factors that vary across polities.

We can see the potential for bias when we consider the role of technical complexity in existing research. Recall that in the literature on Congress, as the policy issue becomes more technically complex, delegation to bureaucrats becomes more attractive. But perhaps the extent to which technical complexity affects delegation strategies depends on the capacity of the legislators to deal with complex issues. Even in the U.S. Congress, which is an extremely professionalized legislature, there is a relationship between technical complexity and delegation. In other contexts, such as the U.S. states or other countries, legislatures often are less professionalized and as a result are probably less able to deal with technical issues. Does this variance affect legislative strategies? If so, leaving this factor out of our explanations might mislead us in our understanding of other variables.

Similarly, many scholars have emphasized that mechanisms other than statutes exist for controlling bureaucrats, including the courts, appointments, budgets, regulations and decrees, and reorganizations, among others. But the nature of these alternative mechanisms varies from polity to polity. How does the nature of such alternative mechanisms affect the strategies politicians adopt in efforts to shape bureaucratic autonomy in policymaking? We cannot address this question theoretically or empirically without a comparative focus.

We believe it will be valuable to redress these biases. This process has already begun to some extent in recent studies of delegation across the U.S. states. Volden (2002b), for example, investigates the factors that influence the states' design of welfare programs. Potoski (1999, 2000) examines the institutional mechanisms that states use to influence environmental policymaking. De Figueiredo (1997) identifies political factors that predict whether or not a state will allow a line-item veto. And for more than a decade, Teske (e.g., 1990, 2001) has provided thoughtful analyses of how institutional factors that vary across states have affected state-level regulation in a variety of areas. In cross-national research, Carey and Shugart (1998a, 1998b) argue that the delegation of decree authority to executives is most likely to occur when a strong veto exists and the judiciary is independent of the executive. Bernhard (1998) shows that the incentive of legislative majorities to delegate fiscal policymaking to independent central banks is influenced by the committee structure in the legislature.[30]

None of this research, however, focuses on the central role of statutes in policymaking processes. Alone among comparative researchers, Moe and Caldwell (1994) discuss how the design of statutes relates to the broader institutional context. Their general argument is that parliamentary statutes should be less detailed and should impose less cumbersome procedures than statutes in presidential systems, primarily because in parliamentary systems it is much easier for tomorrow's majority to undo today's policy. This claim, however, is not tested empirically, and it ignores the enormous variation that occurs across presidential and parliamentary systems. We know virtually nothing about how the political and institutional context affects the way in which politicians design statutes to constrain bureaucratic autonomy.

Conclusion

At least since the time of Max Weber's classic studies, scholars have voiced concerns about the compatibility of modern bureaucracy with democracy.

[30] Other examples of research in this spirit include Boylan (2000) and Horn (1995).

The central issue has been whether politicians can effectively harness bureaucrats' knowledge and expertise, or whether this very knowledge and expertise allow bureaucrats to usurp the rightful role of politicians in policymaking. If the latter condition prevails, then the possibility for voters to hold politicians accountable for policy outcomes in democratic systems is sharply diminished.

For many years, concerns have been raised that bureaucrats indeed play a disproportionately prominent role in policymaking. Unfortunately, despite the sea of ink spilled on this issue, notions of administrative dominance are conceptually muddled, little evidence exists that would allow us to understand the extent of such dominance, and the practical limitations inherent in providing such evidence are severe. Thus, competing claims remain rampant, with an enormous literature on the administrative state juxtaposed with a substantial literature arguing that politicians do in fact create institutional arrangements that permit effective control of bureaucrats.

But recent developments, particularly in the American politics literature, have fruitfully reoriented scholarly inquiry away from the specific question of whether political constraints on bureaucratic behavior are adequate and toward the theoretical question of how politicians use institutional arrangements to influence the behavior of bureaucrats. These studies have helped us to understand that appointment powers, budget authority, monitoring mechanisms, and, in the United States, the design of legislation itself provide political actors with considerable opportunities to treat bureaucrats as allies rather than as foes in the policymaking process.

In the chapters that follow, we attempt to build on these recent advances in several respects. First, and most importantly, existing institutional theories have been developed primarily in the political and institutional context of single countries (usually the United States). They therefore cannot tell us how features that do not vary within that context affect the way that legislation is used to constrain policy implementation. We therefore want to build our theoretical understanding of how legislation is used by developing a comparative theory – one in which the broad features of the political environment shape strategic incentives. This will help us to understand similarities and differences that exist in policymaking processes across political systems.

Second, we will focus empirically on the nature and role of legislation across a variety of political systems. In existing research on the U.S. Congress, scholars have focused on how structure and process (i.e., administrative procedures) can be used to constrain bureaucrats. In parliamentary systems, scholars have essentially ignored the role of legislation. By looking carefully at the nature of legislation in the U.S. states and in parliamentary systems, we will be able not only to evaluate the applicability of structure and process arguments outside of the U.S. Congress but also, more importantly, to examine other ways in which legislation can be used to influence policy implementation.

Third, as we have noted, the overwhelming emphasis in previous research has been on the ability of politicians to constrain bureaucrats. This will be only an indirect focus of our analysis. As we noted in Chapter 1, we feel that this previous emphasis has obscured the influence of delegation decisions on other aspects of the democratic process. In what follows, we develop and test an explicit formal model of how politicians design legislation. In so doing, we can gain leverage on these broader issues that we believe are inextricably linked to incentives that exist in designing legislative statutes. We return to a more careful discussion of these substantive issues in the concluding chapter of this book.

3

Statutes as Blueprints for Policymaking

When legislative statutes are specific, they make it more difficult for other political actors, especially bureaucrats, to enact policies that differ from those that legislative majorities prefer. Thus, specific statutes allow legislative majorities to limit the policymaking discretion of other political actors, while vague statutes give a larger policymaking role to these other actors. Our main objective in this book is to understand how the political context affects the decision to use statutes to limit agency discretion. In order to achieve this objective, however, we first must carefully investigate the substantive content of statutes themselves in order to gain insights into how they are used to affect discretion during policymaking. Remarkably, since to our knowledge no such investigation has ever been undertaken, we do not really know whether or in what ways statutes differ across parliamentary systems or across separation of powers systems.

We view statutes as blueprints for policies to be constructed. The blueprints may contain instructions for bureaucrats, cabinet ministers, judges, or other actors who create, implement, and enforce policy. There are many different types of blueprints that legislators can adopt. Language can be very vague or specific. It can describe problems or their solutions. It can mandate actions or prohibit them. It can delve into the specifics of a policy itself or focus on the procedures that external actors must follow in making the policy. The broad goal of this chapter is to analyze systematically this dizzying array of possibilities, and to do so across a broad range of political systems. By analyzing a vast amount of legislation across states and countries, we examine the ways in which legislation creates policy and constrains the actions of other actors who are involved in the policy process.

This broader goal subsumes three more specific goals. First, we want to demonstrate that statutes often differ across political systems that are addressing essentially the same issue. In the previous chapter, we noted that scholars of the U.S. Congress often argue that the nature of a policy issue itself will affect the type of statute that is adopted. But if we hold the issue constant, do we still find variation across political systems? The U.S. states, for example, constitute a number of different political systems. Some have divided government, while others have unified government; some have highly professionalized legislatures or alternative mechanisms for control, while others do not. Across these different state-level systems, do we find that legislation addressing the same issue is similar with respect to how much autonomy is delegated to bureaucrats? Likewise, are there differences in the design of legislation that focuses on the same issue across parliamentary systems?

Second, we want to explore the role of policy instructions, which spell out the contours of policy itself, and procedural instructions, which describe the decision-making process that must be followed during agency policymaking and implementation. As we noted in the previous chapter, the research on Congress has emphasized the difficulties associated with specifying precise policy and has underlined the role of procedures in allowing Congress to influence bureaucratic behavior. We also noted, however, that the effectiveness of procedures is debatable and that the evidence of their actual impact on policy outcomes or bureaucratic behavior is mixed. We therefore want to understand the relative role of policy and procedure across diverse political settings. How carefully or precisely are policies and procedures defined in statutes? What is the relative role of each in different types of political settings?

Third, and most importantly, we argue for a simple measure of discretion in legislation. That measure is the length of legislation. We argue that with two statutes that address the same issue, the longer one typically places greater limits on the actions of other actors, because it is filled with policy-specific details that constrain what these other actors can do. Thus, we argue that the length of legislation provides a good proxy for the legislative majority's efforts to control policy implementation. This conclusion is in many ways the most important point of this chapter. In later empirical chapters our statistical tests will control for the nature of policy issues and use the length of legislation to measure discretion in our empirical tests; thus, it is imperative that we establish it as an appropriate measure.

Our approach in this chapter is primarily quantitative, although in this chapter and in Chapters 5 and 7 we also present qualitative evidence. We analyze a large number of statutes, providing quantitative measures of the actual language that they use to limit discretion. In so doing, we are able to address each of the three specific goals just described and to describe noteworthy differences that exist between the U.S. state statutes and the parliamentary ones.

The U.S. States: Policy and Procedure in Statutes

To examine how different U.S. states design statutes on the same general policy issue, we focus on Medicaid, the joint federal-state program that provides coverage for needy populations. The number of people enrolled in Medicaid grew dramatically in the early 1990s, and as a result of this growth and other factors (e.g., the increased costs of new developments in medical technology), the amount of money the states were spending to cover these people was increasing at an extraordinary rate (Rom 1999).[1] Because states have a great deal of discretion, as well as fiscal responsibility, for Medicaid, all state legislatures needed to address this situation, which was rapidly turning into a crisis.

All states therefore faced a similar problem (i.e., increased costs) and pursued a similar goal (i.e., reducing costs). While states used a variety of approaches to curb Medicaid costs, a significant number of them did so by enacting some form of managed care for Medicaid patients. That is, many states began to move Medicaid patients from traditional insurance, known as *fee-for-service* insurance, to managed care systems and health maintenance organizations (HMOs). In the private sector, HMOs and managed care plans had helped to cut costs because, unlike traditional fee-for-service programs, these plans provided doctors and patients with incentives to emphasize wellness and limit expensive tests and the use of expensive technology. Beginning in the late 1980s and especially in the 1990s, state policymakers hoped to harness the same sorts of incentives to reduce costs in the public sector.

Those states that created Medicaid managed care (MMC) programs took very different approaches to creating these programs, and the role of formal statutes varied considerably across the states. As the Texas and Florida examples from Chapter 1 suggest, some states spelled out in minute detail exactly how MMC should work, while other states, like

[1] We provide details regarding these increases in Chapter 6.

Alaska, provided some specifics but also gave state departments of health a fair amount of discretion. Still other states, such as Idaho, gave enormous autonomy to agency policymakers.

To further understand such qualitative differences, we systematically analyze the content of MMC legislation. Our objective is to code the content of these statutes in a variety of ways in order to understand how legislative majorities use statutes to either constrain or allow for discretion during policy implementation. To identify the relevant statutes, we first conducted a search of all state laws using Lexis's Advanced Legislative Service. We searched for general terms and phrases, such as "Medicaid managed care," and also for state-specific names of MMC programs (e.g., MediPass, MC+). We then contacted a range of policymakers, including bureaucrats, staff, and legislators from the various states and, in phone interviews, asked them to identify statutes they considered most significant regarding the MMC system in their state. We used this information to determine which bills were key in the establishment or maintenance of each state's MMC system. We included all the key MMC bills from those states where they were available, as well as a sample of other statutes, including at least one from each state that had passed such a law. In the end, we coded a sample of 67 MMC laws drawn from 35 states, dating from 1989 to 1998. Key bills comprise a majority of our sample.

We are particularly interested in understanding the level of policy precision in the language of statutes, as well as the roles of both policy and procedural instructions. As noted in Chapter 2, scholars of the U.S. Congress have focused heavily on the role of procedures in allowing Congress to control policy implementation processes, and for good reason – previous studies had all but ignored the political importance of such procedures. But acknowledging the importance of procedures does not have to come at the expense of realizing the significance of policy instructions, and there are several reasons to suspect that policy language may have a more significant impact than the specification of procedures on the outcomes of policy implementation. One reason is that procedures are "cheap" and easy to include in legislation. It is not difficult to demand a report or a particular form of consultation, and much procedural language along these lines is so standard that it is included in general statutes that define administrative procedures. It also seems to us that procedural details are less constraining on bureaucrats than policy details. A bureaucrat can comply with the need to write a report or to consult particular groups or to conclude his or her work in a specified time period without being sharply constrained with respect to the policy actually implemented. But if the statute says to do X, the bureaucrat cannot do Y (at least without some risk). In light of these two simple observations, it is not surprising that efforts to uncover an explicit link between procedures and outcomes have produced mixed results.

Policy Details in Statutes

As we saw in Chapter 1, states can use legislation to stipulate explicit features of MMC programs. The Texas legislature, for example, told the bureaucrats who were responsible for setting up the MMC program to increase eligibility for children, to make sure to design programs for children with special health needs, and to favor providers who would continue to provide health care to Medicaid clients even after these clients had left the Medicaid program. Similarly, the Florida legislature provided the agency with some very specific instructions about which clients were required to enroll in MMC and which ones were exempt from the requirement.

We call such stipulations *policy instructions*. Since the observation that legislation can spell out specific policies may seem painfully obvious, it is useful to recall the discussion and literature review in Chapter 2. On the one hand, most studies of bureaucratic control have either explicitly or implicitly downplayed the possibility of using legislation to micromanage which policies are chosen, focusing instead either on the central role of procedural instructions or on the symbolic and credit-claiming uses of legislation. On the other hand, to our knowledge, there exist no studies that have systematically analyzed a wide range of actual legislation for the purposes of describing the extent to which specific policy instructions are used to constrain other actors. We therefore feel it is vital to examine the relative importance of policy-specific instructions in our legislation.

Carefully coding the substantive policy categories provides several significant benefits. First, it allows us to examine the extent to which statutes use very general, nonconstraining language as opposed to more policy-specific language. Second, it allows us to see whether there are systematic relationships between the type of issue and the nature of legislative language. Third, we can see if particular procedures tend to go with specific types of policies.

To examine these issues, we have coded the policy specificity of the 165,000 words in our MMC statutes according to 12 policy categories.[2] For each bill, we proceeded as follows. First, we eliminated all sections of the bill that pertained to matters other than MMC. Next, we divided each bill into sections according to its policy content. And finally, we determined the length of each section (i.e., the number of words contained in the section) and assigned it to one of the policy categories. Most blocks of text were assigned to a single policy category, but in approximately 5% of cases, blocks were assigned to more than one category.

The first policy category, *general policy language*, includes general policy statements and stipulations that place minimal constraints on agency actions. Such language, for example, may discuss the state's broad-based need for a MMC program. These sections also discuss goals for the program, such as making health care more widely available, or reducing costs while not limiting access to medical care. General policy language is related to the overall MMC program rather than to specific policy sub-issues (as defined in the other 11 categories).

The other 11 coding categories consist of specific policy issues that arise in connection with the creation of MMC programs. Language falling into any of these categories is more specific about the parameters of policy than is language in the "General" category, though there of course exists variation in how precisely policy is defined, even within the specific policy categories. We grouped these 11 policy categories into 3 broader umbrella categories, depending on whether the policies pertained most directly to clients or providers or were about other miscellaneous considerations.

Client Categories

Three types of policy instructions focus on clients, or patients, in the MMC system. First, some client-related policy instructions deal with *defining participants*. This type of language defines the client groups that are eligible to participate in the program – in other words, who can (or must) participate in managed care. The instructions in this category do not deal with the health status of prospective clients, as this language is coded in the following category. The groups included under the instructions on

[2] Appendix B provides examples of language coded in each category in order to illustrate the many ways in which legislatures use statutes to set specific policy parameters.

defining participants are based on geographic location or demographic factors such as age and income. Second, the *nature of coverage* category includes language that defines the type of care that must (or must not) be provided, such as those medical procedures and tests that the plan will or will not pay for. Coverage instructions also include provisions for the types of clients that providers must cover (based on their health status), as well as language dealing with co-payments (what proportion of expenses the state will pay for covered services). Third, *client participation* language defines how clients interact with the system. These sections essentially set out the rules of the game for the client and can include provisions about enrollment and disenrollment, marketing, pace of enrollment, and automatic assignment of clients to primary care physicians. Also included in this category are provisions that allow clients to appeal decisions made by the medical care organization (MCO). Provisions for client education are another common component of client participation policy instructions.

Provider Categories

A good deal of the language in MMC statutes concerns these sorts of issues relating to clients and their interaction with the Medicaid system. An even greater number of provisions in legislation, however, deal with the other half of the client–provider relationship. We identify four categories related to the providers of health care. First, the *selection of providers* is important and can be highly controversial. The language in this category includes the criteria that the state will use to determine which MCOs and primary care physicians will be allowed to participate in the state's MMC program. This category includes the legislature's discussion of conditions that health plans or providers must meet in order to be eligible to participate. It also includes language regarding the process of awarding contracts to MCOs, whether through bidding or some other method. This category does not, however, include language about how clients choose a primary care physician, as those sections are accounted for in the client participation category discussed above.

Second, a variety of instructions come under the category of *provider responsibilities and rights.* Instructions in this category can include stipulations that require providers to furnish certain types of utilization reviews (i.e., processes for approving care), assure the quality of the health care provided by the plan, or develop grievance procedures for their clients. One of the most common provider responsibilities, for example, is the requirement to report specific data to the agency. Generally, these stipulations lay out obligations that providers must accept in order to participate in the MMC program. Third, the *paying providers* category includes instructions about paying both the individual primary-care providers and the MCO/HMO plan as a whole. Most MMC programs utilize what are known as capitation rates to pay providers for medical services. This term refers to the rates, set by the state, which impose a limit on how much the state will pay the provider per patient.[3] The last category to deal specifically with providers involves *other providers*, which includes language that defines roles for non-MCO/HMO providers. Instructions regarding other providers are germane when, for example, a client requires services that are not offered within the MCO/HMO network. We include these sorts of instructions about how other providers can be accessed in this category.

Miscellaneous Categories

A number of other policy issues that arise do not fall neatly into either the client or the provider group but are important nonetheless. Furthermore, these cannot be considered "General," as they deal with specific policy issues. These miscellaneous categories address definitions, quality assurance, financial considerations, and privatization.

Just as we saw in Chapter 1 with the example of sexual discrimination in parliamentary democracies, many MMC statutes contain policy instructions that deal with *definitions* of terms. Definitions sometimes are short and vague, allowing bureaucrats to determine the meanings of significant terms. Often, however, they are long, precise, and explicit, so that terms mentioned throughout the bill are unambiguous. In addition, definitions may refer to tangible elements, such as the people who enroll in the managed care program, or to concepts that are essential to the managed care program (such as when clients face limitations on the choice of health care providers). Because these definitions can affect which clients or providers get to participate, which types of medical care are covered, or which sorts of activities are to be funded, they carry major substantive import.

[3] The use of capitation is central to managed care plans. Unlike tradition fee-for-service plans, under which doctors are reimbursed at certain rates for all patient visits and tests (and thus have an incentive to schedule as many visits and order as many tests as possible), capitation provides each doctor with a set amount of money for each patient, regardless of the number of visits and tests (thus producing the incentive to minimize such activities).

Other policy instructions concern *quality assurance*. Quality assurance policy instructions describe the processes that the state will use in order to assess the quality of the MMC program. Under the category of provider responsibilities and rights, we included language that instructed the MCO/HMO to conduct self-tests to ensure the quality of their managed care programs. But the language included in the quality assurance category delineates what the state itself will do, independent of the MCO/HMO, to assure that quality.

Legislation is also used to spell out *financial* considerations. Financial policy instructions give specific instructions with respect to financial goals, targets, and utilization of cost savings. The financial language we coded does not include line-item spending instructions found in appropriation bills, but rather includes provisions set down by the legislature discussing what savings should be achieved through the MMC program and how those savings should be used.

The final policy instruction category deals with *privatization* of portions of the managed care system. This type of policy instruction provides for the delegation of some of the responsibilities of the bureaucratic agency to private concerns. Privatization provisions were rare in our sample.

Analyzing the Data

Several insights emerge from the coding of the legislation into the various policy categories. First, it is useful to distinguish between general policy language, which is the first category, and the more specific language contained in other categories. As noted in Chapter 2, some scholars maintain that legislatures will write general, rather than precise, statutory language because of the problems that are assumed to be associated with writing policy details. The following section from a Washington State statute provides a good illustration of how this sort of general language can be used to provide a rationale for the use of managed care in Medicaid rather than to specify explicit policy details about MMC programs:

(1) The legislature finds that:
(a) A significant percentage of the population of this state does not have reasonably available insurance or other coverage of the costs of necessary basic health care services;
(b) This lack of basic health care coverage is detrimental to the health of the individuals lacking coverage and to the public welfare, and results in substantial expenditures for emergency and remedial health care, often at the expense

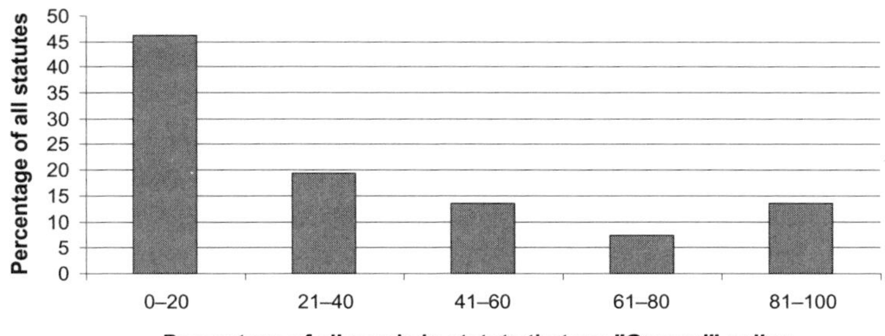

Figure 3.1 The incidence of "General" policy language in statutes

> of health care providers, health care facilities, and all purchasers of health care, including the state; and
> (c) The use of managed health care systems has significant potential to reduce the growth of health care costs incurred by the people of this state generally, and by low-income pregnant women, and at-risk children and adolescents who need greater access to managed health care.

Of course, almost all statutes include general policy language, as legislators sketch the general goals and objectives underlying legislation. But we can see in Figure 3.1 that the relative role of this legislation is small in most statutes. Only 13.4% of the 67 statutes have more than 80% of their words coded as "General," and only 7.5% have between 61% and 80% of their words coded as "General." In contrast, nearly half (46%) of the statutes have less than 20% of their total words coded as "General." Thus, although legislators sometimes write laws that use quite general policy language that places few constraints on implementation, in our data they are much more likely to focus their attention on describing specific aspects of policy.

Table 3.1, which breaks the data down by specific issue category, provides further insight into the different types of policy language included in statutes. The middle column presents the total number of words in our dataset assigned to each category.[4] As in Figure 3.1, we see that policy-specific statutory language is much more prevalent than general language. Only 21% of all codings are in the "General" category, with the rest falling into one of the policy-specific categories. It is also clear that the state

[4] Some double counting occurs because in some cases it was impossible to create text blocks that focus on a single policy category. Thus, the total number of words is less than the sum of the words in all the categories.

Table 3.1. *Policy Language in Medicaid Managed Care (MMC) Legislation*

Specific Category	Total Number of Words in All Statutes	Mean No. of Words/Statute (Std. Dev.)
General Policy Language	**36,485**	**545 (699)**
Client Issues	**49,085**	**717 (1,148)**
Defining participants	6,101	91 (171)
Nature of coverage	25,515	381 (657)
Client participation	17,469	261 (617)
Provider Issues	**58,302**	**852 (1,760)**
Selection of providers	12,698	190 (402)
Provider responsibilities and rights	29,848	445 (1,337)
Paying providers	13,738	205 (479)
Other providers	2,018	30 (122)
Miscellaneous	**32,463**	**485 (979)**
Definitions	12,470	186 (375)
Quality assurance	8,003	119 (288)
Financial	11,874	177 (675)
Privatization	116	2 (14)

legislators are able to write specific language on a wide range of policy issues, as many of the 11 narrow policy categories are the subject of substantial legislative activity.

The same basic story emerges from the rightmost column of Table 3.1, which provides averages across statutes. Again, we find a predominance of

Table 3.2. *Correlation Matrix of Three Main Policy Categories*

	Client Words	Provider Words	Miscellaneous Words
Client words	1.0		
Provider words	.79 (<.001)	1.0	
Miscellaneous words	.43 (<.001)	.45 (<.001)	1.0

Note: p-values are given in parentheses.

policy-specific language and a propensity of legislators to include specific language across a wide range of issues. But as we underlined in our earlier qualitative discussion, there is also considerable variation across the states with respect to how much detail is included across statutes in these different policy categories. For each policy category, the standard deviation in the number of words is much larger than the mean, which reminds us that on the same policy, some statutes provide considerably more policy-specific guidance than others.

Table 3.2 presents the correlations of word length across the main policy categories. We see that the number of words in one policy category is highly correlated with the number of words in another policy category. This suggests that when legislators decide to write policy details into statutes, they tend to do so across a variety of issues rather than selectively on specific issues. We are not, then, picking up issue-specific incentives to write policy details across these three broad categories.

The point thus far is clear: in the MMC statutes, language about specific policy topics is much more prevalent than very general policy language. The legislation contains a great deal of language that describes the policy that should be implemented, and it does so across a wide range of issue areas. This language is not merely general language that stresses "the importance of proper health care to the people of the great state of Minnesota" or proposes to "increase the effectiveness of managed care in the state." Rather, it is language that deals with specific issues having to do with clients, providers, and miscellaneous considerations. At the same time, there is considerable variation with respect to how much policy detail different statutes include on the same issue. This variation, however, tends to be greater across statutes than across issue areas within statutes. Thus, when legislators have a propensity to write policy details into statutes, they do so across a variety of issues. But it is not true that they undertake this effort on all statutes.

Procedural Instructions

A central theme of the literature on the U.S. Congress is that the incorporation of agency decision-making procedures into legislation is an important strategy that members of Congress use to control implementation. Procedures, recall, are nonpolicy instructions about how the decision making by executive agencies should proceed. By *nonpolicy*, we do not mean to imply that the procedures themselves have no impact on policy, but rather that the procedural language does not describe what policies should look like. Examples of such *procedural controls* include deadlines for program implementation, requirements for reports to the legislature, defining groups that must be considered in decision-making processes, and so on.

In MMC, procedural instructions would affect the manner in which agencies develop and implement programs. The legislation that we collected and read does show considerable variation with respect to the types of procedures that are created for agency decision making. Utah, Illinois, and Rhode Island, for example, all created special commissions to play a role in Medicaid policymaking, but they took quite different tacks with respect to how these commissions are composed. Utah's Senate Bill 158, for example, puts substantial appointment discretion in creating an advisory committee in the hands of the state health commissioner:

> (2) Immediately after the effective date of this section, the commissioner shall appoint a Health Benefit Plan Committee. The committee shall be composed of representatives of carriers, employers, employees, and health care providers and producers.
>
> (3) The committee shall serve as an advisory committee to the commissioner and shall recommend services to be covered, copays, deductibles, levels of coinsurance, annual out-of-pocket maximums, exclusions, and limitations for two or more designated health care plans to be marketed in the state.

Rhode Island's Senate Bill 980 (1993), on the other hand, takes much more care in delineating how an advisory committee will be composed, focusing on appointment powers in the legislature, party composition, and the role of specific state administrative agencies:

SECTION 4. A special advisory commission is hereby created consisting of nine (9) members; two (2) of whom shall be from the house of representatives, not more than one (1) of whom shall be from the same political party to be appointed by the speaker and two (2) of whom shall be from the senate, not more than one (1) from the same political party to be appointed by the majority leader; one (1) of whom shall be the director of the department of health, or his or her designee; one (1) of whom shall be the director of the department of human services, or his designee; one (1) of whom shall be a member of the governor's policy staff, to be appointed by the governor; one (1) of whom shall be the president of the RI Chapter, American Academy of Pediatrics; and one (1) of whom shall be the chairperson, Rhode Island Health Center Association. The purpose of the commission shall be to advise the department of health and the department of human services of the state of Rhode Island in the design and implementation of the RIte Track and RIte Start programs as established by this act.

And in Illinois, Senate Bill 776 creates a council that will focus specifically on the narrow issues of co-payments in the health programs. Like the Rhode Island law, it carefully distributes the power to appoint members of the Council, and it also defines several of the committee's decision-making procedures:

The Illinois Department shall establish a Medicaid co-payment council to assist in the development of co-payment policies for the medical assistance program. The Medicaid co-payment council shall also have jurisdiction to develop a program to provide financial or non-financial incentives to Medicaid recipients in order to encourage recipients to seek necessary health care. The council shall be chaired by the director of the Illinois department, and shall have 6 additional members. Two of the 6 additional members shall be appointed by the governor, and one each shall be appointed by the president of the senate, the minority leader of the senate, the speaker of the house of representatives, and the minority leader of the house of representatives. The council may be convened and make recommendations upon the appointment of a majority of its members. The council shall be appointed and convened no later than September 1, 1994 and shall report its recommendations to the director of the Illinois department and the general assembly no later than October 1, 1994. The chairperson of the council shall be allowed to vote only in the case of a tie vote among the appointed members of the council.

Thus, just as we find variation in the level of policy discretion found in statutes, we find variation in how carefully procedures are defined. In order to examine systematically the types of procedures that are written into legislation and to assess their importance, we coded procedural instructions in similar fashion to our coding of policy instructions. Based on our reading of the statutes and the previous literature, we identified 12 specific procedural categories that fall into 4 broader groups. Examples of language containing these sorts of controls can be found in Appendix C; here we present a brief description of each type of procedure.

The first category, ex ante procedural controls, affects the implementation process before final policy decisions are taken.[5] Some ex ante controls involve *information requirements*, such as language that specifies which groups must be considered or consulted when the agency makes decisions about the MMC program. A common example found in many statutes is the mandate that local health care providers and the public be allowed to have input at certain stages during the implementation of the managed care program. The second type of ex ante control is a legislative *proposal requirement*, under which an agency can take no action until it has gotten clearance from the legislature. The final type of ex ante control involves *study requirements*. Pilot programs, which are commonly designed to test the MMC program in certain areas before it is fully implemented statewide, are the most common form of study requirements.

The second category consists of ex post controls, which are activities that occur after an implementation decision has been taken. One important type of ex post control is a *reporting requirement*, which instructs an agency about what types of information must be reported to the legislature and when these reports must occur.[6] One of the most common examples of this type of instruction is a requirement for the managed care agency to report annually to the governor and the legislature on levels of enrollment and utilization in the program. Another type of ex post control involves the establishment of an *appeals process* for providers who are participating in the system and have grievances.[7] Of the different procedures we examined, this one perhaps comes closest to blurring the distinction between policy and procedure because language establishing appeals processes often has a strong policy component – for example, by stating the criteria that must be used to decide particular kinds of appeals.

[5] The controls in this category – especially those having to do with information requirements – are the sorts of procedures that McCubbins, Noll, and Weingast (1987) have in mind when they discuss the legislature's desire to mirror the environment, stack the deck, and put the agency on autopilot.

[6] The main difference between *proposal requirements* and *reporting requirements* is the timing of the interaction between the agency and the legislature. With reporting requirements, the agency can perform its duties, but afterward (i.e., ex post) it must report to the legislature.

[7] The appeals coded under this section are for providers only. Appeals for clients are included in the *client participation* category of the policy instructions.

Third, agent controls are those that affect which agents take certain actions. Legislation may give authority over agencies to either legislative or nonlegislative committees. In the MMC context, a legislative committee could have proposal powers, veto powers, or oversight responsibilities directly over the bureaucratic agency. Nonlegislative committees are often special task forces formed to monitor or make recommendations about the managed care program. Furthermore, the legislature can spell out *staffing requirements*, which specify or fund staffing within the agency. These instructions may include descriptions of the actual positions to be included in the MMC project or they may explain who has the power to appoint staff members. The final procedural instruction in this group involves the *creation of a new agency or department.* This type of procedural instruction delineates where a newly created MMC agency or special department is situated in the executive branch of the state government.

Fourth, there is a *general* procedural control category that does not fit well into the aforementioned categories but that is commonly found in legislation: routine boilerplate that places *time constraints* on implementation activity. Such procedures tell the bureaucratic agency in clear terms the amount of time it has to implement parts of the MMC program or how long it can operate without future action from the legislature (e.g., via sunset clauses).

How prevalent are procedural instructions in MMC legislation? Before answering this question, it is important to bear in mind that in these statutes, the procedural language and the policy language are often inextricably intertwined. Consider the following example from Massachusetts (1997, ch. 47):

> (c) Within said fund, the division shall establish a separate account for the insurance reimbursement program component of the MassHealth demonstration program established by section 9C of chapter 118E. This separate account shall consist of amounts transferred from the Uncompensated Care Trust Fund, any federal funds transferred from the Children's and Seniors' Health Care Assistance Fund established by section 2FF of chapter 29, and any funds as may be appropriated for deposit into this account. The division shall administer this account and disburse funds from this account for the purposes of said insurance reimbursement program component of said MassHealth program. Funds deposited in this account shall be kept separate and not be commingled with funds of the uncompensated care pool established pursuant to subsection (d). The comptroller is hereby authorized and directed to effect the transfers authorized by this subsection pursuant to a spending plan filed by the division of medical assistance with the secretary of administration and finance and the house and senate committees on ways and means.

This text block has a clear policy category – financial – and it also creates a reporting requirement, which is a procedural instruction. But the reporting requirement is intermingled with other very precise instructions about how the agency should treat funds for different categories of clients.

Another example of this intermingling occurs in Oklahoma's House Bill 1860 (1997):

> On or before July 1, 1998, a proposal for a Medicaid waiver to implement a managed care pilot program for participants with long-term care needs shall be developed and presented to the Joint Legislative Oversight Committee established in section 1010.7 of title 56 of the Oklahoma statutes. The pilot program shall provide a continuum of services for participants, including but not limited to, case management, supportive assistance in residential settings, homemaker services, home-delivered meals, adult day care, respite care, skilled nursing care, specialized medical equipment and supplies, and institutionalized long-term care. Payment for these services shall be on a capitated basis. The Joint Legislative Oversight Committee shall review the waiver application for the pilot program on or before December 1, 1998. In no instance shall the waiver application be presented to the Health Care Financing Administration prior to the review by the committee.

This text block provides policy details about the nature of medical coverage and the use of capitated payment systems in Oklahoma's managed care program, but the policy instructions are closely intertwined with a procedure that requires a report to a Joint Legislative Oversight Committee.

It is important to bear in mind that the intermingling of policy and procedure – like the level of policy details in statutes – varies across (and within) statutes. Earlier in this section, we saw that Illinois and Rhode Island each passed statutes that created special commissions. Both of these statutes included explicit instructions about the composition of these commissions. At the same time, however, they varied quite substantially with respect to how many policy details were specified in the language that created the commissions. The Illinois law went on to define a number of important policy constraints on the actions of the commission:

> The council shall be guided by the following principles as it considers recommendations to be developed to implement any approved waivers that the Illinois department must seek pursuant to this subsection:
>
> (1) Co-payments should not be used to deter access to adequate medical care.
> (2) Co-payments should not be used to reduce fraud.
> (3) Co-payment policies should be examined in consideration of other states' experience, and the ability of successful co-payment plans to control unnecessary or inappropriate utilization of services should be promoted.

> (4) All participants, both recipients and providers, in the medical assistance program have responsibilities to both the state and the program.
> (5) Co-payments are primarily a tool to educate the participants in the responsible use of health care resources.
> (6) Co-payments should not be used to penalize providers.
> (7) A successful medical program requires the elimination of improper utilization of medical resources.

The Utah law put similar specific policy constraints in place. In contrast, the Rhode Island statute, though detailed with respect to the composition of the committee, did nothing to narrow the policy scope of its mandate. There exists, then, considerable variation not only in how procedures are defined, but also in how various procedures are intertwined with policy mandates.

It is consequently very difficult in the MMC statutes to clearly and meaningfully separate procedural language from policy language. We therefore began by using policy content to delineate each text block. Then, once the policy category was identified and assigned, we coded whether the text block also included any procedural instructions. Just as some text blocks address more than one policy, some also have more than one procedure. We should note that this lumping together of policy and procedure is not only necessary from a coding perspective but also desirable from a conceptual one. That is, as we discussed earlier, we cannot and should not treat the role of procedures as independent of the way in which policy is specified in a statute.

We began by examining the general incidence of procedural language in statutes. We did so both by examining the raw number of words and the number of text blocks with specific procedures. We used text blocks in addition to word counts because, as we noted, when we coded each bill, we began by dividing it up into blocks of text and then coding each block as belonging to one of the policy categories discussed earlier. Next, we determined whether the block contained any procedural instructions. As a result, many of these blocks contained more than one procedural component. Thus, when we divided the number of words that were given a procedural code by the total number of words, we were double-counting in the numerator.[8] Examining text blocks allowed us to avoid this problem

[8] This is more of a problem for procedural instructions. Because we divided the text of each bill by policy topic, very few groups of text have more than one policy code, but many have more than one procedural code.

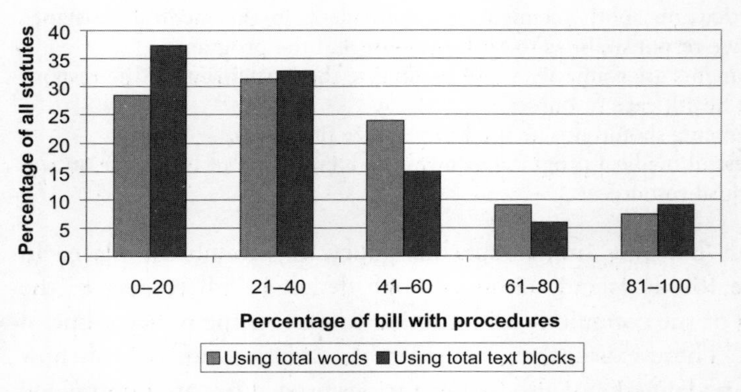

Figure 3.2 The incidence of procedures in MMC bills

by noting merely whether each block of text contains any procedural codes.

In Figure 3.2, we can see that although the role of procedural language varies quite a bit across statutes, many statutes have very little legislative language that contains procedures. For 28% of statutes, fewer than 20% of the words in the statute have any procedure attached to them. For only about 7% of the statutes, by contrast, more than 80% of the words have a procedural component attached to them. The same general story holds if we use percentage of text blocks rather than percentage of total words in the legislation: nearly 40% of the statutes have procedural content in less than 20% of their text blocks, and fewer than 10% of the statutes have more than 80% of their text blocks with procedural content. If we aggregate the statutes, we find that 33% of the total words in our sample, and 23% of the text blocks, have a procedural code attached to them.

Table 3.3 breaks down the data by procedural type. One fact that is immediately obvious from the data is that certain procedures are very rarely used. In particular, statutes rarely create new agencies (or departments within agencies) to implement managed care programs, and they rarely create specialized committees that lie strictly within the legislature. Another finding from the table is that although the other procedures are all employed with some frequency, three procedures are used most widely. Within the ex ante group, informational requirements are by far the most common. This finding is consistent with the arguments made by

Table 3.3. *Procedural Controls in MMC Legislation*

Type of Control	Specific Categories	Total Number of Words with This Procedure	Percentage of All Words with This Procedure	Percentage of All Text Blocks with This Procedure
Ex Ante Controls	Informational Requirements	14,670	8.9%	6.0
	Proposal Requirements	4,290	2.6	1.3
	Study Requirements	5,752	3.5	2.7
Ex Post Controls	Reporting Requirements	8,143	4.9	3.0
	Appeals Process	2,939	1.8	1.1
Agent Controls	Nonlegislative Committees	3,650	2.2	1.2
	Legislative Committees	265	0.2	0.2
	Staffing Requirements	1,313	0.8	0.6
	Creation of New Agency/Department	302	0.2	0.1
General Controls	Time Constraints	32,509	19.7	11.6

McCubbins, Noll, and Weingast (1987), who claim that when legislators are uncertain about which policies they want to adopt, they will ensure that bureaucrats are exposed to information from the groups that they care about. Within the ex post group, reporting requirements are the most common. And by far the bulk of procedural language is simple boilerplate that establishes time constraints.

One could argue that these time constraints seldom create clear legislative control over the nature of policies. Often, legislation will describe a policy, and then at the end of the description will include time constraints that state something to the effect that "This policy will take effect July 1, 2000," or "The agency shall complete its study by April 11, 1995." Such language can influence policy because it precludes delay. But this language differs qualitatively from that describing the other types of procedures because it creates no clear bias in policymaking processes toward the

Table 3.4. *Policy Type and Procedural Choice*

	Percentage of Text Blocks with Procedural Type			
Policy Type	Ex Ante	Ex Post	Agent	None
General	16.1	6.8	6.7	72.7
Client	7.6	2.5	0.2	90.2
Provider	7.8	3.7	0.4	88.8
Miscellaneous	4.8	2.4	2.4	91.1

Note: The cells give the percentage of all text blocks that have both the given policy and procedural codes.

legislators (other than to eliminate the possibility of delay). If one were to take the position that these time constraints should not be treated as procedural mechanisms, then the actual incidence of procedures declines rather dramatically in our data. In fact, the total amount of legislative language that includes procedures is roughly halved when we eliminate the boilerplate concerning time constraints.

Table 3.4 describes how different types of procedures are used in different policy areas. If we look at the specific policy categories, we find that procedures are not used very frequently at all – they are used in only approximately 10% of all text blocks – and that the ex ante procedures are used roughly twice as often as any other procedural type. In the general policy text blocks, by contrast, procedures play a much more prominent role. More specifically, about 27% of all text blocks receive some procedural code. And the use of all types of procedures is much greater when no specific policy is being described.

A clear story begins to emerge from our analysis of procedures. As a purely empirical matter, they are much less prevalent in legislation than are specific policy descriptions. Furthermore, they tend to be most prevalent when policy is defined generally rather than specifically. In many respects, this finding is consistent with previous research that argues that procedures can be substitutes for policy. At the same time, however, the use of procedures seems less prevalent than some of the previous discussion suggests. And even when statutes are general and policy is vaguely defined, procedures remain a relatively small percentage of total legislative language, probably because procedures themselves have a smaller and more uncertain influence on policy implementation than does the actual specification of policy.

Parliamentary Systems and Labor Policy

We now turn to a small set of data on labor legislation in parliamentary systems and ask the same questions we asked about the MMC data in the U.S. states. How specific is the policy language in the statutes? Are the types of procedural instructions found in parliamentary legislation the same as those found in our MMC laws? What is the relative prevalence of policy as opposed to procedural language?

It is impossible for us to address these questions in as systematic and detailed a way as we did for the states. This is partly because we do not have the same sort of natural experiment that requires a wide range of political systems to address the same issue at roughly the same time. Moreover, even if one could find such an issue, across the 19 countries we analyze in this book, statutes are written in 10 different languages. Thus, we are more limited in the types of analyses we can do. We can, however, draw on the International Labour Organization's Natlex database to obtain a small set of labor statutes to analyze.[9] In particular, from Natlex we obtained English-language copies of 30 labor-related statutes from 12 different countries. We use this small cross section of statutes to examine whether the broad patterns we find in the cross-national labor laws are similar to those we find in the cross-state MMC laws.

Before conducting our quantitative analysis, however, we first read these various laws to see whether different countries were dealing with similar issues in different ways. We found numerous examples showing that they were. Our example in Chapter 1, which showed the different approaches that Ireland and Germany took in defining sexual harassment, provides one such instance that we drew from these laws. And just as we saw, in that case, that one country (Ireland) provided a much more detailed and specific definition of sexual harassment than did the other country, we also found many examples in other areas where some countries provided detailed instructions about a specific policy, while others provided much more general language that allows bureaucrats to make policy decisions. We discuss one of these other policy areas – the nature of gender discrimination in the workplace – in more detail in Chapter 7.

We also found many examples of procedural differences in these statutes. Both France and Ireland, for example, use legislation to create a special organization that is charged with aspects of implementing the

[9] The bills were downloaded from http://natlex.ilo.org/scripts/natlexcgi.exe?lang=E.

gender discrimination law. France, however, almost totally abdicated authority over implementation to civil servants in the French Council of State. Article 17 of Law 83–935 creates the "Conseil supérieur de l'égalité professionnelle entre les femmes et les hommes." But the article is very vague and short, containing only three sentences. The first sentence creates the organization and places it under the jurisdiction of several ministers (the ministers of women's rights, labor, and employment and professional training). The second sentence gives a very vague mandate to the Conseil, stating that it should participate in defining and implementing policy regarding professional equality between men and women.[10] Finally, the third sentence assigns the Council of State the job of filling in the details regarding the role and functioning of the new Conseil supérieur.[11] Thus, though the legislation establishes some political control over the implementation of the law by placing the Conseil under specific ministers, the details of how the major state organization should implement the goal of professional equality between men and women is left to civil servants. If one goes to the Code du Travail (Partie Réglementaire – Décrets en Conseil d'Etat), Chapitre 2, one finds seven articles that have been made by decree in the Council of State. These articles spell out in detail what the Conseil supérieur shall do, who shall be on it, how it should be organized, and what it must report.

The Irish legislation on the same subject stands in sharp contrast. Part V of the Employment Equality Act sets up an Equality Authority to deal with all aspects of discrimination. The act is 6,000 words long, and every aspect of the Authority seems to be carefully defined. The act, for example, lays out who is on the Authority and how they are chosen, what the functions of the Authority will be, how the Authority will be organized, what support staff it will have, what types of reports it will make to whom and when, how it will be financed and what sorts of financial accountability it will have, and how Irish citizens must respond when contacted by the Authority, to name a few examples.

Article 47(5) provides a useful example of the extraordinary detail found in this section of the Act:

[10] "Ce conseil est chargé de participer à la définition, à la mise en oeuvre et à l'application de la politique menée en matière d'égalité professionnelle entre les femmes et les hommes."

[11] "Un décret en Conseil d'Etat détermine les conditions d'application du présent article."

At a meeting of the Authority:
(a) the chairperson shall, if present, take the chair,
(b) in the absence of the chairperson or, if the office of chairperson is vacant, the vice-chairperson of the Authority shall take the chair, and
(c) if and so long as:
(i) the chairperson is not present or the office of chairperson is vacant, and
(ii) the vice-chairperson of the Authority is not present or the office of vice-chairperson is vacant,
the members of the Authority shall choose one of their number to take the chair at the meeting.

The members of the legislative majority obviously wanted to spell out exactly who gets to sit in the chair!

The Irish legislative majority also used legislative detail to ensure that the government would retain firm control over this administrative body. Article 41, for example, states that the minister for social, community, and family affairs will name all members of the board (whereas the French government is represented on the Conseil supérieur, but has no say over the composition of much of the board). And Article 44(3) states that the minister "may at any time, for stated reasons, remove an ordinary member of the Authority from office."

Coding the Parliamentary Statutes

As with the statutes from the U.S. states, it is valuable to further explore the differences that exist across countries in the labor statutes. Our coding system for the Natlex data is necessarily a bit different than that used with the MMC. First, we do not code the specific policy topics of the text blocks because the statutes are not all about the same policy. The statutes include, for example, an Australian employment act, an act to consolidate the Canadian labor code, a New Zealand human rights act, an Italian law on immigration control, a Swedish act against ethnic discrimination, a Norwegian act on unemployment benefits, and a Danish act to protect union members from dismissal, among others. All of this legislation directly or indirectly affects labor, but there is no possibility of carefully coding policy subcategories, or of coding the mapping between policy type and procedure. Second, reading these bills reveals a clear and important difference from the U.S. state statutes: procedure and policy are not so carefully intertwined, and the role of procedure is much smaller. Thus, we are able to distinguish policy words from procedural ones and are not forced to link procedural codes to policy text, as in the case of the MMC statutes.

To code each statute, then, we simply separated the policy language from the procedural language. For the policy language, we coded whether it was general or specific (in the sense described with respect to MMC), and for the procedural language we coded the type of procedure. This coding system causes the number of words about procedure to be much lower than in the case of the MMC legislation, since here only the procedural words are counted (and not the policy words associated with them). Thus, the results are not directly comparable to those presented in the section on MMC. However, given that we are dealing with such a small and nonrandom sample of statutes in the case of labor policy, our goal was not to replicate the MMC study, but rather only to see whether similar trends emerge.

Data for all statutes are summarized in Table 3.5. Two very clear themes emerge. First, there is a predominance of policy language. For one Norwegian statute, "only" 84% of the language is coded as policy, with the other 16% falling into the procedural category. For the rest of the statutes, at most 8% of a statute is coded as procedure, and typically the percentage of procedural language is minuscule, often less than 1%. Thus, although our coding system for the parliamentary statutes understates the role of procedures (relative to the MMC coding scheme), it seems that these procedures play a much smaller role than we find in the U.S. state legislation. This finding is consistent with Moe and Caldwell's (1994) argument that statutes in parliamentary systems do not encumber civil servants with a large number of procedural requirements.

Second, the data in Table 3.5 suggest that the policy language is typically very specific. In only 4 of the 30 statutes is more than 10% of the language coded into the "General" category, and for many items of legislation in our sample, only a very small fraction is "General." And for many statutes, the percentage of "General" language is extremely small – again, often less than 1%. This is much less consistent with Moe and Caldwell's argument that parliamentary statutes give wide policy discretion during policy implementation.

Table 3.6 breaks down the procedural language according to procedural type. Of course, in interpreting these numbers, it is important to bear in mind that the total amount of procedural language is very small. With that caveat in mind, we found in the parliamentary statutes a somewhat different distribution of procedural types. First, several of the procedural

Table 3.5. *Policy and Procedural Language in Parliamentary Statutes*

Country	Total Policy Words	Policy Words That Are "General"	Percentage of Policy Words That Are "General"	Procedural Words	Percentage of Procedural Words
Australia	22,114	110	0.50%	975	4.22%
Canada	4,773	226	4.73%	36	0.75%
Denmark	2,309	96	4.16%	112	4.63%
Denmark	3,482	40	1.15%	86	2.41%
Denmark	756	118	15.61%	18	2.33%
Denmark	3,850	33	0.86%	0	0.00%
Denmark	7,694	0	0.00%	32	0.41%
Denmark	1,477	35	2.37%	18	1.20%
Denmark	6,072	48	0.79%	288	4.53%
Denmark	484	15	3.10%	26	5.10%
Finland	5,516	163	2.96%	24	0.43%
Finland	9,204	56	0.61%	695	7.02%
Germany	5,476	157	2.87%	281	4.88%
Germany	5,210	59	1.13%	36	0.69%
Germany	20,668	42	0.20%	502	2.37%
Ireland	32,094	248	0.77%	1,051	3.17%
Ireland	9,260	149	1.61%	364	3.78%
Italy	17,199	113	0.66%	1,511	8.08%
New Zealand	11,032	100	0.91%	98	0.88%
Norway	2,697	0	0.00%	42	1.53%
Norway	1,962	268	13.66%	377	16.12%
Norway	25,440	462	1.82%	119	0.47%
Norway	6,156	0	0.00%	40	0.65%
Spain	3,546	545	15.37%	136	3.69%
Sweden	1,491	98	6.57%	97	6.11%
Sweden	5,130	737	14.37%	10	0.19%
Sweden	3,535	0	0.00%	178	4.79%
UK	8,870	222	2.50%	141	1.56%
UK	82,574	149	0.18%	274	0.33%
UK	12,168	147	1.21%	0	0.00%

categories – proposal requirements, study requirements, and legislative committees – are empty. Second, time constraints are relatively prominent compared to the other procedures, though not nearly so much as in the MMC data. In fact, the most prominent procedures are reporting requirements, which represent 29% of all procedures in our data.

Table 3.6. *Procedural Controls in Parliamentary Legislation*

Type of Control	Specific Categories	Total Number of Words with This Procedure	Percentage of All Procedural Words
Ex Ante Controls	Informational Requirements	1,484	16.8%
	Proposal Requirements	—	—
	Study Requirements	—	—
Ex Post Controls	Reporting Requirements	2,578	29.2
	Appeals Process	1,465	16.6
Agent Controls	Nonlegislative Committees	976	11.0
	Legislative Committees	—	—
	Staffing Requirements	225	2.6
	Creation of New Agency/ Department	229	2.6
General Controls	Time Constraints	1,870	21.2

In our parliamentary data, we also were able to code the delegation of rulemaking authority. Almost every statute contains some language that authorizes a minister or ministry to make rules. A 1993 Danish statute, for example, states:

2) In the case of a period of specially arranged job training as under Section 22, para. 2 or para. 3 (compare para. 2), where the employment service or the commune dispatches the unemployed person to work with a general educational organization etc., the educational organization etc. pays out a sum for the work performed to the employment service or the commune. More detailed regulations regarding the amount of this sum are laid down by the Minister of Labour after discussion with the Minister of Social Affairs.

Similarly, a 1993 Finnish statute states:

The Ministry of Labour shall issue further provisions on the circumstances in which a work permit may be granted without requesting a statement from the Employment Office to a person who has been issued a residence permit on other grounds than work-permit consideration.

The impact of such language is difficult to quantify because, in many instances, the authority of ministers to take such measures is implicit, even if there is no language that expressly gives the minister such authority. This

Table 3.7. *Policy and Procedure in Statutes from U.S. States and National Parliaments*

	Percentage of Policy Language That Is "General"	Percentage of Language in Statute That Is Procedural[a]
U.S. states on MMC	22.1	34.5
National parliaments on labor law	1.3	2.3

[a] In the MMC data, procedural codes are attached to text blocks with policy codes, whereas in the parliamentary data, we separate out the procedural from policy text. See text for discussion.

is specifically true in many civil law countries and, as we discuss in more detail in Chapter 7, is usually not true in common law countries. It is also not clear whether this language should be treated as policy or as procedure. It is clearly not a procedure that constrains, but rather one than enables. We have thus separated such language from the data presented earlier. In our 30 statutes, 3,678 words contain this type of delegating legislation, which represents only 1.1% of the 333,484 words that we have coded. Thus, this language that expressly delegates rulemaking autonomy to ministers is a very small percentage of all language.

In sum, there are some clear parallels between the labor legislation and the MMC legislation. First, as other studies have pointed out, legislation does contain procedural instructions that can be used to constrain agents. Second, while these procedural details are important, they are much less prevalent in statutes than are policy instructions. And third, when legislatures write about policy, the instructions are about specific policy topics and are not merely general language about goals, objectives, or guidelines.

We also found, however, rather significant differences between the parliamentary and state legislation on each of these issues, which are summarized in Table 3.7. In particular, though policy-specific language is much more prevalent than general language in both sets of data, general language is much more common in the U.S. state data. Second, as we have noted several times, differences in our coding scheme (discussed earlier) make it impossible to compare directly the incidence of procedural language across the two types of data. Still, given the order of magnitude of the difference, it seems likely that procedural language plays a bigger role in the U.S. states than in the national parliamentary systems.

These two findings make intuitive sense. First, with respect to "General" language, the legislatures in many of the U.S. states that we examine have relatively low levels of capacity, making it very difficult for them to write specific policy instructions under any circumstances. In the parliamentary context, by contrast, legislation usually is drafted in cabinets occupied by the most knowledgeable and experienced party leaders. Moreover, these party leaders have at their disposal the entire state apparatus, making it much more likely that they have the resources to craft careful policy details. We return to this central issue of legislative capacity in subsequent chapters.

Second, with respect to procedures, it is not surprising that they play a larger role in countries with separation of powers systems than in parliamentary systems. In parliamentary systems, as we discuss in more detail in Chapter 7, cabinet ministers sit atop administrations during policy implementation, and they are constantly responsible to a majority in parliament. Thus, incentives to use procedures to constrain implementation are much weaker than in the U.S. states. Once legislation is adopted in a presidential system, it is the executive agency that implements policy, and legislative opportunities to influence decision making in these agencies are relatively few compared to what we find in the parliamentary systems that lack separation of powers. As noted, we return to both of these points later in the book.

Policy Discretion and the Length of Legislation

The preceding sections demonstrate that some legislation contains quite detailed policy descriptions, while other legislation on the same subject is much more general. We also found variation in the role of procedures, but discovered that procedures seem to play a minor role, relative to policy instructions, in all contexts. These discussions, we believe, suggest an answer to the difficult measurement problem we face in efforts to conduct cross-system tests of the extent to which parliamentary statutes, or statutes in the U.S. states, delegate policymaking autonomy to other actors.

Obviously, this is not an easy task. The most impressive efforts in this regard are by Epstein and O'Halloran (1999). But as we noted, even this state-of-the-art approach did not use actual legislation, but rather relied on *Congressional Quarterly's* year-end summaries of statutes. Their measure consisted of two components. First, for each bill, they identified the percentage of the policy areas described by *Congressional Quarterly* where delegation occurs. A score of 100% on a long bill, then, would represent a lot of discretion. Second, they created an index of procedural constraints and used a formula to subtract the constraints from the percentage of the bill that delegates.

We must take a different approach to measuring delegation. First of all, because our statistical analysis in later chapters will include thousands of different statutes, many of which (in the case of labor policy) are written in languages other than English, we cannot code the policy content of each bill. And unfortunately, there is no cross-state or cross-national equivalent of *Congressional Quarterly*'s year-end summaries. But because our theoretical argument points out the necessity of conducting a comparative empirical analysis, we need to find some measure that we can use to operationalize legislative discretion across this vast array of legislation. And second, because Epstein and O'Halloran's measure focuses on procedural constraints, it cannot measure the amount of policy precision, which we have argued is the most important component of whether statutes allow for – or constrain – discretion. For both of these reasons, we need to utilize an alternative measure that will allow us to compare statutes.

The proxy that we use is the length of statutes. Our qualitative and quantitative investigation of a huge number of statutes suggests that the more words a legislature puts into legislation on the same issue, the more it constrains other actors who will implement policy on that issue. Similarly, the fewer words it writes, the more discretion it gives to other actors. The earlier comparison of Idaho's and Texas's MMC statutes provides a stark example of how this proxy operates, as does the gender equality legislation from Ireland and France and the many other items of legislation we have described. Even when legislative language develops procedures, longer statutes put less authority in the hands of policy implementers, as we saw in the comparison of the Illinois and Utah language creating special commissions.

At one level, this makes intuitive sense. Longer statutes on the same topic are more likely to tell agencies what to do, and shorter ones give them more leeway. At the same time, we realize that counting the number of words in legislation and using this as a measure of discretion may be controversial (although see Lutz 1994). Thus, in this section, we attempt to bolster further our argument that statute length – on the same topic – is a reasonable proxy for discretion.

In order to demonstrate that length of legislation is a good proxy for legislative constraint, we begin by building on the findings of the previous sections. Our qualitative examples in this and other chapters, drawn from places like Idaho, Texas, Germany, Ireland, and France, show that there is a great deal of variation in the specificity of legislative language across both parliamentary and separation of powers systems. And our quantitative analysis of a large amount of legislation confirms our more anecdotal and impressionistic evidence. The legislation we coded consists in large part of instructions about specific policy areas, and not of general language that has no specific policy content. Such specific policy language is also much more prevalent than procedural provisions that tell agents how to go about making policy but not what sort of policy to make. This latter point is especially important because if statutes consist mostly of general language, or if statutes consist mostly of procedural language, then length is not a good proxy for discretion.

While these conditions are important, in order to demonstrate convincingly that longer legislation acts as a useful and appropriate proxy, we must demonstrate two additional conditions. First, we must show that longer legislation does not consist of mostly general language. Second, we must show that longer legislation does not contain proportionally more procedural language.

Statutes can be long for a variety of reasons. A legislature might, for example, use statutes to address specific policy topics and to provide instructions to other political actors about what policy is supposed to look like and how it should be implemented. Of course, statutes might also be long simply because they consist of filler and meaningless generalities. In reading over legislation, we certainly came across numerous examples of such language. States and countries frequently use legislation to spell out very general goals, to take noncontroversial stances, or to set themselves up for future credit-claiming. This sort of language occurs especially frequently in the statutes' preambles.

If longer legislation consists mostly of this sort of general language, then we cannot use length as a proxy for discretion. In such cases, longer legislation is simply that – longer – and no meaning can be attached to the length. On the other hand, if length has meaning and can be used to measure discretion, then it must be the case that as statutes get longer, the proportion of language categorized as "General" decreases.

This is obviously not an issue in our parliamentary data, where very little of the language is general. To test whether this is the case in the MMC data, we use individual statutes as our unit of analysis. We look both at our entire sample of MMC statutes and at the smaller set of statutes identified as key bills. In the first column of Table 3.8, we report the

Table 3.8. *Bill Length and Bill Specificity*

Statutes	Relationship between the Total Number of Words and the Proportion of Words Coded as "General"	Relationship between the Total Number of Text Blocks and the Proportion of Text Blocks Coded as "General"
Full sample	−.27 (.027)	−.24 (.047)
Key	−.45 (.015)	−.37 (.046)

Note: Top number is Pearson's r; number in parenthesis is two-tailed level of significance.

correlation between the total number of words in the bill and the proportion of "General" language in the bill. In the second column, we report the correlation between the total number of blocks of text in the bill and the percentage of blocks of text categorized as "General."

The findings are clear. For both the full sample and key bills, the correlation between the length of a statute and the proportion of a bill that is "General" is negative and significant. In other words, as statutes get longer, they consist more and more of specific policy instructions and less and less of general statements. In one respect, this is not particularly surprising. Some of the general language tends to come at the beginning of statutes, and such preambles or introductions should not be expected to be much longer in longer legislation. At the same time, however, many other general sections occur in other parts of bills, and thus it is significant to learn that as statutes become longer, it is the more specific parts that are growing in length. This finding lends additional support to the use of length as a proxy for discretion, since it indicates that longer statutes are longer because they provide more details about the policy to be implemented.

A similar test examines whether longer statutes contain proportionally more procedural language. Again, such a test is irrelevant in parliamentary systems, where very little language is procedural. But in the MMC data, it could be the case, for example, that as statutes become longer, legislatures are more apt to fill them with more procedural controls. While this would indicate some level of control, it would give us less indication that length is a good measure of discretion, since it is difficult to assess the degree to which such provisions act to constrain agents. In addition, it would mean that the length is not necessarily due to the presence of additional policy directions.

We therefore examine whether the proportion of words in statutes that are procedural is correlated with the total number of words in the statutes. In other words, as length increases, do statutes gain proportionally more procedural codes? The answer, it turns out, is no: there is almost no correlation between the size of a bill and the percentage of the bill that consists of procedures. Thus, as legislation gets longer, it does not contain proportionally more procedural provisions.[12]

It is, of course, possible to think of factors that can affect length without affecting discretion. Statutes, for example, might in one sentence refer to other laws that greatly restrict discretion. Thus, there are clearly additional issues regarding how to use length in operationalizing a cross-system measure of discretion in statutes. We take up these issues in the discussion of our specific tests later. We hope at this stage, however, to have convinced the reader that as legislation on a particular topic becomes longer, it is extremely likely that this increased length is accompanied by an increase in the amount of language that defines the precise boundaries of policy. And it is these specific boundaries on policy that most clearly constrain the types of choices that are made during policy implementation.

Conclusion

Legislative statutes are blueprints for policymaking. In some cases, legislatures provide very detailed blueprints that allow little room for other actors, such as bureaucrats, to create policy on their own. In other cases, legislatures take a different approach and write statutes that provide only the broad outlines of policy, which gives bureaucrats the opportunity to design and implement policy.

In the next four chapters, we will present and test a theory that explains why legislatures sometimes use statutes to constrain agency autonomy but at other times issue broad grants of discretion. Before doing so, however, it has been essential to first undertake a systematic analysis of the amount of policy detail in legislative statutes, a task which, surprisingly, has never

[12] The correlation between the number of blocks in a bill and the percentage of blocks with procedural provisions is .05 ($p = .68$). The correlation between the number of words in a bill and the percentage of words with procedural provisions is .03 ($p = .83$). Results for key bills similarly are small and insignificant.

previously been done. In other words, before explaining the causes of variation in discretion, we wanted to establish in what respects and to what extent such variation exists. Thus, in this chapter, we looked at MMC statutes from the U.S. states and labor statutes across parliamentary democracies. Furthermore, we looked at both the policy and the procedural instructions in these laws and examined whether longer statutes are qualitatively different from shorter statutes.

Our results can be summed up easily. First, and most importantly from the standpoint of the rest of this book, when comparing laws on the same topic, the length of a law serves as a useful, appropriate proxy for the extent to which it constrains agency policymaking. Simply put, longer statutes provide more detailed instructions, and hence provide greater constraints on the actions of bureaucrats and other political actors. Longer statutes do not simply consist of general language, but instead provide instructions about specific policy areas. Second, while procedures do play a role in these statutes, it is clear that laws – especially longer laws – consist mostly of policy-specific language. When procedural language is put in place, it is often attached to specific policy instructions. Finally, we found similar patterns in both the cross-state and cross-national contexts. The parliamentary statutes exhibited a wide range of specific policy instructions and also a great deal of variance in the amount of discretion they allow for. And even more so than in the case of U.S. state legislation, procedural instructions were secondary to policy instructions in the parliamentary context.

4

A Comparative Theory of Legislation, Discretion, and the Policymaking Process

We now turn to the main analytic task of the book, which is to develop a theory about how politicians design statutes that will affect agency discretion. Like previous arguments, our theory is built on the simple premise that politicians are motivated by policy considerations. The policy motivations could stem from electoral considerations – politicians may want to produce the policy outcomes that will get them reelected. Alternatively, politicians might simply have an intrinsic interest in policy itself, either for selfish or altruistic reasons. Regardless of their origin, these policy motivations create a challenge for politicians, who must decide how to use legislation in the pursuit of desired policy outcomes.

In Chapters 1 and 3, we provided examples of the ways in which different legislatures can take quite different pathways to making policy on the same sorts of issues, with some legislatures at some times writing very detailed statutes and other legislatures at other times writing vague, general statutes. To explain such differences, our theory focuses on the political environment in which legislators find themselves. As noted in Chapter 2, two important elements of this environment have been carefully investigated by previous researchers. The first is the extent to which politicians' policy goals and preferences diverge from those of bureaucrats (e.g., Epstein and O'Halloran 1994, 1999; Martin 1997). As divergence increases, so do incentives to use details in statutes to micromanage policy implementation. That is, when politicians have reason to suspect that bureaucrats will choose policy outcomes they dislike, these politicians will not delegate broad discretion through vague legislation, but rather will delegate narrow discretion through specific legislation. The second element is the technical complexity of the policy issue. Many policy areas are very complicated, and bureaucrats often spend their careers developing policy expertise in narrow policy domains. Politicians may attempt to utilize this expertise by writing vague legislation that allows bureaucrats substantial latitude in determining policy details on complex issues.

As in previous theories, these factors comprise central elements of our theory. Policy uncertainty can create incentives for politicians to write vague statutes that delegate policymaking responsibility to expert bureaucrats. And policy conflict between politicians and bureaucrats can create incentives for politicians to write specific statutes that limit the discretion of bureaucrats who cannot be trusted. Still, although a distrust of bureaucratic motivations may provide the incentive for politicians to write detailed legislation, variation in this distrust is often inadequate for explaining differences that we see in statutes across different political systems. To account for these cross-system differences, we must examine other factors in the political environment that influence the ability and incentives of politicians to write detailed statutes. These factors are the focus of our theory.

Even if politicians have the initial incentive to write and pass detailed statutes (because, for example, they do not trust the bureaucracy to choose the "right" policy), their ability to do so is determined by other factors. The first of these factors is *legislative capacity*, which affects the costs to politicians of *drafting* detailed legislation. One cost is informational. Politicians may need to do considerable work in order to have enough information to draft a detailed bill. But other factors affect legislative capacity as well. Even if the politician were fully informed, writing a detailed bill has considerable additional costs, central of which is the consumption of time, both on the floor of the legislature and away from it. In Chapters 6 and 7, we discuss more carefully the political and institutional factors that affect legislative capacity. Here it is important to note that politicians may find themselves in the position of wanting to write detailed legislation (because they distrust bureaucrats) but being ill equipped to do so. This issue of capacity is scarcely on the radar screen of congressional scholars, who study delegation in one of the most active and professionalized legislative bodies in the world. But it is an issue in many other settings where issues of political control over bureaucrats are no less salient. In the United States, for example, there is a great deal of difference in legislative capacity across state legislatures, with some legislatures having very low levels and others having very high levels of capacity.

While having the legislative capacity to write detailed laws is important, politicians also must be cognizant of whether the bill they write will be approved by other relevant political actors. The difficulty of passing optimal legislation depends on the *bargaining environment*, or the constitutional arrangements, that specify the number of actors who must consent to the passage of legislation. In effect, when more institutional actors have authority to propose or veto legislation, there are greater institutional obstacles to passing legislation. In a Westminster system like Great Britain, a governing majority in a lower house of parliament can unilaterally determine the content of legislation. This stands in sharp contrast to a bicameral presidential system, where two chambers must agree to a legislative proposal that then must receive the assent of the president or governor. In this second type of system, even if a legislature has a high level of legislative capacity, allowing it to write detailed legislation, it may be frustrated by other actors in its efforts to include policy details in laws. Thus, even given the incentive to write detailed laws, a legislature might choose not to do so because it realizes that other institutional actors will refuse to agree to such legislation.

Finally, we contend that there is one additional variable that affects whether or not politicians will choose to adopt detailed statutes. Legislation, we must bear in mind, is hardly the only constraint on bureaucrats. Furthermore, bureaucratic actions do not solely determine policy outcomes. If the political system is one that allows politicians to keep recalcitrant bureaucrats in line without writing detailed legislation, then the incentives to use legislation as a policymaking instrument should be diminished. In other words, if politicians can depend on other nonstatutory features of the political environment to help produce bureaucratic actions that are congruent with their preferences, this diminishes the extent to which precise statutory language is necessary for obtaining desired policy outcomes. The converse is also true: politicians may trust bureaucrats to implement desired policies but may also worry that other political actors, particularly judges, may subvert bureaucratic decisions. Such possibilities may increase the need for specific policy instructions in laws. Since these nonstatutory mechanisms influence bureaucratic decisions and policy outcomes, they need to be accounted for in any theory of legislation and delegation.

To sum up briefly, first, politicians often will have the incentive to use policy details in legislation to limit the discretion of bureaucrats. Second, their ability to act on this incentive will be conditional on a number of other factors that vary across political systems. Our theory, which elaborates the influence of all of these factors, is developed more fully in a formal model contained in Appendix D. In this chapter, we describe the model and its main results using language that requires no specific expertise in modeling. In so doing, however, we stick closely to the actual model; that is, we discuss in detail our model's basic assumptions, the intuitions about optimal strategic behavior in the model, and the links between these intuitions and the core hypotheses that we will test in the remainder of this book.

In what follows, we flesh out our basic argument about how these elements of the political context affect the role of legislation in policy-making processes. We begin by describing the key players in the model, their motivations, and the structure of their interactions. We consider three different versions of the model, which correspond to different types of political systems. We then develop our central hypotheses about how the political and institutional context affects the design of statutes.

Designing Legislative Statutes: Players and Core Assumptions

Our goal is to develop a straightforward and simple framework for thinking about how the comparative institutional context affects delegation and discretion. The very process of modeling naturally requires us to abstract away from many details that may affect the design of legislation at specific moments in specific places. But such abstraction, of course, is the goal. We are not trying to describe all the factors that might affect the level of detail that we should find in any given piece of legislation. Instead, we are trying to develop ceteris paribus arguments about basic patterns and relationships to look for between the variables described previously and policy discretion in statutes.

Players and Assumptions

In our theory, there are two types of players, "Politicians" and "Bureaucrats." Politicians author legislation and in this way determine the level of policy discretion in a statute. Thus, Politicians are usually legislators, although we allow this to vary according to the political system. In our model of a political system with an executive veto, for example, there are two Politicians – a Legislator and a President. In parliamentary systems, the Politician can be thought of as a pivotal party in the government majority, as we discuss in more detail in Chapter 7.

Once the Politician adopts a statute, the Bureaucrat reads it and then implements a policy. The policy outcome is determined in part by the statute that the Politician designs and in part by the way in which the Bureaucrat implements this policy. Like the term *Politician*, the term *Bureaucrat* is obviously highly stylized here. There are many actors who affect policy implementation after statutes are adopted, including not only bureaucrats in the classic sense but also presidents, governors, cabinet ministers, courts, and other nonlegislative actors. We discuss the implications of this fact when we operationalize tests of our theory. In this chapter, however, one should simply view the Bureaucrat as an agent who plays a central role during policy implementation after statutes are adopted.

We make a number of assumptions about the motivations and actions of the players. To begin with, we assume that the Politician and the Bureaucrat are motivated by policy outcomes. Although each actor chooses a policy, he or she has preferences over the outcomes that result from these policy choices and wants to achieve his or her most preferred policy outcome. We will return to this shortly, but for now it may be useful to think of *policy* as what is spelled out, in more or less detail, in legislation and during implementation and *outcomes* as what happens in the real world once a policy is adopted and implemented.[1]

We also assume that the Politician's and the Bureaucrat's policy preferences may diverge. The Politician, for example, may want to leave no stone unturned in efforts to improve gender equality in the workplace, whereas a Bureaucrat may want to allow discrimination complaints only under limited conditions. Consistent with our earlier discussion, situations where preferences diverge in this manner provide the Politician with the incentive to use legislation to define policy in detail, thus minimizing the likelihood that the Bureaucrat will choose a policy that the Politician dislikes.

One key assumption we make is that the Bureaucrat is better informed than the Politician about the repercussions of particular policy choices. Consider a Politician who has some policy goal, or outcome, that she wishes to achieve. She may know her preferred eventual outcome but may not know which statute will best help her to achieve this goal. A state legislator, for example, may want to trim 8 million dollars from the health care budget. She may know that she wants to do this by forcing all Medicaid clients into some form of managed care program, but there may

[1] Thus, *policy* is interchangeable with *policy choices*, *policy implemented*, *statutes*, and *legislation*. Policy *outcomes* are synonymous with *outcomes*, *goals*, and *repercussions*.

be different forms and features of managed care to choose from. We assume that the Politician may be uncertain about what outcome will actually ensue when particular policies are chosen. Later, we talk about how this uncertainty is specifically captured by our model. Unlike the Politician, who may be uncertain about the outcomes that specific policies will produce, the Bureaucrat knows the consequences of these policy choices.[2] As discussed in Chapter 2, this idea that bureaucrats have more technical expertise than politicians is standard in the literature on modern democracies, and the relative expertise of bureaucrats is often a central motivation for politicians' delegating policymaking powers to bureaucrats in the first place. The director of the Department of Health, for example, is likely to possess considerable knowledge about how the state health care system works, as well as the staff available to work on specific policy questions. Ideally, the Politician will design legislation so as to take advantage of this expertise.

Two additional assumptions about the actions of the Politician and the Bureaucrat are central to our theory. First, we assume that designing a statute is costly to the Politician. These costs depend on both the extent to which the Politician limits discretion and the general capacity of the Politician to write detailed bills. Returning to the example in Chapter 1, compared to the short and general German law on gender equality, the extremely detailed Irish Gender Equality Act would have taken a great deal of time and energy to draft, to debate in committee, and to debate on the floor. Moreover, the actual level of these costs should depend on the capacity of the Politician. In a political system where politicians who draft statutes are less qualified, possess fewer resources, or enjoy fewer opportunities to consider legislation, it will be much costlier to write detailed statutes. Our theory thus includes a variable that describes the Politician's capacity to write details. As this capacity increases, the cost of setting a specific limit on discretion declines.

Note that we distinguish between policy uncertainty and the costs of writing detailed legislation, and we make no assumptions that these are correlated. Clearly, many of the costs that legislators face are informational, as legislators need to become informed in order to figure out which policy they wish to adopt. But as we discussed earlier and elaborate on

[2] We do not believe, of course, that bureaucrats actually have perfect knowledge about policy outcomes. Rather, this assumption is a straightforward way to capture what we do believe to be true: that bureaucrats generally have more policy expertise than politicians.

further in subsequent chapters, many costs of drafting detailed bills are unrelated to policy uncertainty. Thus, while costs and technical uncertainty may be correlated, they need not be.

Second, we assume that the Bureaucrat has a choice about whether to implement the policy chosen by the Politician. In other words, the Bureaucrat, like the Politician, is a strategic political actor who will make choices that are predicated on achieving his most preferred policy outcome. The catch for the Bureaucrat is that if he is caught implementing a policy that the Politician does not like – if, in other words, he chooses not to comply with the statutory instructions he receives from the Politician – he will pay a price. We discuss this in more detail later in this chapter, but we mention it at this point in order to stress that the Bureaucrat, like the Politician, hopes to achieve his most preferred outcomes. Both players will act strategically, however, and will take potential costs into account when striving to achieve these outcomes.

Thus, our model makes a number of assumptions about the Politician and the Bureaucrat. Both players want to achieve their most preferred policy outcomes. The Politician is less knowledgeable than the Bureaucrat about the repercussions of policy choices and faces the additional hurdle that writing detailed legislation is costly. The Bureaucrat, on the other hand, knows which outcomes will result from which policy choices, but he also knows that if he chooses a policy that produces an outcome at odds with what the Politician wants, he may pay a price for doing so.

Anyone who studies policymaking in the political systems that we examine would quickly accept the idea that bureaucrats have greater levels of policy expertise than politicians. Researchers also would certainly accept the argument that drafting legislation can be costly. And it is clear that bureaucrats have policy preferences of their own, but if, in implementing these policy preferences, they make choices that run counter to the directions they have received from elected politicians, they may suffer consequences. Yet, while all of these things make sense intuitively and are representative of the policymaking process, only the notion of information asymmetry has been included explicitly in previous models of delegation. Thus our model presents an advance over previous models and takes steps toward being more realistic by including these other features.

Finally, before moving on to discuss the different versions of the game, we need to discuss an additional assumption and an empirical implication of one of our other assumptions. First, we assume that if no policy change occurs, then the status quo is retained. The status quo in our model represents the expectations of the players about the policy outcome that will result if no new legislative action is taken. It is an outcome that has been determined by previous laws, exogenous shocks, court decisions, and any other factor that has affected policy in the past. Since our primary focus is on how statutes are designed, not on whether policy changes, we will not pay a great deal of attention to the role of the status quo in our analysis.

Second, following our discussion in Chapter 1 of the induced preferences of bureaucrats, and anticipating our empirical tests in Chapters 6 and 7, we should note that we take a narrow and stylized view of the Bureaucrat's policy preferences. In particular, it would be impossible to obtain even minimally accurate measures of the actual preferences of bureaucrats in the wide range of political systems that we study empirically. But we recognize that in all political systems, certain political actors stand at the apex of nearly every bureaucratic hierarchy and thus are privileged in their opportunities to influence policy implementation. In deriving our empirical tests, we therefore assume that the preferences of these privileged political actors strongly influence the policy preferences of bureaucrats. A governor, for example, often has substantial control over who gets appointed to head particular agencies, and often can punish bureaucrats for taking actions that are not in the governor's interests (e.g., by reassigning or even terminating them). Similarly, cabinet ministers often have substantial control over the actions of civil servants who work in the ministers' departments.

This working assumption – that the preferences of the bureaucrats are induced by the interests of a privileged politician – is entirely unnecessary from a theoretical perspective. But given the constraints we face with our data, it is crucial from a practical, empirical perspective. Furthermore, it is an assumption that we feel comfortable making after conducting numerous interviews with bureaucrats and other policymakers. We return to this issue in our empirical chapters, as well as in our concluding chapter.

The Game in Different Political Contexts

We examine the interaction of the players in three different political contexts in order to explore the effects of different types of political systems on statutes and discretion. These three models share many features, including the fact that there is only one Bureaucrat who implements policy and that the policy space is one-dimensional. Variation exists in the number, preferences, and institutional prerogatives of the Politicians.

We explore how the constitutional system – more specifically, the way in which the system identifies which players must agree on legislation – affects statutory construction by examining three models that differ in their assumptions about the distribution of proposal and veto opportunities. In our *Parliamentary model*, one Politician unilaterally establishes the contours of legislation. This model depicts the case where no significant institutional checks exist on the majority in the lower house. We thus can think of a Politician in this model as the median member of parliament, for example, or as the leader of the majority party in a parliamentary system, or as the pivotal member of a majority coalition.[3] In the *Veto model*, there are two Politicians, one (e.g., a legislative majority, as in the Parliamentary model) who has the power to propose legislation and one (e.g., a president or governor) who either accepts or vetoes legislative proposals. This model is useful for understanding policymaking in presidential systems that are unicameral, or that are bicameral with a unified legislature opposing the executive. Finally, in the *Bicameral model*, we examine the influence of institutional conflict between chambers in a bicameral system. In this version of the model, two Politicians have the power to propose policy. They have different policy preferences, and they must both agree on the content of legislation before a bill can be adopted. This model is most useful for examining bicameral bargaining in presidential systems where different parties control the two chambers.

Stages of the Game

Each of these models – the Parliamentary model, the Veto model, and the Bicameral model – has three distinct stages. In the following sections, we discuss each of these stages and elaborate further on the strategic interaction in the model.

Stage 1. In the initial legislative stage, the Politician (or Politicians) decides whether to adopt a new statute that delineates the set of policies that the Bureaucrat can implement. As we observed in earlier chapters,

[3] In Chapter 7, we discuss why multiparty coalition governments should *not* be viewed as having more than one pivotal legislative actor.

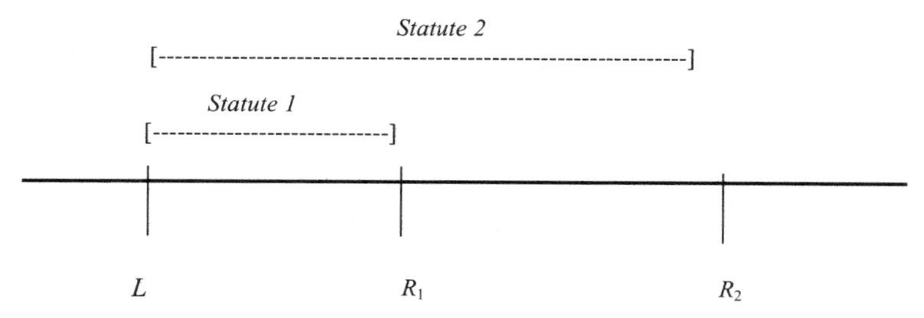

Figure 4.1 Policy discretion in statutes

there is considerable variation in the degree to which statutes actually limit the types of policies that bureaucrats can implement, and we capture this variation in our single policy dimension by allowing the Politician(s) to specify in the statute the left and right boundaries on policy.[4] Figure 4.1 depicts examples of two statutes, one that gives considerable discretion to the Bureaucrat and another that gives much less. Both statutes have a left-most boundary at L in the figure. Statute 1 has a right boundary at R_1. Thus, if Statute 1 is adopted, the Bureaucrat can comply with the statute only by implementing a policy in the interval between L and R_1.[5] Statute 2 has a right boundary at R_2, which is far to the right of R_1. This statute gives the Bureaucrat considerably more discretion than Statute 1 because the Bureaucrat can comply with the statute by implementing any policy between L and R_2. Note that a bill gives *no* discretion if the right boundary equals the left boundary (i.e., $L = R$). The central goal of our model is to understand when the Politician will adopt bills that give more or less discretion.

Stage 2. Once the Politician adopts a statute, the process turns to policy implementation, which is the domain of the Bureaucrat. In this second stage, after a new law is passed, the Bureaucrat implements a policy. As we discussed earlier, the Bureaucrat knows much more than the Politician about the repercussions of the policy choice. To capture this asymmetry in policy-specific expertise, we assume that there exists a mapping from

[4] This modeling approach is closely related to that chosen by Epstein and O'Halloran (1994, 1999).

[5] Compliance in this setting is defined as choosing a policy that falls within the bounds set by the Politician.

policies to outcomes and that while the Politician is uncertain about the mapping, the Bureaucrat is not. In other words, the Bureaucrat knows which outcomes will result from which policy choices, but the Politician does not. This is, of course, an oversimplification, but it captures the noncontroversial idea that bureaucrats in modern democracies have more information and knowledge about policies than do elected politicians.

Returning to the Medicaid examples, policies might be related to different modes of paying doctors and outcomes might be expressed as dollars saved in health expenditures. The mapping states how many dollars will be saved from each policy choice. We follow existing models in capturing these two dimensions (policy and outcomes) in a single-dimensional model. We do this by assuming that after a policy is implemented in our single dimension, the outcome will be a mapping that is a specific direction and distance away from the original policy. The distance may be zero, in which case the outcome equals the policy, or it may be positive.[6] We assume that the Bureaucrat knows the direction and distance, and that the Politician may be uncertain about this direction and distance.

How might we think intuitively about the mapping between policies and outcomes? One way would be to compare what happens when the distance is zero with what happens when it is positive. In the first scenario, policy choices lead to perfectly predictable outcomes. In the second scenario, however, the link between policies and outcomes is not so straightforward or obvious. In the first scenario, for example, a policy that is designed to increase enrollment in MMC programs might do exactly that. Thus, the policy and the outcome will be the same. In the second scenario, however, the policy might have some side effects that were not anticipated by those with limited information. It may be, for example, that the attempt to increase enrollment might also result in less money from doctors, thus decreasing doctors' incentive to participate in MMC and in turn decreasing the options for patients to enroll in managed care programs. In such a situation, the policy that is chosen might result in something other than the intended outcome. Importantly, only the Bureaucrat has the information to know about this potential repercussion.

Figure 4.2 illustrates how this policy uncertainty can affect the game. Suppose there are two possibilities:

[6] In other words, given a policy, x, and an outcome, y, there is a relationship $y = x - \varepsilon$, where $\varepsilon \in \{0,1\}$.

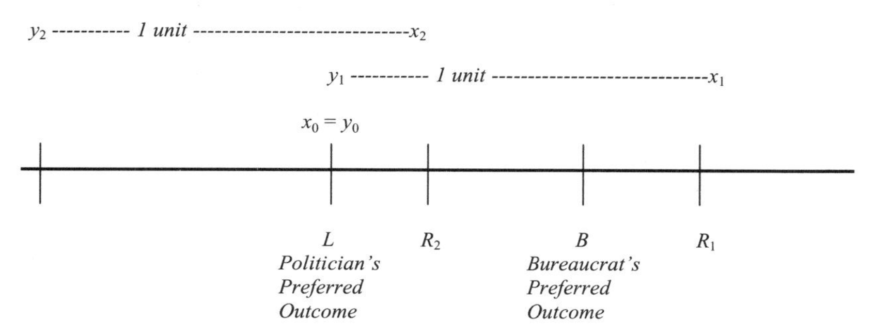

Figure 4.2 The Politician's policy uncertainty

(a) the policy implemented by the Bureaucrat is also the policy outcome (i.e., the distance is zero) or
(b) the outcome is one unit to the left of the policy implemented by the Bureaucrat.

Under the first scenario, the Politician would want the Bureaucrat to implement the policy corresponding to *L*, the Politician's ideal point. Referring to the figure, the Politician would want the Bureaucrat to implement policy x_0, which would yield an outcome, y_0, at the same point. In the second scenario, the Politician would want the Bureaucrat to implement a policy that is one unit to the right of the Politician's ideal point. In the figure, this means that the Politician wants the Bureaucrat to implement x_1, which yields an outcome of y_1, the Politician's preferred outcome.

In our models, we assume that the Politician believes with some probability that (a) is true and believes with some probability that (b) is true. If either probability is 1, then the Politician suffers no policy uncertainty. But as the probability of (a) moves to 0.5, the Politician's uncertainty about which policy produces the best outcome increases. The Bureaucrat, on the other hand, knows with certainty whether (a) or (b) is true, and thus knows which policy will achieve the desired outcome.

This policy uncertainty can lead to two types of mistakes by the Politician. One type of mistake occurs when the Politician gives the Bureaucrat too much discretion. Suppose that the Politician believes that (b) is likely and thus wants to allow the Bureaucrat to implement x_1. This requires the Politician to adopt a policy with a right boundary at R_1 in Figure 4.2. But suppose that despite the Politician's belief, (a) is the true state of the world. In this case, the Bureaucrat, whose preferred outcome is to the right of the Politician's in this example, will implement a policy at B, which yields an outcome at B. By giving the Bureaucrat too much discretion, the Politician has allowed the Bureaucrat to choose a policy that yields an outcome at the Bureaucrat's ideal point and far from her own. This possibility, of course, is a common one that motivates so much research on control of bureaucrats.

The other type of mistake occurs when the Politician fails to grant sufficient policy discretion. Suppose that the Politician believes that (a) is very likely – in other words, that the outcome is likely to equal the policy implemented. Given this belief, the Politician will want to constrain the Bureaucrat by adopting a right-side boundary that is very close to the Politician's ideal point, such as at R_2 in Figure 4.2. If in fact the Politician is mistaken and (b) describes the true state of the world, then suboptimal outcomes can occur. Suppose that the Bureaucrat complies with the statute by implementing x_2, which yields the outcome y_2. In this case, both the Bureaucrat and the Politician would have preferred a statute that allows the Bureaucrat more discretion. Given such an opportunity, the Bureaucrat could have chosen a policy that would have yielded a policy that the Politician (and the Bureaucrat) would prefer to y_2. Because of the Politician's mistaken beliefs about the link between policies and outcomes, however, the Politician gave the Bureaucrat too little discretion.

This second type of mistake is especially notable, because it points out that the Politician can hurt herself by giving the Bureaucrat too *little* discretion. If the Politician makes this sort of mistake, it can lead to a policy that is, from the Politician's viewpoint, suboptimal. In other words, the Politician can, under certain conditions, be better off when she delegates greater responsibility to a more well informed Bureaucrat.

Finally, note that when the Bureaucrat implements a policy, he knows both the nature of the statute that has been adopted by the Politician and the consequences associated with implementing various policies. In choosing which policy to implement, the Bureaucrat must decide whether to comply with the statute by choosing a policy that is within the boundaries set by the Politician. One objective of our analysis is therefore to determine whether or not a Bureaucrat will comply with the intent of the statute. We assume that if a Bureaucrat does comply with the statute, he cannot be punished, regardless of the outcome. On the other hand, if the Bureaucrat implements a policy that is outside these boundaries, then we assume that the Bureaucrat may be punished. We return to this point later in this chapter.

Stage 3. Policy outcomes are seldom determined exclusively by the content of statutes or the actions of bureaucrats. In recognizing that *nonstatutory factors* influence policy outcomes, in the third and final stage of our model, the political system responds to the action taken by the Bureaucrat. In some contexts, for example, the authors of statutes have ample opportunity to monitor and correct the actions of agents after legislation is adopted. This might occur when legislatures can veto rules adopted by agencies or when it is easy for cabinet ministers to use informal means to influence the actions of bureaucrats. In other contexts, the authors of statutes can rely on others to enforce their wishes. In some parliamentary democracies, for example, cabinet ministers can fill in the details of laws through the regulations they adopt. Similarly, judges often make decisions that influence agency actions and policy outcomes. And, of course, many parliamentary systems have developed nonlegislative avenues for creating and implementing policy in particular areas. Independent central banks, for example, often play a major role in determining the specifics of monetary policy. And in labor policy, which will be the substantive focus of some of our empirical tests, corporatist policymaking arrangements influence the incentives to use statutes for controlling bureaucratic agents.

A central assumption of our comparative theory is that politicians, when they write statutes, take into consideration how features of their political system, like those just described, affect policy outcomes. There are clearly a huge variety of political factors that affect ultimate policy outcomes, some of which may be mostly within the immediate control of politicians (e.g., legislative vetoes or ministerial regulations) and some of which may be mostly outside the immediate control of politicians (e.g., independent central banks or judges). Furthermore, as we mentioned earlier in this chapter, the existence of such features will influence the Politician's incentive to write policy details into statutes.

Rather than trying to examine all these different factors specifically, our model includes a single parameter intended to tap how favorable the nonstatutory environment is to the Politician. Specifically, we make the very simple assumption that after the Bureaucrat acts, one of two things occurs. Either no nonstatutory factors intervene to influence the policy outcome or such factors do intervene, shifting the policy outcome to the Politician's preferred policy. In the first case, the Bureaucrat is never sanctioned if the policy he implements does not comply with the statute, but in the second case, if the Bureaucrat has implemented a policy that is outside the boundaries set by the statute, he will be punished and must pay a cost. Both the

Politician and the Bureaucrat know the likelihood of these two different events.

This likelihood has straightforward implications for the design of statutes and the implementation of policy. We would expect, for example, that if a Politician knows that courts will vigorously protect the interests of politicians, then she will have fewer incentives to pay the cost of micromanaging bureaucratic behavior through the design of legislation that gives the agency little discretion. Similarly, if a Bureaucrat knows that nonstatutory factors are unlikely to intervene, the risk of implementing a policy that is inconsistent with a statute will decline, making such behavior more attractive.

We recognize that our approach to modeling these nonstatutory factors oversimplifies in many respects. The model assumes that the probability of nonstatutory factors moving policy to the Legislator's ideal point is the same as the probability of the Bureaucrat's being caught in noncompliance. It also assumes that this probability is exogenous and that it is thus unrelated to the actions of the Bureaucrat or the design of the statute itself. And it assumes that if nonstatutory factors operate, that they only move the policy to the Legislator's ideal point (rather than somewhere else in the policy space). We feel that more careful modeling of institutional variation in the nonstatutory environment is an important topic for future research, an issue we discuss in Chapter 8. But we also feel that our approach, in spite of its limitations, provides a straightforward way to investigate a host of nonstatutory factors. That is, by including an exogenous variable in the model that taps the extent to which the Politician needs to rely on policy details to obtain desired policy outcomes, we can attempt to link, both theoretically and empirically, the design of statutes to a wide range of nonlegislative institutional factors.

The Bureaucrat's Implementation Decision

Having outlined the stages of the game and the basic assumptions on which we build our theory, we now describe the logic of the model. We begin at the end, with the action of the Bureaucrat, who faces the same incentives in each of the three models. We need to understand the Bureaucrat's incentives because his expected reaction to different types of legislation will influence the optimal level of discretion for the Politician(s). We describe the Bureaucrat's decision in general terms – that is, without specifying whether he is playing the Parliamentary, Veto, or Bicameral game –

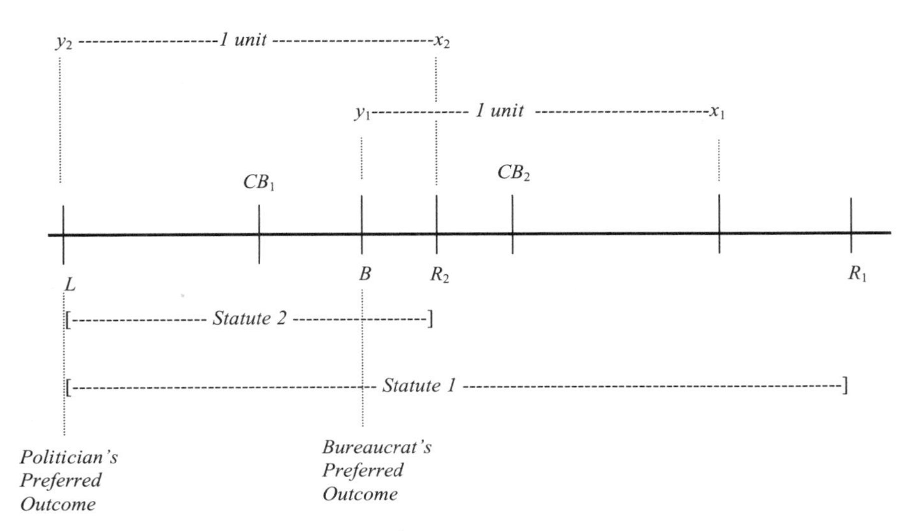

Figure 4.3 The Bureaucrat's implementation strategy

because the logic of his actions is quite general. In the following sections, we make use of the arguments in this section for each of the three versions of the model.

The Bureaucrat obviously would like to implement the policy that yields the outcome he most prefers. If the Bureaucrat's policy expertise informs him, for example, that the outcome will be one unit to the left of the policy that is implemented, then the Bureaucrat will ideally select a policy one unit to the right of his ideal point. In Figure 4.3, for example, if the Bureaucrat knows that the policy outcome will be one unit to the left of the policy that is implemented, then he would like to be able to implement a policy, x_1, that is one unit to the right of his ideal point and consequently yields y_1 as an outcome. If the statute allows sufficient discretion (as does Statute 1 in the example), then the Bureaucrat's implementation strategy will yield the Bureaucrat's most preferred policy.

The difficulty for the Bureaucrat occurs when the policy he wants to implement is outside the set of policies allowed by the statute. In Figure 4.3, for example, this occurs when Statute 2 has been adopted. In this case, the Bureaucrat faces a dilemma. If he adopts his most preferred policy, x_1, he may be caught and sanctioned, since this policy is outside the set of policies described by the statute. Alternatively, he could adopt a "safe" policy, one that is consistent with the statute. In the figure, the optimal safe policy for the Bureaucrat is at x_2, which is within the bounds allowed by Statute 2. By adopting this policy, he obtains a policy outcome, y_2, which, although far from his ideal point, is the best outcome he can obtain for which he cannot be punished.

The optimal choice for the Bureaucrat obviously depends on the probability of sanctions for the risky policy and the magnitude of these sanctions. These variables create a point that we call the *compliance boundary*, which captures the idea that the Bureaucrat will be forced to make a strategic calculation when faced with a statute that does not allow him to safely achieve his most preferred policy outcome. On the one hand, he can comply with the statute. Doing so, however, means that the policy outcome will be some distance from his ideal point, a distance that will increase as the statute becomes more restrictive. On the other hand, the Bureaucrat can implement the policy that yields his preferred outcome, regardless of what the statute specifies. While such noncompliant behavior might lead to a better outcome for the Bureaucrat if he is not caught, there is some probability that he will be caught and sanctioned. And if this happens, the final policy outcome could end up even further away from his ideal point than the outcome he could have produced had he complied with the statute.

In order to decide which policy to implement, the Bureaucrat will compare the net benefits from noncompliance to the benefits he would obtain from simply (and safely) complying with the statute, and if the latter exceed the former, then he will comply with the law. The compliance boundary is the point at which these combined benefits and costs of noncompliance are equal to the benefits of compliance. The Bureaucrat is exactly indifferent between implementing a law that is at the compliance boundary (thereby avoiding any risk of sanction) and implementing a policy that yields the Bureaucrat's most preferred policy but that also risks sanction.

More generally, the Bureaucrat will comply with any law that has a right boundary above (to the right of) the compliance boundary and will not comply with any law that has a right boundary below (to the left of) the compliance boundary. Furthermore, as the risk of being caught or the penalty for noncompliance increase, the compliance boundary moves away from the Bureaucrat's preferred policy. Alternatively, as this risk and penalty decline, the Bureaucrat has less to risk from implementing a policy that is inconsistent with the statute, and the compliance boundary therefore moves toward the Bureaucrat's most preferred policy. Hence, the compliance boundary reflects important information about the probability of being caught in noncompliance and the penalty for this noncompliance, and thus about the Bureaucrat's behavior.

In Figure 4.3, for example, if either sanctions or the probability of getting caught are reasonably large, the compliance boundary may be relatively far to the left of the Bureaucrat's ideal point, perhaps at CB_1. In this situation, the right boundaries of Statutes 1 and 2 are both above CB_1, which means that the Bureaucrat prefers complying with either statute to implementing a policy that yields the Bureaucrat's ideal point (but risks sanction). CB_2 depicts a compliance boundary where sanctions or the probability of getting caught (or both) are lower than those associated with CB_1. In this case, the Bureaucrat will comply with Statute 1 but will not comply with Statute 2, which has a right boundary below the compliance boundary.

The Bureaucrat's response to any statute is therefore straightforward. If the statute allows sufficient discretion so that its right boundary is above the compliance boundary, the Bureaucrat will implement the policy that he most prefers from among those policies that comply with the statute. If the statute limits discretion too much, and thus has a right boundary below the Bureaucrat's compliance boundary, he will take a chance and risk sanctions by implementing the policy that yields his most preferred outcome. In effect, if the potential benefits of choosing a noncompliant policy outweigh the risks and potential costs of doing so, then the Bureaucrat may choose to ignore the statutory instructions he receives. This, in turn, implies that the Bureaucrat is more likely to follow the Politician's instructions if the political system is likely to catch noncompliant behavior and if the potential benefits of such behavior are low.

Several observations about the Bureaucrat's strategy are helpful for understanding the strategic incentives in the model. First, the location of the compliance boundary depends not only on the probability of nonstatutory factors moving policy and the magnitude of sanctions, but also on the relationship between policies and outcomes. In Figure 4.3, for example, we assume that the Bureaucrat knows that the outcome will be one unit to the left of the policy that is implemented. If instead the Bureaucrat knows that the outcome will be equal to the policy implemented, the compliance boundary will move to the right. Obviously, then, the Bureaucrat's compliance boundary depends on the relationship between policies and outcomes, which only the Bureaucrat may know with certainty. The Politician's policy uncertainty thus affects the nature of the statute she adopts and can lead to noncompliant behavior.

Second, the compliance boundary can be below the Politician's ideal point for one or more states of the world – that is, for one or more of the possible mappings from policies to outcomes. If in our models the compliance boundary is above the Politician's ideal point for all states of the world, then there will exist many situations in which the Politician can never write a statute that will lead to her preferred policy outcome. For example, if there is a state of the world such that outcomes and policies are identical, then the Politician cannot write a statute that yields her most preferred policy when the compliance boundary is above her ideal point. This cannot occur, however, if the nonstatutory mechanisms are sufficiently effective, the Bureaucrat's ideal policy is not too extreme, and/or sanctions for noncompliant behavior are minimally deterrent.

In some situations, it might be reasonable to assume that none of these conditions are satisfied. It may be the case, for example, that during democratic transitions – when the state apparatus remains dominated by individuals loyal to the previous authoritarian regime – it is impossible for new governments to write statutes that will induce bureaucrats to implement the government's preferred policy. In the mature and stable democracies that are our focus, however, this seems highly unlikely. In such systems, there typically exist legitimate judiciaries that can discipline recalcitrant state officials. There are very real sanctions for breaking the law. And there exist competitive selection mechanisms that usually ensure that bureaucrats are not policy extremists (e.g., Aberbach, Putnam, and Rockman 1981). Our analysis therefore focuses on cases where there always exists some statute that *could* produce compliant behavior. This does not imply that compliant behavior will always occur, however, because our Politician's uncertainty can lead her to write a statute that limits discretion too much.

Third, on this point, our assumption that bureaucrats can *choose* whether to comply with statutes stands in contrast to previous theories discussed in Chapter 2. Those models invariably assume that statutes define the possible policies that bureaucrats can implement and thereby preclude, by assumption, the possibility that statutory instructions may be ignored. In our theory, the Bureaucrat chooses whether or not to comply with statutes, and both compliant and noncompliant behavior can emerge in equilibrium. We believe that this is a more appropriate assumption about agent behavior, given that even in mature democracies, agents are often discovered to have taken actions that are not in compliance with statutes. It also allows us to examine factors that lead to noncompliant behavior.

Finally, our analysis of the Bureaucrat's implementation strategy provides an important insight about the Politician's optimal statute. Most importantly, it will never be optimal for the Politician to adopt a statute that the Bureaucrat is certain to ignore (i.e., that has a right boundary below the Bureaucrat's compliance boundary for all states of the world). This is true because adopting a statute that limits discretion is costly. Why would the Politician want to pay these costs if there is no chance that the Bureaucrat will pay attention to the policy constraints inherent in the statute? The Politician would clearly prefer to adopt a vague, low-cost statute that allows the Bureaucrat to implement the policy she most prefers than to adopt a low-discretion, high-cost statute that results in exactly the same policy outcome.

This observation reminds us that one strategy that is always available to the Politician is to adopt the least costly, highest-discretion statute possible. Such a statute, which allows the Bureaucrat to implement any policy he desires, will obviously result in a policy outcome that corresponds to the Bureaucrat's most preferred policy. Alternatively, the Politician can pay the costs of limiting discretion in an effort to move the final policy away from the Bureaucrat's most preferred policy and closer to the Politician's. We want to understand the factors that increase the likelihood that the Politician will want to pay the costs of adopting a low-discretion law.

Legislation and Discretion in the Parliamentary Model

Our expectation about the circumstances under which an increase in policy conflict should lead to an increase in the adoption of low-discretion statutes depends on the level of legislative capacity. Recall that the Politician must pay a cost to adopt a low-discretion law and that this cost is a function of legislative capacity. Obviously, the relative value of adopting a low-discretion law will increase as legislative capacity increases (and thus as the costs decrease).

To see the different possibilities about how policy conflict and legislative capacity can interact to influence legislative statutes, it is useful to consider some examples. In these examples, we make a number of assumptions for simplicity. First, there is no policy uncertainty; both the Politician and the Bureaucrat know that the policy outcome will be whatever policy the

Bureaucrat implements. Second, nonstatutory factors do not exist and will not affect outcomes. Third, the Bureaucrat will comply with the statute. Finally, there is at least some conflict between the Politician and the Bureaucrat.

First, consider two extreme laws, a very-high-discretion law that allows the Bureaucrat to do whatever he wants and a very-low-discretion law that forces the Bureaucrat to implement a very specific policy. If a very-high-discretion law is adopted, the Bureaucrat will implement *B*, the policy he most prefers; and because nonstatutory factors do not exist, this policy will also be the final outcome. Correspondingly, a statute that gives the Bureaucrat no discretion will force the Bureaucrat to implement the Politician's favored policy, and this will produce an outcome at *L*, the Politician's ideal point. If we assume that the Politician's policy utility decreases linearly as the policy moves away from her preferred outcome, then the policy gain from adopting the low-discretion statute is the distance from the Legislator's ideal point to the Bureaucrat's ideal point. That is, if the Bureaucrat and the Politician have only a small degree of conflict over policy, where *L* and *B* are close together, then there is only a small benefit to writing the low-discretion statute; but if the policy conflict is great, with *L* and *B* being far apart, then the benefits of the low-discretion statute are large.

If the low-discretion law were costless, the Politician would always want to adopt it, since it yields her preferred outcome. But typically it will not be costless to craft precise policy details in a statute. The question for the Politician, then, is whether the benefits of the low-discretion law outweight the costs of producing such a law.

In Figure 4.4 we illustrate how the answer to this question can be dependent on both the amount of policy conflict and the costs of writing a low-discretion law. In this figure, we present three potential policy preferences for the Bureaucrat, with B_1 representing the shortest distance from *L* and thus the least amount of conflict, B_3 representing the most conflict, and B_2 being in the middle. In addition, we depict several levels of costs, which correspond to various levels of legislative capacity. As we know, writing a detailed low-discretion law is not easy, and some Politicians – those with low capacity – will face very high costs in writing such a law. Others, however – those with high capacity – will find that these costs are actually fairly low. In our figure, c_1 depicts the lowest costs and highest capacity, while c_6 represents the highest costs and lowest capacity.

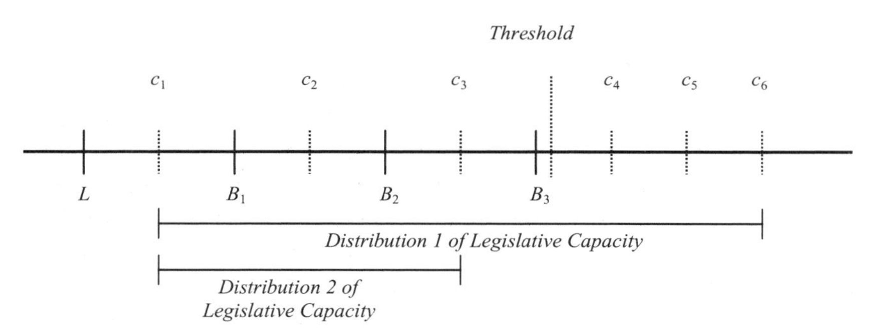

Figure 4.4 Policy conflict, legislative capacity, and discretion in legislation

Recall that in our example, the outcome will always be located at either the Politician's or the Bureaucrat's ideal point. Assume, for example, that the Bureaucrat has a preferred policy at B_1. If the Politician adopts a low-discretion statute, the Bureaucrat will implement L, but if she adopts a high-discretion statute, the Bureaucrat will implement B_1. The crucial factor for the Politician who is deciding between these two laws, and the two outcomes these laws will produce, is the cost of the low-discretion law. If the Politician has a high level of capacity, she will face a low cost in writing a detailed statute. If the cost of the low-discretion statute is c_1, then for this relatively high-capacity Politician, the policy benefit from the low-discretion statute (i.e., the distance from L to B_1) is greater than the costs (i.e., the distance from L to c_1). But if legislative capacity is lower, with costs, for example, at c_2, the costs of the low-discretion statute exceed the benefits, and we should expect the Politician to adopt the high-discretion statute. Thus, as costs increase from c_1 to c_2 – that is, as legislative capacity decreases – the adoption of low-discretion laws becomes less likely.

The same intuition operates with respect to policy conflict. If the costs of a low-discretion statute are fixed at c_2, then the benefits of the low-discretion statute do not exceed the costs when the Bureaucrat's ideal point is located at B_1. Since the costs of writing the low-discretion law exceed its benefits, a Politician faced with this scenario will opt instead for the high-discretion law. But if the Bureaucrat's ideal point is at B_2, the policy benefits of the low-discretion law increase. Thus, holding capacity fixed (with costs of a low-discretion statute equal to c_2), an increase in policy conflict from B_1 to B_2 leads to the adoption of a low-discretion as opposed to a high-discretion statute.

A tempting inference to draw from these examples is that all else equal, increases in legislative capacity and policy conflict should lead to increases in the adoption of low-discretion statutes. In fact, however, as we move from the model to empirical predictions about how policy conflict and legislative capacity influence the design of statutes, two related but distinct hypotheses can be derived from the model. On the one hand, the model can predict the direct effect of policy conflict and legislative capacity. That is, all else equal, more legislative capacity and more policy conflict should lead to more low-discretion legislation. On the other hand, the model also suggests an interactive effect of legislative capacity and policy conflict. The interactive hypothesis suggests that there exists a *threshold* of policy conflict that must be surpassed before we expect the level of legislative capacity to influence discretion in legislation (or, identically, there exists a legislative capacity threshold that must be surpassed before policy conflict influences discretion). As we will demonstrate shortly, determining which of these two formulations is appropriate is an empirical rather than a theoretical question because we cannot know, ex ante, where the threshold lies.

To see this, return to Figure 4.4. Assume that we have collected data on discretion in statutes from a large number of political systems, and that our measures of legislative capacity and policy conflict vary across these statutes and political systems. Figure 4.4 depicts three different possible levels of policy conflict. It also depicts two possible distributions of legislative capacity. The main difference between these two distributions is that Distribution 1 has a much wider range of legislative capacities. In Distribution 1, the range of costs for adopting low-discretion statutes is from a low of c_1 to a high of c_6. In other words, in this distribution there exist a wide range of legislative capacities within these systems, ranging from those with very high capacity (e.g., c_1) to those with very low capacity (e.g., c_6). In Distribution 2, on the other hand, these costs range only from c_1 to c_3. Thus, Distribution 2 consists of a set of political systems with high legislative capacity and the attendant small costs of adopting low-discretion laws.

To understand when our model should lead us to look for interactive effects, consider Distribution 1 in which there is a wide range of legislative capacities. If the costs to our political systems were arrayed along the continuum described by this distribution, we would be unlikely to uncover direct effects of policy conflict and legislative capacity on discretion because many of the political systems have insufficient capacity to *ever* adopt a low-discretion statute. In other words, their costs of designing a low-discretion statute exceed the policy benefits for any level of policy conflict. Since the policy gains from low-discretion laws must exceed the costs in order for the politician to adopt such a statute, the highest possible level of conflict creates a threshold. If a political system has legislative costs of low-discretion statutes that exceed this threshold, then changes in capacity and changes in policy conflict will never affect the decision to adopt a low-discretion statute. As the costs of adopting low-discretion laws decrease from c_6 to c_5, or from c_5 to c_4, for example, there is no effect on the adoption of low-discretion laws because in either case, even if conflict is at its highest, the costs of low-discretion laws exceed the policy benefits. By the same logic, obviously, if costs are somewhere above the "threshold," then changes in policy conflict – say from B_1 to B_2 or from B_2 to B_3 – would have no effect on the adoption of low-discretion statutes.

Among the group of political systems that have relatively high capacity (e.g., costs below the threshold), the story is different. Among these systems, increases in conflict or capacity are much more likely to have a direct effect on the adoption of low-discretion laws. As we move from low conflict (B_1) to medium conflict (B_2) for example, many systems will adopt low-discretion statutes (e.g., all those systems whose costs are to the left of B_2), and others that will adopt low-discretion statutes as we move from medium conflict to high conflict. Similarly, if we hold conflict constant, as capacity increases in this range (e.g., as costs of low-discretion legislation decline from c_3 to c_2 or from c_2 to c_1), so does the likelihood that the costs of low-discretion laws will be smaller than the policy benefits.

This discussion demonstrates that whether we should look for direct versus interactive effects of policy conflict and capacity depends on empirical rather than conceptual factors. If the location of the threshold implies that a significant number of political systems will never have the resources to adopt low-discretion laws (as in Distribution 1), then direct effects will be zero for many systems and thus will be difficult to uncover. Instead, we should expect an interactive effect, with capacity (alternatively, policy conflict) having an effect only after we exceed the necessary level of conflict (alternatively, capacity). In other words, to uncover the influence of capacity on discretion, capacity must be interacted with conflict. By contrast, if the location of the threshold is such that most systems have enough capacity to respond to the highest levels of conflict (as in Distribution 2), then

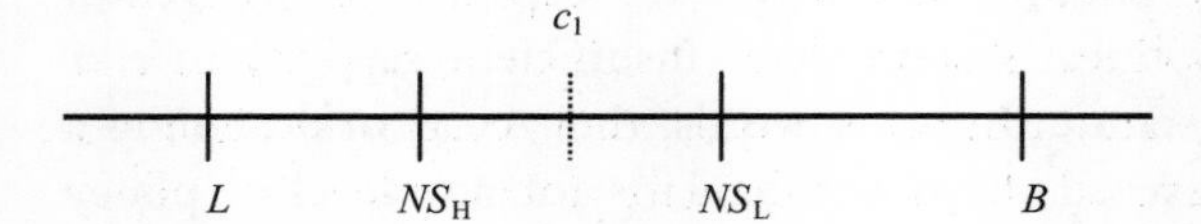

Figure 4.5 Nonstatutory factors and discretion in legislation

the model predicts direct effects of policy conflict and capacity. The practical problem we face is that we do not know, ex ante, where the threshold is in our distribution of capacity and policy conflict. Since we cannot observe where the threshold lies, a logical approach is to simply test for both types of effects. We can then learn from the data the extent to which the lowest-capacity legislatures are able to respond to incentives that might exist to create low-discretion laws. We return to this issue in Chapters 6 and 7.

To this point, we have focused only on legislative capacity and policy conflict. Recall that regardless of the level of discretion that exists in a bill, nonstatutory factors will, with some probability, help the Politician achieve her desired outcome. The Politician therefore realizes the full benefits of a low-discretion law only when nonstatutory factors are inoperative. That is, even when policy conflict and legislative capacity are such that the Politician has an incentive to engage in writing a low-discretion law, the value of the low-discretion law relative to a high-discretion law decreases as nonstatutory mechanisms become more reliable for the Politician.

Figure 4.5 gives the intuition for this result. As earlier, assume for simplicity in this figure that adopting a low-discretion statute yields the Politician's most preferred policy. Now further assume that with some probability, factors such as judicial intervention or legislative oversight move the policy to the Politician's ideal point, independent of the language in the statute. When such factors lurk as a possibility, the outcome from the high-discretion statute will be either the Politician's preferred outcome (when such factors operate) or the Bureaucrat's preferred outcome (when such factors do not operate). Since the Bureaucrat's preferred outcome is at *B*, the expected outcome from the high-discretion statute will be somewhere between *B* and *L*. Figure 4.5 depicts two possible expected outcomes. At NS_L the nonstatutory factors operate with relatively low probability, and at NS_H these factors operate with relatively higher probability (moving the expected outcome closer to the Politician's preferred outcome). The figure also depicts the expected cost, c_1, of adopting a low-discretion statute.

If nonstatutory factors are operating with low probability (producing the expected outcome at NS_L), the Politician benefits from adopting a low-discretion statute. This is true because the gains from moving from an expected outcome at NS_L to a guaranteed outcome at L exceed the costs of doing so. But if nonstatutory factors are more effective, yielding an expected outcome at NS_H, this is no longer the case. Instead, the Politician is more likely to get her desired outcome independent of what she writes in the statute, lowering the relative value of the low-discretion statute. Thus, nonstatutory factors create a substitution effect. As these factors become more reliable, the Politician will be less inclined to pay the costs of a low-discretion statute.

Legislation and Discretion in the Veto Model

We have discussed rather carefully how policy conflict, legislative capacity, and nonstatutory factors influence the decision to adopt a low-discretion statute in the Parliamentary model (where the Politician unilaterally determines the level of discretion in the statute). Increases in policy conflict or legislative capacity increase the relative value of low-discretion statutes, though our specific expectations about whether these effects are direct or indirect depend on the distribution of legislative capacity in the political systems that we study. Increases in the reliability of nonstatutory mechanisms, by contrast, decrease the relative value of low-discretion statutes.

We now turn to the effects of these variables in the Veto model, where a President must consent to the adoption of any new statute. Importantly, all of the insights from the Parliamentary model carry over to the Veto model. When an executive veto exists, we find that the relative value of low-discretion statutes increases as policy conflict between the Politician and the Bureaucrat increases, as legislative capacity increases, and as nonstatutory factors become less reliable. These are, of course, the same findings that emerged from the Parliamentary model.

It is not hard to see why the logic of the main results in the Parliamentary model carries over to other institutional contexts. Consider the Veto model, where there exists one Politician (e.g., the legislature) that adopts a policy and another Politician (e.g., the President) that has a veto prerogative. We assume that the President and the Bureaucrat have the same preferences. In some situations, the threat of the veto has no effect on behavior. If the status quo is to the left of the Politician in any of the preceding figures, for example, any policy that makes the Politician better off also makes the President better off. Thus, there are no credible veto threats and the Politician's strategic incentives are the same in the two models.

For some locations of the status quo, no new policy can be adopted. This might occur, for example, when the status quo is between the President and the Politician. In this case, the veto obviously does not affect the level of discretion in statutes that are adopted, but it does affect whether any policy change occurs.

Finally, if the status quo is relatively far to the right of the Bureaucrat in any of the preceding figures, the basic strategic incentives will be the same as in the Parliamentary model. In particular, there will exist some statute that has the optimal level of constraints given the Politician's belief about the location of the compliance boundary. As in the Parliamentary model, the Politician will propose this only if her legislative capacity is sufficient. Given a particular level of legislative capacity, the relative value of the low-discretion statute will increase as policy conflict between the Politician and the Bureaucrat increases. And this relative value of the low-discretion statute will decrease as nonstatutory factors become more reliable for the Politician.

A noteworthy additional insight that emerges from the Veto model is that the threat of the veto can never lead to less discretion, but in some cases it will lead to more discretion than we would find in the Parliamentary model. That a veto can never lead to less discretion is rather obvious. It cannot be the case that adding a constraint on the amount of discretion that the Politician can adopt will lead her to adopt statutes with less discretion than she would want in the absence of this constraint. The result that a veto can lead to more discretion is somewhat subtler, but the logic is easy to see in Figure 4.6.

For simplicity in conveying the idea, assume that (a) all the players in the model know that the final policy outcome will be the same as the policy the Bureaucrat implements; (b) the Politician has sufficient capacity to adopt any statute she wishes; (c) the Bureaucrat sufficiently fears sanctions that he will comply with any bill; and (d) the Politician and Bureaucrat prefer different policy outcomes. If there were no veto, a Politician who could act alone would implement a low-discretion bill with a left and a right boundary at L, her most preferred policy. The President, however,

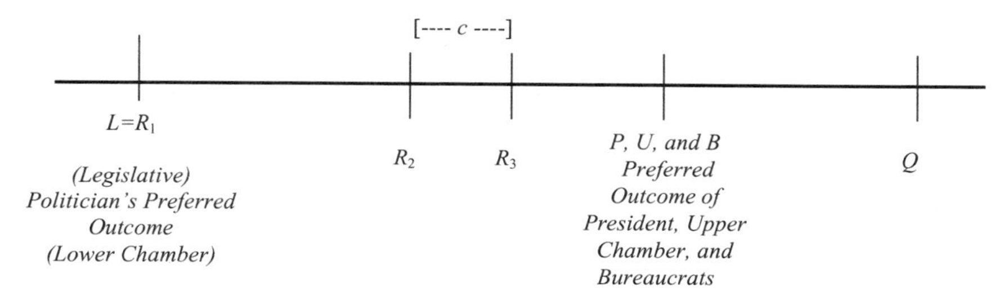

Figure 4.6 Vetoes, bicameral bargaining, and discretion in legislation

would realize that he prefers the status quo, Q, to this outcome and would veto such a bill. Thus, in the Veto model, the Politician must give the Bureaucrat leeway to implement a policy that the President will accept. This might be a policy, for example, with an upper bound at R_2, because in such a case, the Bureaucrat would implement R_2. Hence, the existence of the veto causes the Politician to give the Bureaucrat more discretion, since in the absence of such discretion, the President would prefer Q to the legislatively induced policy outcome.

Legislation Discretion in the Bicameral Model

Our last theoretical argument concerns the bargaining environment. Our model shows that when bicameral bargaining is necessary, the discretion in statutes cannot decline and often will be greater. We can see the logic in Figure 4.6.

Assume that if bicameral bargaining is necessary, both the Upper and the Lower Chamber can make policy proposals, and they do so sequentially. If the first proposal is met with a counterproposal by the other house, then the two chambers must pay a bargaining cost associated with the opportunity cost of delay. The well-recognized result of such models (e.g., Baron and Ferejohn 1989) is that a privileged actor in the model can always extract the bargaining costs from the other actor, taking a policy payoff in lieu of paying the inefficient bargaining costs. In this model, the chamber that shares the preferences of the Bureaucrat is always privileged because this chamber prefers more discretion to less.

To see this, assume in Figure 4.6 that the bargaining cost of a counterproposal is given by c. Furthermore, assume, for simplicity, that neither chamber pays any other cost of making a proposal. Finally, assume that the Upper Chamber has made a policy proposal and the Lower Chamber now has to decide whether to pay the bargaining costs of making a counterproposal. In this case, the best proposal the Lower Chamber can make is R_2, since the President would veto anything that is worse. Proposing R_2 yields an outcome of R_2 but also entails a cost, c. Thus, the Upper Chamber can take advantage of this in its initial proposal. It can propose R_3 as an upper bound on policy, for example. This policy will be accepted by the Lower Chamber because it prefers a policy outcome at R_3 and zero bargaining costs to an outcome at R_2 that has bargaining costs c. Thus, the Upper Chamber has extracted the bargaining costs from the Lower Chamber in the form of increased legislative discretion. This, of course, is but one example, but the result is more general. For any level of bargaining costs and any order of proposing, the ultimate bill cannot give less discretion and often will give more.

Institutional Context and Policymaking by Statute

Our models describe how the level of discretion in legislation should vary with specific features of the political and institutional context in which politicians find themselves. The arguments are easily summarized:

- As policy conflict between politicians and bureaucrats increases, or as legislative capacity increases, the relative value to politicians of low-discretion statutes increases.
- Whether the model predicts a direct or interactive effect of these two variables on discretion depends on the distribution of legislative capacity and policy conflict among the political systems that are analyzed. If there are a large number of political systems that never have sufficient capacity to adopt a low-discretion law, then we should expect interactive effects (where, for example, legislative capacity influences the design of statutes only if the level of policy conflict is sufficiently high). By contrast, if a large number of political systems have high legislative capacity, the effects of these two variables should be direct.
- As the ability of politicians to rely on nonstatutory factors to achieve policy objectives increases, the relative value of low-discretion laws declines.
- These results hold in parliamentary and presidential systems.

- In presidential systems, bicameral conflict often leads to more discretion.

These results are highly intuitive. When elected politicians trust bureaucrats to make the "right" policy choices – that is, the policy choices that produce the outcomes they prefer – we should expect these politicians to write vague statutes and to give bureaucrats broad grants of policymaking authority. In addition, we should expect the propensity of politicians to micromanage the policymaking process in legislation to be affected by their capacity to do so. Incentives to place policy details in legislation also should decrease if the politicians can rely on nonstatutory means to achieve their objectives. And if there is disagreement between two legislative chambers that are constitutionally vested with the power to write legislative language, then the chamber that wants clear policy constraints in legislation will face greater difficulties placing this language in legislation than when unconstrained by the other chamber. In short, by looking at the interaction of incentive and capacity, and by acknowledging that both incentive and capacity are affected and determined by broad features of the political system, we can come to understand how the political context affects the extent to which policy details are spelled out in legislation.

Though these results are highly intuitive, the model has helped bring into sharp relief subtler issues related to the interactions between the central variables in our model. We find, for example, that previous arguments about policy conflict – such as those focusing on divided government in presidential systems – cannot be applied willy-nilly, independent of the broader institutional context. Divided government might lead to incentives to write low-discretion laws, but this effect might differ across political systems. How we uncover and evaluate such effects depends fundamentally on the nature of our political systems, and in particular on the distribution of legislative capacity and policy conflict across political systems.

The model is useful because it also provides a clear logic about issues that are substantively important but difficult to examine empirically. In this chapter, we have focused on the insights of the model with respect to legislative discretion, which is our central empirical focus. But the model also speaks to other issues as well, such as the factors that affect the propensity of bureaucrats to comply with statutes, the ability of the legislative majority to obtain desired policy outcomes, and the responsiveness of political systems to the need for policy change. We return to these issues in Chapter 8. Before doing so, however, we turn to the main empirical task at hand, which is to test the theoretical arguments developed in this chapter about discretion in legislation.

5

Legislation, Agency Policymaking, and Medicaid in Michigan

Like every other U.S. state, Michigan faced an explosion in Medicaid participation and costs in the early 1990s. From 1990 to 1994 alone, the number of persons eligible for Medicaid grew nearly 25%, from 1,173,384 to 1,464,923.[1] Much of this growth was due to new federal guidelines that increased the number of persons eligible for Medicaid.[2] Partly as a result of this increased participation, during this same time period total expenditures increased from $2,078,412,202 to $4,103,376,419, or 97.4%. By 1995, Medicaid expenditures consumed 20% of the state's budget.

In this chapter we explore a case study, based on extensive interviews with key participants from the state legislature, the Michigan Department of Community Health, and affected interest groups, of Michigan's attempt to bring these costs under control while maintaining sufficient standards of care for Medicaid clients. While a case study like this has some clear benefits, as we will discuss, it also suffers from a significant restriction that we readily acknowledge up front. A focus on any single state precludes us from exploring the influence of some of the most important elements of our theory: namely, the institutions, or rules, that vary across political systems. To be more specific, we cannot examine how behavior in Michigan was influenced by alternative mechanisms for control or by

[1] Figures in this paragraph are from Fairgrieve (1995).

[2] Federal mandates in this time period included (a) pregnant women and their newborn children up to 185% of the poverty level, (b) children under age six up to 133% of the poverty level, (c) children up to age nine below 100% of poverty level, and (d) 12 months of transitional Medicaid coverage for AFDC recipients who leave AFDC because they get jobs.

legislative capacity, as these remained constant in Michigan during the period we examine. Thus, we clearly cannot, and do not, treat the evidence from this case study as a test of our theory.

We can, however, use a single-state case study to accomplish several other significant things. First, although we cannot examine the influence of alternative mechanisms for control, or legislative capacity, we can focus on the variables in our theory that might vary within a system and that do vary over time in our Michigan case study. These variables, both of which were identified as central to our theory in Chapter 4, are policy conflict between the legislator and the agency and bicameral bargaining. We investigate the causal relationship between each of these two factors and the way Michigan legislators addressed the issue of Medicaid policy. In addition, focusing on a specific policy in a specific state allows us to show how legislatures use policy language, and not just procedural language, when constraining bureaucrats. Thus, the case allows us to examine whether some of the mechanisms posited by our theory do indeed work in the way our argument says they do and to determine whether the theory describes the behavior of politicians in actual bargaining processes.

Second, the case study helps us to motivate some of the decisions we make in the quantitative empirical tests we offer in Chapter 6. In particular, the case study illustrates why divided party government provides a good measure of the level of conflict between legislators and bureaucrats, and why divided party control of legislative chambers provides a suitable measure of the level of bicameral conflict. It also has implications for how to gather data from the states to measure our dependent variable. Consistent with our more aggregate findings presented in Chapter 3, the case study demonstrates that longer statutes are more specific and provide greater constraints on the actions of bureaucrats.

Finally, the case study serves as an important reminder of the substantive importance of understanding how the level of discretion in statutes is determined. As noted in Chapter 2, the lion's share of research on this subject has centered on the questions of whether legislatures control agencies and whether such control (or the lack of it) is good or bad. Our case study of Michigan shows how legislatures attempt to design statutes in order to constrain discretion and, more importantly, what factors affect this design. It also illustrates an important implication beyond that of discretion: transparency in public policy decision making. We return to these general issues in the conclusion.

The Beginning of Managed Care in Michigan

We begin with a brief history of Michigan's experience with Medicaid, which dates back to 1966. Like every other U.S. state, Michigan initially contracted with insurance companies to process Medicaid claims. But soon thereafter, the state's Department of Social Services (DSS) decided to phase out the role of insurance companies.[3] By 1972, the DSS had taken over Medicaid entirely and had become responsible for all aspects of the system, including billings and contracts.

A significant change in the Medicaid program took place in 1973, when some HMOs in the Detroit area approached the state with a proposal to introduce some of the principles of managed care into the state's Medicaid system. In response, the state decided to implement the beginnings of a managed care framework for Medicaid participants who lived in Wayne County, the region in southeast Michigan that contains most of the Detroit metropolitan area.

Over the next two decades, the state's use of managed care continued to evolve. The primary form of managed care that the state used was what is known as a *gatekeeper system*, wherein access to specialists was restricted and patients had to be referred to specialists by participating primary care physicians. In time, the state also began to adopt other sorts of cost containment strategies and developed other kinds of managed care arrangements, such as a physician-sponsored plan in Wayne County. In addition, Republican John Engler, upon becoming governor following the 1990 election, had the state expand the use of HMOs beyond Wayne County to the rest of the state.[4] By 1991, virtually all eligible participants in Wayne County were enrolled in managed care arrangements, and by 1994 a large proportion of AFDC and Supplemental Security Income (SSI) recipients also were enrolled in managed care.

In general, however, Michigan's use of Medicaid managed care (MMC) was rather limited prior to the 1990s. The state's program mainly utilized

[3] Blue Cross/Blue Shield and Traveller's were the first companies to be involved, and they processed primarily long-term care claims.

[4] The physician-sponsored plan was developed in 1981 by the Michigan Medical Association and the Michigan Osteopathic Society. The Clinic Plan was also developed at this time. Clinics function as HMOs but are not necessarily licensed as HMOs. These plans were voluntary at first, but eventually were made mandatory for most groups other than spend-down populations with sporadic eligibility, people paying for long-term care, and those who were also eligible for Medicare.

the gatekeeping system and did not affect payments, which remained on what was essentially a fee-for-service basis. In such systems, health care providers, such as doctors or hospitals, are reimbursed at a given rate for any and all actions they take when treating a patient. The more frequently a patient visits a doctor, or the more tests the doctor orders for a patient, the more money the doctor receives. A more common managed care approach uses a capitation system in which providers are paid a set amount for each patient, regardless of how often the patient is seen or how many treatments and tests the patient needs.

Under a fee-for-service approach, doctors have no incentive to choose less expensive treatments or limit the number of tests for any given patient; indeed, as many health policy analysts have pointed out, their incentives under such a system are to provide as *many* tests and the *most* expensive treatments available. Under a system of capitation, however, the incentives are reversed. Since a doctor receives the same amount for a patient – a capitated amount – whether he or she sees that patient once a year or ten times a year, the doctor has an incentive to limit the patient's use of the health care system. Although Michigan eventually moved, as we shall see, to a capitation system for Medicaid, initially it relied mostly on gatekeeping to keep costs down.[5]

To keep tabs on the MMC system, the Michigan legislature created a classic "fire alarm" system (McCubbins and Schwartz 1984). More explicitly, it created a committee to monitor the system and then appropriated $30,000 – which, as one staffer put it, "was real money back then" – directly to this committee. The legislature also stipulated that the monitoring committee should be chaired by groups that were advocates for Medicaid clients. The idea, of course, was to make sure that the use of managed care would not lead to a reduction in service or quality. To monitor the system, the committee would, for example, take a monthly sample of enrollees, call them, and ask them questions about the level of service. Committee members and staffers also would pose as Medicaid clients and call doctors' offices to ensure that someone was accepting calls from Medicaid clients and that these clients were allowed to make appointments. An analyst who served in the bureaucracy at the time recalls the way in which this monitoring committee worked:

[5] Under Michigan's Clinic Plan, there was capitation for outpatient services but not for inpatient hospital services, which accounts for the vast majority of spending.

In other words, we turned over to the advocacy community the right to look at everything we did. And they looked at a lot – they'd call the new enrollees to see how things were going, they'd call doctors to make sure they were complying with rules. And then they'd alert us and the legislature when things were wrong.

Thus, the monitoring committee used its funding to check closely whether the system was working and whether the state bureaucracy was running the system in accord with the legislature's preferences. In addition, the same analyst argued that although such an approach might seem intrusive, some also saw it as necessary:

The whole thing of managed care was so new, and so fearful, that in order to get it through, we pushed on. Everything was challenged by the legislature (and the monitoring committee). And if there was a problem, the legislature found out right away, real-time. We knew we liked managed care; so we said if we have to go slower, then that's okay.[6]

Furthermore, while this committee was nominally outside of the legislature, there was very little doubt about whether it sided more with the legislature or the bureaucracy.

Everything we (DSS) tried to do was challenged by [Democratic Representative] Hollister and these monitoring committees. Technically, the committee reported to DSS, but in reality it functioned as an arm of the legislature.

In essence, heading into the 1990s, managed care had a well-established foothold in the Michigan Medicaid program. Although the state was not using a capitation system, which was the primary cost-saving technique traditionally used by managed care organizations in the private sector, it was using other features of managed care, such as gatekeeping and physician-sponsored organizations. In addition, although the bureaucracy was given a great deal of authority to implement Medicaid policy, the legislature, with the help of the monitoring committee it had created, was keeping tabs on how well this system was serving its constituents.

Michigan and Medicaid Managed Care in the 1990s

In response to the increasing costs and growing population of the early 1990s, the state conducted a study to learn of its possible options. It soon

[6] Another bureaucrat added that "[the move to] managed care was not done on a slam-dunk basis, as it has been in other states. Instead, we moved slowly."

came to the conclusion that moving to a capitation system held the most promise for reducing costs while maintaining service. Of course, this decision raised a host of technical issues that the state needed to address. While some of these issues had arisen under the gatekeeping system that was in place, others were new and were more specific to the capitation approach. For example, should enrollment in MMC be optional or mandatory? If mandatory, for whom? There also were questions about the role of consumer involvement, grievance procedures, and the use of utilization review, which determines whether a procedure for a patient will be covered by the plan. And two basic issues needed to be resolved: first, how the state should determine which health care providers should be allowed to participate, and second, how much these providers should be paid.

One example of a technical issue that was debated in detail in the mid-1990s concerned an issue central to the cost-saving mission of managed care: what price should be paid to participating health care providers for each enrollee? The state's dilemma was that it wanted to set prices as low as possible, but if it set the prices too low, the costs of participation would exceed the benefits and no plan would want to participate. Yet if prices were set too high, the state would not be able to realize all of the potential gains of the capitation system. Thus, there would be dangers in setting the prices either too high or too low. As one civil servant stressed to us, "There is so much money involved here [in Medicaid], you can never make a small mistake. A twenty-dollar spread per client per month between the low and high bid . . . adds up to millions and millions of dollars." Indeed, with 500,000 enrollees, this $20 difference multiplies into $10,000,000 per month or $120,000,000 per year.

There was, however, an alternative to having the state set prices itself. The state realized that although it did not know the marginal costs and benefits faced by the providers, someone else did – namely, the providers themselves. These providers knew better than anyone else what the true costs were. The question then became how to get this information from the providers. Furthermore, in order for these providers to know the costs and benefits of participation, they would have to know exactly what services they would need to provide. And this, needless to say, would require addressing all the technical issues just discussed.

Of course, how to structure the managed care program was not just a technical question. Just as importantly, or perhaps even more importantly, it also was a political question. As pointed out in the previous chapter, in order to understand whether a legislature will give the agency broad discretion or limited discretion, we need to take a look at the political context.

What was the political context in Michigan in the early and mid-1990s as the debate over MMC began in earnest? Starting in 1992, Republicans controlled both the legislature and the executive branch. The governor, John Engler, was a conservative Republican who, during his election campaign, advocated welfare reforms that emphasized the personal responsibility of individuals.[7] Joining him in the state government in Lansing was a legislature in which Republicans controlled both chambers.

How did these political actors go about setting up a capitated managed care system in Michigan? In April 1996, the Department of Community Health (DCH) began preparing the "Request for Proposals" (RFP) that would define how managed care entities could bid to provide services to Medicaid patients and that would determine how contracts would be awarded. The DCH's main objective was to design the RFP so that it would assure quality while stimulating competitive prices. Individuals at DCH began looking at other states to learn what was in and what was out in covering aspects of health care such as mental illness, substance abuse, dental care, long-term care, and so on. They then had to decide how to set the price. A leading participant in this process said that

> [t]he governor, the legislature, and the director of the budget all agreed on the importance of keeping costs in check. And everyone recognized that the state basically had no idea if past rates reflected market prices. They also know that the HMOs which had been serving Medicaid patients had the highest profit margins in the state.

Based on this information, the politicians decided to use a competitive bidding process to determine prices. Under this process, the state would solicit bids from interested health plans, and these plans would bid, or propose, the price that they would accept. While in principle this was an appealing approach, in practice the Michigan politicians could not learn much from other states, because very few states had done actual bidding. Wisconsin, for example, had a two-step process where in the first step, any HMO could try to demonstrate that it passed muster on quality, and in the second step, an HMO approved in the first step could bid at the state-established price. Instead of adopting this approach, the Michigan DCH

[7] Engler's primary program in this area was known as Work First; it required welfare recipients initially to volunteer to receive benefits and later to work – first 20 hours a week and then 30 – in order to continue to receive benefits.

decided to establish a *bid corridor*, whereby the state established a lowest price, to rule out unacceptable quality, and a highest price, which was created based on past experience. The decisions on the parameters of the bid corridor were made by state fiscal agencies, and HMOs then were free to bid within this corridor. All plans that were in the bid corridor and that were deemed qualified were accepted.

During the next several months, elected and appointed officials conducted an ongoing series of discussions to determine what the priorities of the capitation program should be. These officials wanted, for example, to figure out how to include doctors who had previously participated in Michigan's gatekeeper plans, to encourage weekend hours, to encourage conveniently located primary care offices, and so on. The problem was to figure out how to put these public commitments on paper. To accomplish this, DCH created a 30-point incentive system. Health care plans submitting proposals could receive up to 30 points for including provisions in their proposals that accomplished goals valued by various participants in the RFP process. Figure 5.1, which is taken from the RFP, describes the incentive system. One state employee involved in this process said that the biggest of these incentives, worth five points, was inserted into the plan by the director of DCH himself. This director, appointed directly by Governor Engler, shared the same values as Engler concerning the encouragement of individual initiative and responsibility among welfare recipients. As the DCH employee put it, the director, like the governor who appointed him, "felt it was important to change the culture or philosophy of individual behavior." Thus, the RFP reviewers could award five points to plans that included "[i]nnovative strategies to incorporate health promotion messages stressing personal responsibility."

The scores of the plans did not affect their opportunity to offer their services since, as mentioned earlier, all qualified bids were accepted. Instead, the discretionary points were used to deal with another technical issue that arose from the implementation of this system: what to do about Medicaid clients who did not voluntarily choose a plan? Some sort of automatic assignment process was needed to deal with such people, and the bidding process was designed for this process. The assignment process would first assign individuals to the plan with the highest total of these 30 discretionary points; next, when this plan was full to capacity, to the second highest plan; and so on. Since it was estimated that up to 120,000 eligible participants would not sign up voluntarily, this 30-point plan created substantial incentives for the various plans competing to provide services.

Step 3. Evaluation of Attributes to Meet the Unique Needs of the Medicaid Population (30 points per evaluator)

Existence of local agreements for coordination and collaboration with local health departments (3 points maximum)

Existence of local agreements for coordination and collaboration with adolescent or school-based health centers, family planning agencies, substance abuse coordinating agencies, or other local health agencies or community based organizations (2 points maximum)

New capacity for Medicaid enrollment (3 points maximum)

Evidence of a prior relationship with the Michigan Medicaid program that demonstrates positive performance in contract matters such as marketing practices, submission of periodic reports and responsiveness to suggestions for improvement (2 points maximum)

Providers that offer evening and week-end hours (3 points maximum)

PCP locations close to public transportation (2 points maximum)

Provisions to meet the cultural and linguistic needs of the people targeted for enrollment (2 points maximum)

PSP providers on network panel (4 points maximum)

Innovative strategies to incorporate health promotion messages stressing personal responsibility (5 points maximum)

Formal dental referral or delivery arrangements to expedite care for enrollees (2 points maximum)

FQHC or RHC participation in its provider network (2 points maximum)

Figure 5.1 The 30-Point Incentive Plan in Michigan's RFP

The DCH received 24 responses to the RFP, including 250 boxes, or about two tons, of material. The Joint Evaluation Committee, composed of individuals from DHC, as well as the insurance and budget bureaus, was in charge of evaluating these responses. To this end, it employed Medstat, a private consulting firm, for technical assistance on the systems reviews. State bureaucrats did the rest.

As this brief history illustrates, the decision to introduce capitation into MMC in order to control costs led to a large number of thorny technical questions, the answers to which require a vast amount of expertise. How do you find the correct price that an MCO should be paid for each patient under a capitation plan? Which plans should be allowed to participate? If you use a bidding process to determine MCO participation, how should it be structured? Should Medicaid recipients be required to enroll in a managed care program? If they are required to enroll, yet do not do so, how should they be assigned to a program? Clearly, for state legislators to answer all these and numerous other questions themselves would have required a significant commitment of resources.

Policymaking under Unified Government

The legislation concerning the bidding process, shown in Figure 5.2, gives almost complete discretion to the DCH. This discretion, we should bear in mind, is on a very important process that would ultimately affect over one million citizens of the State of Michigan and that involved billions of dollars. The statute, adopted in 1996, stipulates that competitive bidding must be used, and it describes some of the features that are valued or preferred, such as annual open enrollment. But it contains very little language that actively limits agency discretion. In effect, then, the legislature chose to allow the state bureaucrats to design the system that would organize this multi-billion-dollar program.

This broad grant of discretion does not imply that the bidding process is without important policy content. Indeed, the RFP, which runs 77 pages plus appendices, not only describes how the actual bidding process will be structured but also spells out detailed substantive policies about both patients and providers. We have noted some of these in the discussion of the 30-point incentive system. But there is much more policy than this in the RFP. The document states (among many other things)

- which individuals are eligible and must enroll in a capitated plan
- the procedures for the enrollment of Medicaid clients
- the scope of the comprehensive benefit package
- how certain types of special coverage must be provided (such as emergency services, immunizations, or out-of-network services)
- how the confidentiality of patient records must be kept
- how payments will be made to the plans, the necessary administrative structure and services to be provided by the plans, rules for marketing, and data reporting requirements, among others.

Sec. 1643. (1) The department may develop a program for providing services to medical assistance recipients under a full-risk capitation arrangement, through contracts with provider-sponsored networks, health maintenance organizations, and other organizations. The department shall award contracts under the program at least every 5 years based on a competitive bidding process. In developing a program under this section, the department shall consult with providers, medical assistance recipients, and other interested parties. The following provisions shall be considered in any program:

In determining eligible contractors, the department shall consider provider-sponsored networks along with health maintenance organizations, and other organizations. All eligible contractors shall meet the same standards for quality, access, benefits, financial, and organizational capability.

The department may make separate payments directly to qualifying hospitals serving a disproportionate share of indigent patients, and to hospitals providing graduate medical education training programs. If direct payment for GME and DSH is made to qualifying hospitals for services to Medicaid clients, hospitals will not include GME costs or DSH payments in their contracts with HMOs.

(2) In the event that changes to federal statutes are not enacted to permit development of a proposal for full-risk arrangements pursuant to subsection (1), the department shall submit a plan for holding fiscal year expenditures within the appropriated amounts through established policy consultation process prior to implementation.

(3) Whenever economical and feasible, the department shall give preference to programs that provide a choice of qualified contractors and at least an annual open enrollment in the program.

Figure 5.2 Michigan's 1996 legislation: Moving toward a capitation system

These are all important policy components of the state's MMC plan. Yet these important policy decisions, which could have been written into law by the legislature, were made by bureaucrats in the DCH, and they were made by these bureaucrats because the Republican-controlled legislature trusted the Republican governor's agency to make these decisions. There were many issues that were important to Republicans involved in state government, the most conspicuous one being the 30-point plan. Yet the Republicans in the legislature chose to allow Engler's DCH to design this plan in the RFP rather than set it out in legislation.

In fact, a number of the policies addressed in the RFP were seen as important by many of the Republicans in government. In general, in the area of Medicaid policy, Democrats tend to favor stronger government involvement and pay more attention to issues concerning Medicaid clients and their rights, while Republicans tend to favor less government involvement and focus on issues related to health care providers and their rights. In the RFP we saw examples of both Democratic issues (e.g., the scope of benefits, special coverage, how enrollment should work) and Republican issues (e.g., having provider participation determined by a bidding process rather than by an agency, information about payment to plans). Thus, we can reject the idea that Republicans in the legislature did not provide policy-specific details in legislation because they were not concerned about policy issues or because they favor less of a role for government. They could have used legislation to spell out many issues related to providers and to clients but chose instead to delegate such responsibility to the DCH.

Our interviews with the key participants probed the causes of the broad grant of discretion. The dominant theme that emerged from these interviews was that the presence of unified government allowed Republicans in the legislature to trust the agency to make these important decisions. During the adoption of the statute, the Republicans controlled the governorship, as well as both houses of Michigan's bicameral legislature. When Republicans controlled both legislative chambers as well as the executive branch, the legislature felt comfortable granting broad discretion to the bureaucracy. As one participant explained to us:

> Prior [to the Democratic takeover of the House of Representatives, which occurred following the November 1996 elections], managed care and how it works – the intricacies – legislators didn't have the time to figure it out. With the Republicans, they trusted the administration to do it right – they thought the administration was well-meaning.

One prominent Democratic legislator went even further in discussing the extent to which the legislature did not determine policy:

> We didn't do anything to affect the bidding process because we gave that up (to the agency). We can only speak to the agency through legislation. We never call them to ask them how they wanted to do it. The director of the agency is extremely independent of the legislature. Once he got the authority, he saw no need to come back (and consult with the legislature). There was no specific boilerplate about the bid process because it was well underway. The language was only oversight.

This legislator added that the legislature "abrogated authority over Medicaid managed care" when it first came up. The reason it did so, stressed this legislator, was that the Republican Party controlled both chambers, as well as the governor's office, and Engler made it clear that he wanted control of the reforms. A number of high-ranking bureaucrats agreed with this assessment and issued the following opinions:

> The governor wanted control . . . and he wanted his agency to control implementation. The administrations' philosophy [was] "Damn the legislature, we're going to do whatever we want to do."

> We basically assume legislative endorsement in this state and proceed on our own. This administration's style is not very inclusive with respect to the legislature. It decides what it wants to do, and then does it.

> I don't know if it's term limits, or what in blazes is going on. Take the Children's Health Initiative. They didn't consult the legislature at all. They just moved money around. There was no role for the legislature. . . . No one was consulted on a one hundred forty million dollar program. They're going to have a hearing after they've decided what to do, and only because HCFA [the federal Health Care Financing Administration] said to.

Why didn't the legislature do more? In large part because they didn't need to. High-ranking Republicans in both chambers supported Governor Engler in general and his approach to public aid programs like Medicaid in particular. And Republicans controlled both chambers. The end result was that "whenever Havemann [the head of DCH] wanted to do something, he'd just do it" – and he could do so because the Republicans controlled all branches. This did not sit well with all legislators, of course. One Democratic legislator complained that in the 1995 and 1996 bills

> [W]e ceded our responsibility to the agency. . . . I felt that these decisions rightfully belonged in the hands of the legislature. Instead, we get a really rapid process. No discussions of the criteria for selecting providers. It was all rushed. The essential bottom line was saving dollars.

As many of the preceding quotes suggest, it is crucial to recognize in this context that the issue of conflict between legislator and agency is intimately tied to control of the governor's office. The governor himself was able to exercise substantial discretion over the DCH's policymaking and the implementation process. The DCH was in fact created by an executive order issued on January 31, 1996, by Governor Engler. The executive order consolidated the Department of Public Health, the Department of Mental Health, and the Medical Services Administration, the state's Medicaid agency. The Office of Drug Control Policy and the Office of Services to the Aging were consolidated with DCH in subsequent executive orders.

While the standard explanation of efficiency was invoked in justifying this consolidation, it was clear that there were also political reasons underlying Engler's order. From the point of view of Democrats in the legislature, in particular, the move was part of the ongoing battle with the executive branch.[8] A staffer for the Senate Fiscal Agency pointed out that one effect of having a variety of activities consolidated with DCH is that it has become

> more difficult for the fiscal agency to provide succinct overviews to legislators; it's harder to synthesize than when it came from separate and delineated agencies. It has become more difficult to get information. . . . DCH is *much* more powerful now than before the consolidation.

A colleague from the House Fiscal Agency agreed with this assessment. He complained that because he was now dealing with a different set of people than he had before, and because the reorganization had led to a lack of institutional memory and even different styles of policymaking, "In general, it's more difficult [to obtain information]."

Some Democratic legislators were even more explicit in pointing out the problems that the reorganization created for the legislature and in talking about the political roots of this reorganization:

> It's a problem to know who to ask for information. . . . You'd think you could pick up the phone and call to ask questions, but now you don't know who to ask. Early retirements have gotten rid of a lot of people who you could depend on to help you out. Now you have to work through the legislative liaison. There's been a shutdown of the flow of information. It's the first time that anyone can remember restrictions of the flow of information from individuals in the agency.

> Today it's much more secretive. They've closed off information, except from official channels like liaisons and the director. Ten years ago I went there regularly, talked to them about what they were doing, had lunch, things like that. They would call. I would call. Now, under Engler, there's a hatchet person who controls the flow of information (in each department). People I talked to for ten years couldn't talk to me anymore.

[8] Engler was able to reorganize the executive branch using an executive order because the Michigan constitution allows for such actions, subject only to a two-house negative veto.

We're not sure what they're doing [at the agency], information is so filtered. People there are afraid to talk to you.

Perhaps most telling was an anecdote related to us by a former DCH official concerning a meeting between a prominent Democratic representative who served on a committee charged with overseeing the DCH and the head of the DCH, James Havemann:

[The legislator] and Havemann were having a meal together in April and she said, "We should get together and talk." And his reply was, "I don't know why we need to talk to you. You have no way to stop us if we want to do something."

These views of competitive bidding reflected more generally the legislative process on MMC in 1996. Since control of government was unified, the legislature delegated authority extensively to the agency, granting it broad discretion in coming up with a means by which health care plans would be allowed to participate and in determining the prices. As Figure 5.2 makes clear, the Republican majority in both houses, rather than spending enormous amounts of time and effort to determine exactly how managed care should work, defined only the general contours of such a system, telling the DCH to develop "a full-risk capitation arrangement," giving the agency some guidance about how to choose "qualified contractors," and instructing the agency about payments to hospitals meeting certain criteria. The rest of the details were left to the agency to determine. Through this approach to delegation, the legislature could set the broad parameters of the policy in question but also could allow the bureaucracy to use its considerable expertise to specify the details.

This was true of other parts of the 1996 law, too. The law mentions that "Persons not expressing a preference [for a provider] shall be assigned to a managed care provider" (Sec. 1611) but does not say how such an assignment shall be made. Nor does it say what recourse a patient has if he or she does not like the assignment. At the same time, the legislature did not simply give the DCH blanket authority to make all policy choices. One of the contentious issues in the move to managed care was how plans could be marketed to potential clients. HMOs had been marketing themselves directly to potential clients, but this system had potential for abuse. While some people we interviewed argued that there had been no major problems with this system in Michigan, all acknowledged that there had been problems in other states, such as HMOs signing up people who were not qualified for access to their health plans or providing misleading information to try to attract new patients. Many, however, stressed that direct marketing had been a significant problem in Michigan. One DCH bureaucrat insisted that the ban was driven by the numerous problems that direct marketing had caused in Michigan:

> Direct marketing was a pain in the butt. . . . Clients would complain about it. One reason that it was banned was that it was a statewide problem . . . war stories came out from all over the state.

While HMOs opposed a ban on direct marketing, they realized that they had little support in the legislature on this point.[9] As one advocate for Medicaid clients observed, the likelihood of a ban was increased by "the statewide nature of the problem. Then concern in the legislature broadens. And then it's easier to move something." Furthermore, the agency itself did not fight the ban because, in the words of a House staffer,

> They realized it was not a bad idea. They didn't like being told what to do but decided not to fight this particular fight.

Thus, in Section 1639 of the 1996 law, the legislature instructed the agency how to proceed in this area:

> Medicaid capitated health plans shall not directly market their services to or enroll medicaid eligible persons. The department shall provide or arrange for assistance to medicaid enrollees in understanding, electing, and using the managed care plans available.

Based on this language, the agency could not allow individual firms to advertise themselves directly to Medicaid clients.[10] Once again, however, the legislature did not spell out exactly how such marketing and enrollment should take place. Fitting in with the general approach of the law, the legislature provided the outlines of policy but delegated responsibility for filling in the picture to the agency.

[9] In addition, as one executive at a prominent HMO pointed out to us, they much preferred to compete on quality rather than on the ability of their sales department. Furthermore, their studies showed that the largest HMOs, whose names were already well known to the public, would benefit most from a prohibition on direct marketing.

[10] While there was some disagreement about whether the idea for the ban originated in the House or the Senate, our general sense is that the language emerged from the House. A staffer for the Senate Fiscal Agency argued that "Since the HMOs were also providing care to state employees, to GM . . . we thought that they could handle the direct marketing themselves." On the other hand, while they did not feel that the prohibition made economic sense, "it was accepted as part of the give-and-take of the process."

From Unified to Divided Government

The election of November 1996 provided a new backdrop for the creation of MMC policy. In this election, although Republicans retained a majority in the Senate, Democrats regained control of the House for the first time in several years. As a result, the MMC legislation adopted in 1997 was substantially different from the legislation adopted in 1996.

In Chapter 4, we argued that, all else equal, policy conflict leads to less discretion. If we assume that such conflict will be greatest during divided government, because the legislative majority wants to constrain the executive-dominated bureaucracy, then our model predicts that Michigan's 1997 statute on MMC should contain more precisely defined policy than its 1996 statute.[11] Moreover, the model presented in the previous chapter suggests that bicameral bargaining will make it difficult for the legislative chamber that opposes the executive to succeed in adopting the level of policy detail that it most prefers. Applied to the Michigan case, this suggests that the level of policy details should have been less than what the Democrats would have adopted had they controlled both legislative chambers. We find evidence of both effects at work in the 1997 statute.

In the 1996 law, legislation relating to MMC took 1,276 words. In the 1997 law, these relevant sections totaled 2,066 words. Although neither law was exhaustively detailed, there was nonetheless a significant increase of 62% in length from 1996 to 1997. But as we shall see, the Democrats did not get all that they wanted.

Figure 5.3 provides more details about the changes that were made between 1996 and 1997. Language that was carried over from the 1996 law appears in roman text. The italicized text comes from the version of the bill that was originally written and passed by the House. Text that is both boldface and italicized represents compromise language on issues that initially were raised in the House.[12]

Several features of this legislation are worth highlighting. First, consistent with our discussion in Chapter 3, much of this legislation is policy-oriented. The statute did not simply tell the DCH to "do something";

[11] Michigan, it is worth mentioning, has one of the highest-capacity legislatures in the United States.

[12] In other words, the text that is both boldface and italicized is a revised version of the House language, whereas the text that is only italicized comes directly from the House.

Sec. 1611. (1) The department may continue to implement managed care and may require medical services recipients residing in counties offering managed care options to choose the particular managed care plan in which they wish to be enrolled. Persons not expressing a preference may be assigned to a managed care provider.

(2) Persons to be assigned a managed care provider shall be informed in writing of the criteria for exceptions to capitated managed care enrollment, their right to change health plans for any reason within the initial 30 days of enrollment, the toll-free telephone number for problems and complaints, ***and information regarding grievance and appeals rights.***

(3) The criteria for medical exceptions to qualified health plans shall be based on submitted documentation that indicates a recent *(sic)* **has a serious medical condition, and is undergoing active treatment for that condition, and is undergoing active medical treatment for that condition with a physician who does not participate in 1 of the qualified health plans. If the person meets the criteria established by this subsection, the department shall grant an exception to mandatory enrollment at least through the current prescribed course of treatment, subject to periodic review of continued eligibility.**

Sec. 1635. The implementation of all Medicaid managed care plans by the department are subject to the following conditions:

The department shall require contracted health plans to submit data determined necessary for the evaluation on a timely basis. A report of the independent evaluation shall be provided to the house and senate appropriations subcommittees on community health and the house and senate fiscal agencies no later than September 30, 1998.

A health plans advisory council is functioning which meets all applicable federal and state requirements for a medical care advisory committee. The council shall review at least quarterly the implementation of the department's managed care plans.

Contracts for enrollment services and beneficiary services, and the complaint/grievance procedures are in place for the geographic area and populations affected. An annual report on enrollment services and beneficiary services and recipient problems/complaints shall be provided to the house and senate appropriations subcommittees on community health and the house and senate fiscal agencies.

Figure 5.3 Public Act 94, Michigan acts of 1997: MMC legislation that began with the State House version of the bill

Mandatory enrollment is prohibited until there are at least 2 qualified health plans with the capacity to adequately serve each geographic area affected. Exceptions may be considered in areas where at least 85% of all area providers are in 1 plan.

Maternal and infant support services shall continue to be provided through state-certified providers. The department shall continue to reimburse state-certified maternal and infant support services providers on a fee-for-service basis to be charged back to health plans until such time as health plans have contracts with state-certified providers.

The department shall develop a case adjustment to its rate methodology that considers the costs of persons with HIV/AIDS, end stage renal disease, organ transplants, epilepsy, and other high-cost diseases or conditions and shall implement the case adjustment when it is proven to be actuarially and fiscally sound. Implementation of the case adjustment must be budget neutral.

The department may encourage bids for multicounty regions through the use of preference points but shall not initially require a plan provider to submit a bid for a multicounty region.

(j) Enrollment of recipients of children's special health care services in qualified health plans shall be voluntary during fiscal year 1997–98.

Sec. 1637. (1) Medicaid qualified health plans shall establish an ongoing internal quality assurance program for health care services provided to Medicaid recipients which includes:

Consumer involvement in the development of the quality assurance program and consideration of enrollee complaints and satisfaction survey results.

(5) Medicaid qualified health plans shall provide for reimbursement of plan covered services delivered other than through the plan's providers if medically necessary and approved by the plan, immediately required, and which could not be reasonably obtained through the plan's providers on a timely basis. *services shall be deemed approved if the plan does not respond to a request for authorization within 24 hours of the request. Reimbursement shall not exceed the Medicaid fee-for-service payment for such services.*

(6) Medicaid qualified health plans shall provide access to appropriate providers, including qualified specialists for all medically necessary services.

Figure 5.3 *(continued)*

(11) Medicaid qualified health plans shall develop written plans for providing nonemergency medical transportation services funded through supplemental payments made to the plans by the department, and shall include information about transportation in their member handbook.
Sec. 1638. (2) The department shall report the findings and recommendations of the external quality assurance contractor to the house and senate appropriations subcommittees on community health and the house and senate fiscal agencies by March 31, 1998.
Sec. 1639. (1) Medicaid qualified health plans shall not directly market their services to or enroll Medicaid eligible persons. The department shall provide or arrange for assistance to Medicaid enrollees in understanding, electing, and using the managed care plans available. *Upon request of the Medicaid recipient, such assistance shall be provided in person through a face-to-face interview prior to enrollment when practicable.* (2) Information regarding the available health plans and enrollment materials shall be provided through local family independence agency offices during the eligibility determination and redetermination process, and at other locations specified by the department. *The enrollment materials shall clearly explain covered services, recipient rights, grievance and appeal procedures, exception criteria to mandatory enrollment, and information regarding managed care enrollment broker and beneficiary services.*
Sec. 1640. (2) Medicaid recipients shall be allowed to change health plans for any reason within the initial 30 days of enrollment.
Sec. 1641. (2) The department shall provide for a toll-free telephone number for Medicaid recipients enrolled in managed care to assist with resolving problems and complaints. If warranted, the department shall immediately disenroll persons from managed care and approve fee-for-service coverage. (3) Quarterly reports summarizing the problems and complaints reported and their resolution shall be provided to the house and senate appropriations subcommittees on community health, the house and senate fiscal agencies, and the department's health plans advisory council.
Sec. 1642. [*Note*: This section was vetoed by the governor]

Figure 5.3 *(continued)*

The department shall contract for beneficiary services to assist Medicaid recipients in Medicaid managed care plans to access appropriate health care services. The department may contract with the enrollment counseling service contractor to provide these beneficiary services. The department may also contract with different organizations for beneficiary services to different populations. All of the following apply to this program.

Such organizations shall be private organizations, and shall not be involved in providing, managing, determining eligibility, or accrediting health care services delivered through qualified health plans.

Beneficiary services shall include the provision of information to Medicaid recipients regarding the health plans available to them, their rights under law, how to access services, the complaint and grievance procedures available to them, and if requested, advocate for the recipient in all complaint, grievance, and proceedings.

A report on beneficiary services activities and findings shall be provided to the health plans advisory council and to the house and senate appropriations subcommittees on community health, and the house and senate fiscal agencies no later than January 31, 1998.

Note: Plain italicized text is language carried over from the original initial House version. Bold italicized text is compromise language on issue raised in the House.

Figure 5.3 *(continued)*

rather, it gave the agency specific policy instructions. Furthermore, although the legislation put some procedural requirements in place, by and large the legislature used this legislation to make policy directly. And not surprisingly, given that it was a Democratic chamber that pushed for most of these provisions, the policy-specific language largely serves Democratic constituencies by consisting of consumer protections. For example, the law specifies the following:

- Participants must be informed in writing of the criteria that would make them exempt from participation in a capitated program; of their right to change health plans; and of a telephone number to call with complaints and questions (Sec. 1611(2)).
- Clients cannot be forced to enroll in a capitated plan unless there are at least two qualified health plans in their geographic area (Sec. 1635).

- Enrollment in children's special health care services in MMC plans will initially be voluntary (Sec. 1635).
- The DCH must help Medicaid enrollees choose and use managed care plans and must provide, if requested, personal, face-to-face assistance (Sec. 1639).
- Medicaid recipients shall be allowed to change health plans for any reason within 30 days of enrollment (Sec. 1640 (2)).
- The department must provide a toll-free telephone number for Medicaid clients to call with problems and complaints; and if necessary, the department shall immediately disenroll these clients from the capitated plan and allow them to enroll in fee-for-service plans (Sec. 1641 (2)).

While policy provisions like these formed the vast majority of the law, there were also other provisions that could be classified as procedural rather than policy, such as the following:

- Consumers must be involved in developing a quality assurance program for dealing with complaints (Sec. 1637 (1)).
- The DCH must have its program evaluated by an external contractor and must report the findings of this contractor to the appropriations subcommittees and fiscal agencies in both houses (Sec. 1638).

Even these procedural provisions clearly worked to benefit Democratic constituencies and were put in place because of Democrats' fears that the agency, if left to its own devices, would favor cost-cutting rather than consumers' needs.

The reason these provisions, both policy and procedural, were in the legislation was clear to most of the actors involved. One Democratic leader told us that the election of a Democratic House majority was the impetus behind this change. The Democrats' ascendance caused a basic shift in the philosophy of the House, a shift in a more pro-consumer direction. Furthermore, there was a change in the level of trust between the executive and the legislature. Whereas Republicans in the legislature in previous years were willing to trust the executive branch to come up with policy directives that were to their liking, the newly elected Democratic majority viewed the Republican-controlled executive branch with more suspicion. And controlling one legislative chamber gave the Democrats an opportunity to make some changes they had been trying to implement in the past but had been unable to implement because of their minority status. One participant made this point explicit:

> A key thing is that a lot of these ideas were actually proposed last year; but the Democrats didn't have the majority or the votes to get them written into law.

Some Democratic colleagues concurred with this assessment:

> When Democrats took over the House, that created a new opportunity to influence legislation. You can try to get them to introduce stuff. Another avenue is to get a moderate Republican to do stuff in their Senate caucus.

> The big difference [in the language of the legislation between 1996 and 1997] was that the Democrats took control of the House.

A Republican staffer agreed about the role that Democrats played in crafting the 1997 legislation: "The new Democrats wanted to make sure that all the controls were in." Indeed, the Democrats in the House themselves saw these controls as the last line of defense for Medicaid clients. In their view, the Senate, which still was controlled by Republicans, remained content to let Governor Engler's appointees at the DCH have nearly complete control over the MMC program. As one frustrated Democrat noted, the Senate bill placed no restrictions on the department and the operation of MMC:

> It has absolutely *nothing* in it. It was one sentence. Gave the department total authority. . . . I said, "Wait a minute, I'm not going to give carte blanche. If we have an all-out fight on the floor, we can keep it from passing." There were enough concerns out there about managed care. We threatened an all-out fight. The administration didn't want this to happen on the floor, and they didn't want a bill that we were going to fight, so they asked how they could accommodate us, and we put some very basic consumer protections in the bill. Things such as insisting on a choice of more than one plan.

Of course, even though Democrats had far more leverage in 1997 than they had in 1996 as a result of achieving majority status in the House, they were still limited in what they could accomplish. First of all, House Democrats received little cooperation from their Republican colleagues. As one Democratic staffer recalled:

> The Republicans didn't even participate [in writing the legislation]. The Democrats tried to cooperate with the Republicans, but eventually they said, "If they won't help, we'll do it our own way."

Second, and more importantly, the House faced opposition from the Senate and from the executive branch. Even if the House Democrats had been able to get everything they wanted passed through their chamber, they still faced the fundamental obstacle that exists in all separation of powers systems: a variety of actors, many with different preferences, all need to sign off on the same version of a bill in order for it to become law. As the theory shows, bicameral bargaining constitutes an obstacle when legislators want to write low-discretion laws.

A Senate Democrat described for us the situation in the Senate. Just as the House Democrats were working hard to limit the agency's discretion over MMC, Senate Republicans were working hard to give the agency broad discretion – and, by implication, to prevent the House Democrats from achieving all their goals:

> There is little bipartisan operation in the Senate. Republicans knock things out in caucus and then are unified when they come forward. . . . There's no debate on the floor or in committee. And if anything, Republicans are even tighter since the House went over to the Democrats. . . . Republicans have twenty-two, and they need twenty. They solve everything in the caucus and are then solid on the floor.

In addition, the preferences of the House Democrats were at odds with those of the executive branch:

> The department [DCH] fought tooth and nail against the boilerplate [legislative language] in 1997. They would go into committee and talk about the costs. They lobby legislators. They're on the floor running the caucus. Havemann is John Engler's mouthpiece on the floor. Crossing Havemann is like crossing Engler.

Thus, the House Democrats were in a position where their preferences differed from those of all of the other important political players. Whereas there was general agreement among the Republicans in charge of the Senate, Governor Engler, and the governor's DCH administrators, these Republican politicians had different goals – particularly in terms of patients' rights – than the House Democrats. Consequently, House Democrats wanted to place constraints on the activities of the DCH, and to do so by sinking specific policy prescriptions into legislative concrete.

House Democrats were certainly in a better position to achieve their goals than they had been in 1996, when they had minority status in the House as well as the Senate. After the 1996 election, Michigan's government was no longer under unified Republican control. Instead, the governor and the Republican-controlled Senate needed cooperation from the Democratic-controlled House in order to enact a wide range of laws and policies. Democrats could use this leverage to extract some policy concessions of their own. And as a result, the 1997 legislation is far more detailed than the 1996 legislation. At the same time, while control of one chamber gave the Democrats increased leverage, they were not able to achieve all of their goals. Instead, because they faced opposition from the upper chamber and the possibility of a veto from the governor, they were limited in what they could accomplish. In the end, then, this was an excellent example of how bicameral conflict influences the level of discretion. Under unified government in 1996, the legislature wrote a high-discretion law that gave the DCH broad authority to set policy. Under divided government with a divided legislature in 1997, the new law placed more constraints on the agency. There were not as many constraints as the Democrats would have liked or would have been able to establish with a unified legislature, but there were far more than would have been put in place had they maintained their minority status.

What sorts of goals were the Democrats unable to reach? One of the primary areas in which Democrats ultimately were unsuccessful had to do with language concerning an ombudsman, someone who could help out Medicaid clients who were encountering problems when dealing with the system. The House favored the creation of such a position and in Section 1642 of the bill wrote:

> The department shall contract for beneficiary services to assist medicaid recipients in medicaid managed care plans to access appropriate health care services. The department may contract with the enrollment counseling service contractor to provide these beneficiary services. The department may also contract with different organizations for beneficiary services to different populations. All of the following apply to this program.
>
> Such organizations shall be private organizations, and shall not be involved in providing, managing, determining eligibility, or accrediting health care services delivered through qualified health plans.

The House version of the bill contained language creating such a position and giving ombudsmen the power to act. But the Senate opposed such language and voted it down. The reason for the Senate's opposition, according to a Senate staffer, was that Senate Republicans thought it would place too many constraints on the rest of the agency's MMC activities. House Democrats were able to resurrect this language one more time, getting it passed in the conference committee, but then Governor Engler vetoed it.

Clearly, what went on during the debates over this legislation was a process of give-and-take, or bargaining. Because House Democrats were in a position to achieve some of their goals, but not all of them, they had to focus on some and give up others. They chose to focus on clients' rights, and by and large they were successful in placing all sorts of language in legislation that would act to constrain the agency in this area. At the same time, they had to give up some other things they wanted, such as the creation of an official ombudsman position and more control over the bidding process. One legislator told us that this was the trade-off they explicitly decided to make: "In 1997 [the legislature] could do little to affect the actual bid process, but it worked on patient rights."

Unlike in 1996, then, the Democratic control of the House combined with the Republican executive branch to create an incentive for the majority in that chamber to limit policy discretion in the DCH. At the same time, however, the Republican control of the Senate and the governorship made it impossible for the House Democrats to create all the controls they desired. The policymaking processes boiled down to bargaining. As a Senate staffer pointed out:

> You have to understand the process. It's give-and-take. You move forward in one area, back in another. . . . You need lots of compromise.

Conclusion

In Michigan, partisan control of governing institutions had a clear influence on the design of MMC statutes and on the role of politicians and bureaucrats in the policymaking process. In 1996, due to unified Republican control of government, Michigan's MMC statute was extremely general and vague, granting almost total autonomy to the DCH. This was true even though the Medicaid program consumed over $4 billion of the state's budget each year. The reason for this approach, we were told, was that there was no reason for the Republican majority to tie Governor Engler's hands. They trusted him and his agency.

In 1997, when the Democrats regained control of the House, the approach to legislating on MMC shifted. There were certain features of the program that were hard to change, such as the state's approach for choosing plans to bid for participation in the program or the criteria that were valued by the state in this process. But other features were not as hard to change, and the Democrats succeeded in inserting into statutory law a range of new policy constraints, many of which focused on the standard Democratic goal of improving protections for Medicaid clients.

Two features of this change in the design of statutes are worth noting. First, the constraints that appeared in the statutes were largely narrow descriptions of policy rather than procedural constraints on agency decision-making processes. Procedures were clearly present and nontrivial, but the participants we talked to emphasized the policy restrictions, which represent the lion's share of the new legislative language. Second, although the number of policy constraints rose when the Democrats took over the House, the Democrats were not able to insert all the policy constraints they desired into the statutes. Both our interviews and our examination of the initial House version of the MMC legislation in 1997 make it clear that several of the Democrats' desired policies had to be left out of the final version of the bill.

The Michigan case study therefore nicely illustrates some aspects of our theoretical argument. First, consistent with our model and with existing arguments in the literature, the Michigan case illustrates how conflict between the agency and the legislature affects legislative incentives to use statutes to constrain agencies. When conflict is absent and legislators trust policymakers in the agency, they are likely to design vague statutes that allow the agency to draw on its expertise to make policy. And when conflict is present, legislators who disagree with the agency's policy views will constrain the agency by putting specific wording into legislation. When Republicans in the legislature trusted the Republican governor's appointees in the DCH to do the right thing, they responded by writing vague statutes that allowed the agency to flesh out the details. And when the next election produced divided government, Democratic legislators who worried about the possible choices that the agency might make put policy-specific language, designed to constrain the agency, into the legislation.

Second, the Michigan case shows that in order to understand the design of statutes, we need to consider bargaining processes between legislative chambers in bicameral systems. When a different party controls each chamber, the party favoring the governor has the incentive and ability to block some – but not all – legislative language that ties the hands of the relevant agency. We saw exactly such a pattern emerge in Michigan, where the Democrats, by virtue of controlling one chamber, were able to include some, but not all, of the policy instructions and restrictions that they favored in the legislation. Thus, the case study points to a partisan basis for bicameral conflict. When the Democrats took control of the House, they faced great difficulties in reaching agreement with the Republicans in the Senate. Our interviewees described this conflict in partisan terms, and the policy basis for this conflict rested largely on the extent to which protections should be in place for Medicaid clients.

While the case illustrates and provides examples of how our theory relates to actual politics, it also serves to guide certain elements of a large-*n* study across a large number of states, an investigation that we undertook and describe in the next chapter. The analysis demonstrates, for example, the powerful connection between governors and agencies. In Michigan, the legislature did not view the DCH as an independent and autonomous set of bureaucrats who needed to be controlled, but rather as an agency that was well controlled, albeit by the governor. Indeed, the people we interviewed repeatedly spoke of the DCH and its director as if they were the right hand of Governor Engler. Thus, consistent with much previous research (e.g., Epstein and O'Halloran 1996), the case study suggests that the existence of divided government seems to be a reasonable proxy for the level of policy conflict between legislative and executive agents.

Another way in which the case study serves to guide our large-*n* study is by what it reveals about the potential role of diffusion. Some research on state politics has emphasized that states often learn from each other. On the issue of MMC, there are a large number of resources that legislators and agencies draw on to help them sort out some of the thorny technical issues. Several of our respondents noted that they do look at what other states are doing in order to help design the MMC program, though they also emphasized that each state has its particular program history and program needs, and thus that wholesale borrowing is generally impractical and implausible. This ability to look at what other states are doing suggests that a good control for *issue type* across states is to take a cross section of states at a given point in time. This is desirable because it is simply not the case that the nature of the health care problem is the same, or that it is understood the same way, over a more extended period of time. We will return to this issue in the next chapter.

The Michigan legislation also reminds us that when adopting a new item of legislation, legislators often add to or amend statutes that are already on the books. What is interesting about the 1997 statute in Michigan, for example, is that it added new controls to existing legislation both by adding new language and by modifying existing language (see Figure 5.3). The entire statute, however, was composed largely of existing legislation. This creates the nontrivial practical problem of measuring when new statutory language is actually created. In the next chapter, we describe our answer to this problem, which turns out to be extremely labor intensive and which, for practical purposes, militates against any sort of time series analysis.

Finally, the Michigan case study reminds us of critical issues about how policymaking processes are influenced by the design of statutes. Since the level of discretion is affected by political factors, such as the partisan control of the different branches of government, discretion levels are obviously not policy neutral. When the Michigan MMC statute was vague, the vagueness allowed a specific set of policy values to dominate the policy process – those of the Republicans, especially Governor Engler – with implications, most notably, for the types of client protections that were emphasized in the program (i.e., minimal protections) and the types of health care providers that were favored in the program (i.e., those that created incentives for personal responsibility). We should hardly infer, then, that the specificity of policy language is tangential to understanding the nature of biases in policy outcomes. By empowering and limiting the role of particular agents in the policy process, this level of specificity affects the types of policies that are actually chosen.

By structuring the role of bureaucratic agents in policymaking, the design of statutes also affects how information is incorporated into policymaking processes, and how transparent the policymaking process is to voters and interest groups. When the DCH was completely unconstrained by a majority in either chamber, the opportunity for affected interest groups to influence policymaking processes lay almost exclusively in the executive agency. The Republican majority in the legislature trusted Engler and his political appointees and showed little interest in intervening in the agency's policymaking process. This had the effect of cutting off the legislative venue for interest group and citizen influence over policy. When the Democrats regained a majority in the House, legislative policymaking venue was reopened. Because Democrats could use their majority status to influence debate on the issue, this had the effect of moving the policymaking process into a more open arena, making it more transparent to voters. We return to this and other related substantive issues in Chapter 8.

In concluding this chapter, however, it is useful to remind ourselves of the types of things we cannot learn from a case study. As noted earlier, a central purpose of our theory is to help us understand how the role of statutes in policymaking processes should differ across political systems, such as the U.S. states. The case study has not provided a test of this theory, but rather has illustrated the ways in which some parts of the theory operate. In addition, it provides some insight into the dynamics of policy change, something that is not addressed by our theory, which is essentially static. Although the case study brings into sharp relief the importance of some elements of our theory, it cannot provide insight into how variations in the institutional context – for example, variation in the level of legislative capacity – influence the design of legislation, since this context remains fixed in our case study. Thus, the case study, while valuable because it illustrates parts of our theory and provides a bridge between the theory and large-*n* statistical analysis, cannot help us get at this core issue of institutional context. It is to this issue that we turn in the next two chapters.

6

The Design of Laws across Separation of Powers Systems

Our theoretical argument examines how four factors combine to influence the legislative design of bureaucratic discretion. We explored the role of two of these factors – policy conflict between the legislature and agency and conflict across legislative chambers – in the previous chapter. The issue of policy conflict has been central in studies of Congress and delegation, and our case study of Michigan confirms the importance of divided government. The second issue, bicameral bargaining, has received much less systematic attention, as have the other elements of our theory that could not be explored in the Michigan case study, such as the legislature's capacity to write detailed, constraining laws and the role of nonstatutory policymaking mechanisms.

In this chapter we conduct a systematic empirical test of the main arguments of our theory using a novel data set that looks at all bills affecting Medicaid recipients that were enacted by U.S. states over a two-year period.[1] The data permit a test of the comparative elements of our arguments, as the U.S. states have considerable variation in the theoretical variables we have identified. In addition to using these data to test our theoretical argument, we test alternative hypotheses by operationalizing a number of other factors, including the degree of electoral competition, changes in the partisan control of government, and partisan preferences over the level of governmental activism, that might influence the level of discretion that legislatures choose to allow.

[1] This chapter draws and expands on material originally presented in Huber, Shipan, and Pfahler (2001).

Measuring Discretion

Testing our theory presents thorny measurement problems, many of which we alluded to earlier. There are two general problems worth emphasizing. First, since our goal is to understand how the political context affects the design of statutes, we need to control as best we can for the policy issue. If states have different political institutions and are dealing with different issues, then it will be difficult for us to untangle the effects of the institutions from those of issue type. Second, in order to uncover general relationships between political context and statutory design, we need to look at a large amount of legislation. We certainly concede that on any particular statute, idiosyncratic factors may be at work. Sometimes, for instance, a very short and specific statute will be adopted to deal with a small, politically charged element of a larger issue. Some statutes might utilize more or less general language that is geared toward credit-claiming. Individual-level factors, such as the personnel drafting particular bills or sitting on relevant committees, also may affect the ways that laws are written. Our goal, of course, is not to account for every factor that affects the design of statutes, but rather to explore whether, all else equal, the general relationships described in our theory are present in actual legislation. To uncover these general relationships, we need to conduct tests on a significant amount of legislation.

As noted in Chapter 3, our dependent variable will be the length of legislation. In measuring this length, however, we proceed quite differently in our data from the U.S. states (this chapter) as compared to our data from national parliamentary systems (the next chapter). This is because of the different opportunities and constraints that are present in the data we have for addressing the two issues described in the previous paragraph. In this chapter, we describe how we measure the length of legislation in separation of powers systems while (a) controlling for issue type and (b) amassing a reasonably large sample of data.

We do not test our theory using the MMC data described in Chapter 3. To begin with, the amount of data presented in that chapter is very small. We have an incomplete sample of statutes, and we have at most a few laws from each of the states in that data set. Moreover, several of the statutes in the MMC sample are not entirely new, but rather represent additions or modifications to existing laws. These two factors sharply limit the amount of new legislative language in that data, hindering our ability to uncover the relationships we describe in our theory. Furthermore, the

MMC data cover a wide range of time periods. As we discussed in Chapter 4, the policy issue was evolving rapidly during the late 1980s and the 1990s, with states learning from each other; consequently, focusing on legislation from this entire period would not really control for issue type. That is, a state dealing with MMC in 1993 was not addressing exactly the same policy issues as a state dealing with MMC in 1986. We therefore adopt a strategy for measuring the dependent variable that we feel addresses each of these problems.

Our measure of statutory efforts to limit agency discretion in a state is the total number of new words that the state enacted into law in 1995–1996 (in nonappropriations legislation following the 1994 election) on issues related to any aspect of medical care that is provided to Medicaid recipients. We contend that this issue and time period provide a unique natural experiment, one that gives us an opportunity for meaningful cross-state comparisons. Focusing more generally on Medicaid clearly does not control for issue type as well as focusing on the subissue described in Chapter 3. But we face a clear trade-off: as we narrow our control of issue type, we limit our ability to amass the data necessary for testing the theory. We feel that by focusing on the general issue of Medicaid in 1995–1996, we are able to balance this trade-off in the most effective way possible.

By focusing on medical care that is provided to Medicaid (or medical assistance) patients, we obviously are examining an issue that is similar across states. We are not comparing, say, utilities policy in California with prisons policy in Michigan or with ethanol policy in Iowa. Moreover, this particular issue is one that all states must address, since all states have chosen to participate in the Medicaid program and the federal government mandates a broad set of guidelines. States do not, by contrast, have to adopt MMC within Medicaid but can instead choose other approaches to cost-cutting. Since each state is responsible for setting many important parameters of its overall Medicaid program, including eligibility standards, the scope of services available, payment rates to providers, and methods for program administration, there are considerable differences in the programs across states.

The natural experiment mentioned previously is made possible by two exogenous shocks that created a need for policy action across the states in the same time period. One shock was rising costs (Rom 1999). In the early 1990s, rising Medicaid expenditures and an increase in the number of Medicaid eligibles put Medicaid reform at the top of state political agendas. According to the Health Care Financing Administration (HCFA), total

Medicaid expenditures increased at a rate of 5.9% in the 1980s and nearly 10% in the 1990s, exceeding $150 billion by 1994 (HCFA 2000). The number of individuals eligible for Medicaid across all states also increased, from 23.5 million in 1989 to 36.3 million in 1995 (HCFA 2000). Medicaid spending was of particular concern, however, not just because it was increasing, but because it was becoming a larger share of the states' total health care spending. According to a report by the Congressional Research Service, Medicaid spending as a share of state and local expenditures increased from 1.0% in 1966 to 5.7% in 1990 (Congressional Research Service 1993).

The second shock, more focused in time, concerned changes in politics at the federal and state levels that encouraged states to take up health care and Medicaid reform efforts. After the Clinton administration's unsuccessful attempt at national health care reform, and with the midterm 1994 Republican landslide election, supporters of health care reform largely turned their attention to the states (Leichter 1996; Sparer 1996; Schneider 1997). In addition, in 1993 the Clinton administration had issued new guidelines that encouraged states to seek waivers from federal rules and made it easier to do so (Schneider 1997). Thus, following the 1994 election, not only was there an acute political need to address the provision of medical care to Medicaid and medical assistance clients, but also efforts were made in Washington to increase the ability of states to do so. As a result, we believe that this two-year cross section represents the best possibility we are aware of for making meaningful comparisons across states. And by focusing on the same time period, we control reasonably well for the technical complexity of the issue across the states, as all states had basically the same information during this time period about how to address Medicaid problems.

Two other features of the Medicaid issue are worth highlighting. First, as we showed in Chapters 3 and 5, Medicaid reform is a complex issue in which there is clearly space for legislators to take advantage of agency expertise. Decisions regarding the Medicaid program are many and varied. Policymakers need to decide on reimbursement levels for services. They need to determine eligibility guidelines, including issues such as deciding which groups in addition to those required by federal mandates the state wants to cover. There are regulatory issues for nursing homes and other care facilities. And there are decisions about what types of providers should be allowed to provide Medicaid services. When a state moves to MMC, a whole new set of issues arises. Policymakers need to decide which populations should be moved into managed care arrangements. They must consider whether to implement managed care statewide or on a county-by-county basis. They must decide on a method for selecting managed care organizations to provide services, and negotiate how to educate and enroll the recipients in the new program. These decisions cover a spectrum of informational needs. Thus, state lawmakers clearly face very real costs if they wish to micromanage agency behavior by adopting legislation that limits discretion.

Second, the politics of Medicaid and medical care are extremely contentious and partisan. We saw evidence of this in the Michigan case study: when the Democrats regained control of the House, a battle ensued to increase protections for Medicaid clients. More generally, the vast amount of money at stake makes powerful interest groups representing both providers and recipients acutely interested in this policy area. Providers such as nursing homes, home-health care agencies, community clinics, pharmacists, physicians, and hospitals all vie for available money. Recipients, including the elderly, disabled, and low-income families with children, desire comprehensive services. Muddying the landscape further, with the move to managed care in some form in most states, managed care organizations have joined traditional insurance companies on the scene. Although the politics of Medicaid may vary from state to state, the universal conflict of interest across states guarantees heated political debate and differences in the objectives of the major political parties.

Measuring the Length of Statutes

Statutes vary with respect to how much of their language is new and how much is simply carried over from laws that are already on the books. States also vary in how much legislative language on Medicaid they roll into one statute, as opposed to separating out this language across statutes. Since we would not want to argue that two shorter laws on a topic imply less control than one longer law on the same topic, our dependent variable, *Discretion*, measures how many thousands of new words (i.e., newly added statutory language) were contained in all relevant legislation during the 1995–1996 time period. This total number of words is inversely related to the concept of discretion; that is, as the number of words increases, the amount of discretion that the bill allows for decreases.

Creating this dependent variable is extremely laborious, given the amount of legislation that must be examined. Our first step was to identify relevant legislation in each state by searching Lexis's Advanced Legislative Service database.[2] For each state we used the search terms *Medicaid* and *medical assistance*, which are used interchangeably by states to refer to the Medicaid program, as well as any state-specific names for Medicaid programs (such as *MediCal* in California or *MC+* in Missouri). We retained any nonappropriations bills that turned up in this search that were related to the provision of medical care for Medicaid participants. We then read each statute for relevance, and if it was only partially relevant – for example, if only part of the bill was about Medicaid health care – we edited out the irrelevant portions. This was by far the most labor-intensive part of the process, as we found it necessary to examine millions of words of legislation in order to locate the over 1 million words that were germane to our policy area. After doing this, we used a macro in Microsoft Word to count all the words in the legislation that were new.[3]

We cannot code the substantive content of these bills, given that over 1.1 million words about Medicaid health care were adopted during this time period alone. But in Chapter 3, we argued at length that discretion in policy implementation is most sharply constrained by precise policy language. We further argued that as policy language on the same issue becomes more precise, the length of legislation increases, and we saw evidence of this in the Michigan case study in Chapter 4. Consequently, our measure of the level of policy discretion in statutes is the number of new words of legislation adopted during the 1995–1996 time period in each state. We thus have one observation for each state. Our culling of relevant new words of Medicaid legislation ensures (a) that the statutes we examine represent new legislative language and (b) that this language focuses on the same issue.

It is possible, of course, that some states did not enact much legislation in 1995 and 1996 because they had enacted relevant legislation in previous years. We do not believe this is the case, in large part because of the

[2] We coded legislation for 48 states. We omitted Nebraska from the analysis because it has a unicameral legislature and our theory highlights the difference between unified and divided legislatures. We omitted Virginia because in each year the state legislature passed multiple copies of bills, each containing extremely similar (but not necessarily identical) language. Because of this redundancy, it was impossible to obtain even a moderately accurate count of new words.

[3] Lexis publishes the entire text of adopted acts, but it includes in this text notation that enables users to identify which portions of the text were added and which were carried over from earlier legislation.

Table 6.1. *Total Number of Words of MMC Legislation, by Year*

Year	All Bills	Key Bills
1989	8,909	3,804
1990	848	0
1991	11,761	8,710
1992	985	0
1993	30,678	15,064
1994	5,068	3,388
1995	43,369	24,292
1996	42,128	23,248
Pre-1995	*58,249*	*30,966*
1995–1996	*85,497*	*47,540*

exogenous shocks, described earlier, that caused state legislatures to focus their energies on Medicaid policymaking after 1994. Nonetheless, we are aware of this possibility and control for it in the empirical analysis we present later in this chapter. More specifically, we include some variables that are designed to capture whether there might have been pressure for policy change coming from shifts in partisan control of the government, apart from the need to control agencies.

To further investigate this possibility, we also draw on Chapter 3's more in-depth analysis of MMC legislation. Table 6.1 shows that, overall, states enacted more MMC legislation, as measured by the number of words, in 1995 and 1996 than in any previous years. Indeed, far more legislative detail was created in those two years than in all previous years combined, a finding that holds whether we look at the entire set of coded bills or just those bills designated as key bills.

More importantly, we can analyze whether there is a relationship between the number of words enacted prior to 1995 and the number of words enacted in 1995 and 1996. If there is a negative and significant relationship, then we have reason to doubt whether a focus on the 1995–1996 legislative session alone is appropriate. After all, such a relationship would mean that it is at least plausible that some states enacted shorter, less specific bills in 1995–1996 precisely because they had enacted longer, more specific bills in previous years.

Our analysis, however, shows that this was not the case. For all the states in our sample, we calculated the correlation between the number of words each state enacted prior to 1995 and the number of words enacted by that same state in 1995–1996. Rather than being negative and significant, the correlation was positive and insignificant ($r = .32, p > .05$), indicating that, at least in the area of MMC, states that passed legislation prior to 1995 did not exhibit a decreased level of activity in 1995–1996.

Finally, while all states passed at least some new laws having to do with Medicaid health care, our measure of discretion varies widely across the states. In South Dakota, for example, the government enacted only 216 new words of legislation, while in California the government added 277,496 words. With the exception of California, however, the number of words has a more or less continuous distribution.[4] The average number of words is 24,681; the state closest to this number of words is Louisiana, with 25,602. Not surprisingly, some states that have been identified as policy leaders in the area of health care have produced a large number of new words; New York, for example, produced 61,976, and Minnesota wrote 91,659. Yet other states that also are seen as policy leaders produced very little new legislation (e.g., Florida and Hawaii produced only 9,282 and 3,395 words, respectively). And other states that are not viewed as leaders produced a large volume of legislation (e.g., Arizona, with 101,312).[5] Thus, it is not the case that all states that are policy leaders produce a high volume of detailed legislation or that only policy leaders produce a lot of new words.

Testing Our Theory of Delegation across Separation of Powers Systems

As discussed earlier, our theoretical argument focuses on four variables. To begin with, the existence of *policy conflict* – whether legislators and agencies agree or disagree about policy – affects the incentive, or need, to limit discretion. If legislators and bureaucrats wish to achieve the same objective, then there is no policy conflict and legislators have no incentive to control the agency by undertaking the arduous task of writing detailed

[4] California added more words of new legislation in 1995 and 1996 than did the next three most active states combined (Arizona, Michigan, and Minnesota). In part, this is because California, more than any other state, passes a great deal of county-specific legislation (e.g., to authorize the implementation of Medicaid reforms in various counties).

[5] To identify policy leaders, we relied on interviews and conversations with state-level policymakers, as well as studies of policymaking (e.g., Carter and LaPlant 1998; Paul-Shaheen 1998).

legislation.[6] Second, we must examine the extent to which the legislature has the *legislative capacity*, or ability, to write detailed, policy-specific legislation. Third, we must consider the extent to which the *bargaining environment* – in particular, the existence of bicameral conflict – affects the ability to adopt detailed statutes. And fourth, we must examine whether alternative, *nonstatutory factors* influence affect incentives to use statutes to constrain agency policymaking. Limiting discretion by writing detailed legislation may be a less attractive strategy if the legislature can affect agency behavior through these other means.

We turn now to the task of operationalizing these variables in the separation of powers political systems found in the U.S. states. All of these states have the same basic structure, modeled, not surprisingly, on the national government of the United States. Thus, each has an elected governor who has veto powers over legislation, each has a bicameral legislature (except Nebraska, which we exclude from our analysis), and each is dominated by the two main national political parties, the Democrats and Republicans. But underneath this common structure exists institutional variation that we seek to exploit in our empirical tests.

Policy Conflict

We have noted that policy conflict between legislators and executives plays a central role in theory-building and testing about political control of agencies in the U.S. Congress (e.g., Epstein and O'Halloran 1994, 1999; Bawn 1995; Martin 1997; Volden 2002a, 2002b). And divided government has been the factor most commonly associated with policy conflict. As we saw in Chapter 5's case study of Michigan, divided government should influence the benefits of limiting agency discretion because executives typically have a strong influence on the preferences and actions of leaders in executive agencies. Thus, if the legislature is controlled by one party and the executive by another, we should expect the legislature and the agency to have more divergent preferences than when the executive and the legislature belong to the same party. And if the preferences of the agency diverge from those of legislators, then the immediate benefits of

[6] Our argument rests on the implicit (and, in our view, correct) assumption that legislators are much more concerned about the present than the future. Other studies, however, have focused on incentives of legislators to hardwire future outcomes when they are uncertain about future control of the legislature. Later, we discuss these arguments about political uncertainty and include them in our empirical tests.

specifying details in legislation should be larger than if these preferences converge.[7]

Bargaining Environment

Our theory and our case study of Michigan emphasize the distinction between two forms of divided government. During divided government, the two chambers of bicameral legislatures may themselves be either unified or divided in their opposition to the executive. When the legislature itself is divided, our model predicts that bicameral conflict across the two chambers will limit the extent to which the chamber opposed to the executive can limit agency discretion in statutes. We saw this in fact to be the case in Michigan in 1997. Hence, in order to capture the influence of the bargaining environment and bicameral conflict, it is imperative that our measures account for the difference between divided government with a *unified legislature* and divided government with a *divided legislature*.[8] Although statutes should allow for less discretion under any type of divided government than under unified government, the legislature's ability to write detailed laws should be greater with a unified legislature than with a divided legislature.[9]

Legislative Capacity

The theory laid out in Chapter 4 underlines the need to consider the legislature's capacity to write detailed and specific statutes. Our argument is that, faced with exactly the same issue, legislatures in some political settings

[7] Epstein and O'Halloran (1999) provide convincing evidence to support this argument in the U.S. Congress. Hamm and Robertson (1981) also provide evidence about the impact of divided government on ex post efforts by state legislators to control agencies.

[8] Throughout this chapter, whenever we refer to *unified legislature*, it is implicit that we are referring to a unified legislature in a system of divided government. *Divided legislature*, of course, automatically implies the existence of divided government. For another study that differentiates between these two types of divided government, see Clarke (1998). Clarke shows that budgetary conflict between the legislature and the executive increases under divided government, but only when the legislature is unified.

[9] As we noted, the chief executive may oppose some of the constraints that the legislature wants to implement. Thus, the amount of discretion is relative. A unified government will produce fewer constraints, divided government with a divided legislature will produce more constraints, and divided government with a unified legislature will produce even more constraints. Even in the last case, however, the legislature will not be able to get everything it wants, compared to its ideal, because of the need to obtain the chief executive's signature on the bill.

will face higher costs of limiting discretion than legislatures in other settings. The conflict of interest created by divided government, for example, may create policy gains from writing low-discretion laws, but legislators in each chamber must have the personal ability and motivation to write legislation that will constrain the agency in the ways that legislators desire. Even if the political environment indicates substantial benefits from writing detailed legislation, high costs will limit the ability of legislators to do so.[10]

In this respect, opportunity costs loom large. Not all legislators can devote all of their professional energies to their legislative careers. Although this is not the case in the U.S. Congress, it is the case in many other legislatures, where legislative careers are part-time jobs that are relatively low-paying. If an individual legislator depends heavily for his or her livelihood on activities unrelated to being a legislator, then the opportunity costs of devoting a great deal of attention to legislative responsibilities will be relatively high. In such situations, legislators should be less inclined to attempt to micromanage agencies.

Legislative expertise and ability are also crucial. Legislators must be able to understand which specific policies will produce which specific outcomes and to give precise instructions to agencies about what sorts of policies to adopt. This is achieved in part by attracting high-ability individuals to legislative careers. It is also achieved by retaining these highly qualified people in office, since legislators who have been around a long time gain important knowledge about policies.

Nonstatutory Factors

The final element of our theory that needs to be operationalized across states is nonstatutory factors that influence agency actions and outcomes. Legislators do not have to rely solely on statutory strategies to achieve the policy outcomes they desire from bureaucratic activity. Politicians sometimes can also rely on other features of the political environment to enforce their policy wishes. In some contexts, for example, the authors of statutes have ample opportunities to monitor and correct the actions of agents, such as when legislatures can veto rules adopted by agencies or when it is easy to hold hearings that make agents accountable for their actions. In

[10] Research on U.S. state legislatures suggests that legislative professionalization influences the level of legislative oversight (Hamm and Robertson 1981). Squire (1992), Moncrief (1999), and Carey, Niemi, and Powell (2000) provide useful overviews of the legislative professionalization literature.

other contexts, the authors of statutes can rely on others to influence the actions of agencies. In some political systems, for example, cabinet ministers or administrative law judges can perform this function. This is by no means an exhaustive list, but our more general theoretical argument is that in deciding whether to pay the costs of writing detailed statutes, legislators must anticipate the extent to which the political environment is likely to produce favorable outcomes independent of statutory detail.

We focus on one very direct and important mechanism that legislators use to exercise nonstatutory influence in separation of powers systems: the legislative veto.[11] This, of course, is not the only nonstatutory mechanism available, and later in this chapter we discuss other potential alternative mechanisms for control. But we use it for two reasons. First, the existence of the legislative veto varies across the states, allowing the variation we need for our empirical tests. Other legislative institutions, such as the ability to hold hearings or to vote on budgets, clearly might affect nonstatutory strategies, but they do not vary significantly across states. Second, legislators can clearly anticipate the impact of the legislative veto, because legislators themselves determine its use. Other nonlegislative institutions have a much less predictable impact. Legislators cannot be certain, for example, whether, in the absence of statutory detail, the judicial system will cause the agency to act in ways favorable to the legislature.

Legislative vetoes, then, give the legislature a direct, institutionalized opportunity to veto agency rules (or even to amend such rules, as is possible in West Virginia). Where such institutions exist, and where legislatures are unified (and thus agree on the potential benefits of the veto and can actually use it), the net benefits of specifying precise details in legislation consequently should be low. If no such opportunities for legislative vetoes exist, then incentives to limit discretion will be greater. Thus, when government is divided and the legislature is unified, legislators should be less likely to use legislation to limit agency discretion in situations where legislative vetoes provide opportunities to influence agency behavior.

Measuring the Explanatory Variables

In Table 6.2 we list the primary independent variables from our theory and describe how they are measured. Three of these independent variables are

[11] Ethridge (1981, 1984) demonstrates that legislative vetoes influence actions taken by state agencies.

Table 6.2. *Summary of Presidential Variables and Measures*

Conceptual Variable	Measure
Policy Conflict	
Policy conflict is likely to be greater during divided government, when the party that controls the executive branch does not control both chambers of the legislature, than during unified government.	Dummy variables for divided government (see Bargaining Environment)
Bargaining Environment	
Given divided government, bicameral conflict is likely to be greater with a divided legislature (i.e., when each chamber of the legislature is controlled by a different party) than with a unified legislature (when one party controls both chambers).	Dummy variable for divided legislature and dummy variable for unified legislature (both taking the value 1 only during divided government)
Legislative Capacity	
Capacity increases with the total compensation of legislators.	Yearly level of compensation for the lower house, including per diem expenses (see text for other measures)
Nonstatutory Factors	
The availability of the legislative veto reduces the need for legislatures to rely on detailed laws to compel agencies to make certain kinds of decisions.	Dummy variable for legislative veto (which takes the value 1 if the veto exists and a unified legislature allows it to be exercised)

straightforward to measure. If the governor's party controls only one of the legislative chambers, then *Divided Legislature* takes on a value of 1. Similarly, if the governor's party controls neither of the legislative chambers, then *Unified Legislature* takes on a value of 1. Finally, in states where the legislature has a veto over agency actions, *Legislative Veto* is set equal to 1.

To measure *Legislative Capacity* we use the total amount of compensation, in thousands of dollars, paid to legislators per year. In part, our reasons for using this measure are statistical. Compensation is strongly correlated with other measures of legislative professionalism (e.g., the number of staff or the number of days per session), so including multiple measures introduces an unacceptable degree of collinearity. In addition, using a single-variable measure like this has the advantage of being more straightforward and easily interpretable than a variable that combines different measures.[12]

More important, we have strong substantive reasons for using this measure. Our theoretical argument emphasized the degree to which members need a high level of personal motivation and expertise if they are going to write detailed legislation that will constrain agencies. Legislative compensation works as a strong proxy in this regard. Members who have more experience in the legislature will have higher levels of expertise; higher compensation leads to less turnover and thus more experience.[13] Higher levels of compensation also attract higher-quality candidates in the first place and provide more of an incentive for these candidates to stay in office. Finally, low-paid state legislators generally hold other jobs; therefore, such legislators will face considerable opportunity costs for devoting substantial time to legislative activities. As compensation increases, a seat in the legislature becomes more valuable, which increases the payoff for devoting energy to legislative activities. Thus, because legislative compensation provides a useful single-variable proxy for the types of effects we look for in a measure of legislative capacity, we use *Compensation*, which includes the annual salary plus guaranteed per diem expenses to members of the lower house.

Control Variables

Even within the limited domain of Medicaid, there exist many different types of issues that the legislature can address. Thus, *Discretion* could measure more legislative control or simply more policy change. It is therefore important to control for the factors that could lead to more words independent of the need to limit discretion. To account for the possibility

[12] Collinearity is especially problematic given our relatively small data set and the use of multiple interacted terms. We should note that when we regress other potential measures of capacity on compensation, this single variable explains a large amount of the variance and is strongly significant, thereby supporting our use of this variable as a proxy for capacity. In addition, when we include not only compensation but also the number of committees in our regressions, we obtain similar results. Finally, as we discuss later, when we use an index of professionalism, computed by combining the z-scores of legislative compensation, the number of committees, and the number of staff, our results remain as strong as those reported in this chapter. We omit the number of days in session from this composite measure, in part because on its own (absent the presence of these other factors), we see no reason why it should affect legislative control and in part because of concerns over the reliability of this measure (Stonecash and Agathangelou 1997).

[13] Squire (1988) demonstrates that level of compensation is far more important in predicting the mean years of service than other variables, such as staff size or session length.

that legislative detail is a function of policy change, we need to have some measure of demand for Medicaid policymaking in each state. That is, since legislative attention to Medicaid-related legislation should be influenced by the demand for such legislation, we should expect the number of words to increase with the size of a state's Medicaid program. Thus, the regression models we estimate contain a control variable, *Medicaid Expenditures*, which is the per capita Medicaid expenditures in each state.

Second, changes in the political environment might lead to new policy initiatives. If the legislature switched parties in 1995, for example, we might expect, all else equal, that the amount of legislation will increase independent of the need to control the agency. To control for this possibility, we can include a variety of dummy variables that measure changes in the partisan composition of government. We would also note, however, that if we are correct about the importance of the exogenous shocks with respect to Medicaid, then such partisan changes might not predict *Discretion*, because these shocks should prompt all states to take some action, regardless of recent changes in the partisan composition of the legislature.

Third, one might expect that in political systems where control of the government regularly switches between the two parties, politicians might be more likely to write detailed legislation whenever they are in power. This idea is similar to Moe's (1989) concept of *political uncertainty*. Moe argues that political majorities are uncertain about whether they will continue to be in power in the future, and this uncertainty gives strong majorities the incentive to write detailed legislation in an effort to lock in the policy outcomes they desire. One could interpret this argument to imply that the greater the level of uncertainty about future control of government, the greater the incentive to use legislative details to structure future agency behavior. While this is a plausible interpretation, the theoretical impact of political uncertainty is not completely clear. Moe himself does not treat political uncertainty as a continuous variable. Instead, he points out that such uncertainty is inherent in politics, and thus its impact on political strategy is always present.[14] Moreover, de Figueiredo's (1998) model of political uncertainty indicates a weak link between the level of uncertainty and incentives to lock in agency behavior. Given the ambiguity about the theoretical relevance of political uncertainty in the context we consider, we will estimate models both with and without variables measuring political uncertainty.

[14] However, the idea that political uncertainty can vary is both implicit in and consistent with Moe's argument.

Fourth, it is possible that the length of legislation is simply a function of partisan preferences. Since Democrats favor a more activist role for government while Republicans favor a more reduced role, perhaps Democrats simply write longer laws. We examine whether such a trend emerges in our data.

Fifth, features specific to the executive may influence the level of discretion in legislation. In particular, the legislature's decision to delegate broad discretion to the agency may be influenced by the bureaucracy's level of professionalism. All else equal, a legislature may be more willing to give broader discretion to an agency that has a higher level of competence. Thus, we test whether bureaucratic professionalism influences the level of discretion in statutes. In addition, we examine several variables related to the governor's institutional power to see whether they influence the way in which the legislature delegates to the agency.

Finally, we examine other state-specific factors that may affect the length of legislation. In particular, we investigate whether the interest group environment may have a systemtatic effect on the level of discretion in laws. We also check to see whether the state's political culture influences statutory discretion.

The Empirical Tests

The dependent variable in our empirical tests is, as described previously, *Discretion*. In order to make the results more readable, we divided the total number of new words by 1,000; thus, our dependent variable is measured in terms of thousands of words. A positive coefficient for the independent variables indicates longer statutes and thus greater effort to limit agency discretion. The main independent variables, as described in the previous section, measure the various forms of divided government, legislative capacity, legislative vetoes, and a variety of control variables related to the size of the Medicaid program, recent political change, political uncertainty, the professionalism of the bureaucracy and powers of the governor. We estimate the models using ordinary least squares (OLS) and use a simple linear model, both because our theory does not suggest that other functional forms are more appropriate and because the results are easily interpreted.[15]

[15] Results obtained using negative binomial regression are nearly identical to those reported here.

We initially present the estimates of our statistical models using the nonsouthern states (a restriction we relax later).[16] Scholars have widely recognized that southern Democrats are more conservative than Democrats elsewhere in the country, causing the policy differences between the Democrats and the Republicans to be smaller in the South than elsewhere. Consequently, divided government in the South is much less likely than elsewhere to measure genuine conflict of interest between the legislature and the executive. When divided government occurs in the South, it usually consists of a Republican governor and a conservative Democratic legislature. While this technically would be categorized as divided government, the policy differences between the two branches are often not nearly as great as the differences in nonsouthern states (Erikson, Wright, and McIver 1993).

In all the equations reported in the remainder of this chapter, we also include two control variables. First, as discussed earlier, we include per capita *Medicaid Expenditures* to control for the overall level of Medicaid policymaking activity in each state. Second, we include a dummy variable to account for the large amount of legislative activity in California.[17] We expect both of these variables to be positive and significant.

The discussion in Chapter 4 suggests two possible ways to test the effects of policy conflict and legislative capacity. One is to enter each variable directly, which is particularly appropriate if the distribution of legislative capacity is such that there are very few political systems with low levels of capacity (as in Distribution 2 in Figure 4.4, for example). The other is to look at the interactive effects of divided government and legislative capacity (as in Distribution 1 in Figure 4.4). If there are a large number of political systems that have little policy conflict or insufficient capacity to adopt detailed legislation (for any level of conflict), then whether each of these variables matters will depend on the value of the

[16] The southern states that we initially exclude are Alabama, Arkansas, Florida, Georgia, Louisiana, Mississippi, North Carolina, South Carolina, Tennessee, and Texas. We also exclude Virginia for reasons detailed elsewhere in this chapter.

[17] As noted earlier, the number of new words enacted by the government of California far exceeds that of any other state. While we add a dummy variable to account for this extreme volume of legislation, we hasten to add that the results of our analysis remain substantially the same when we simply omit California from the empirical analysis. Excluding California from the analysis causes the goodness-of-fit measures to fall, of course, but they remain respectable. More importantly, the significance (or insignificance, as the case may be) of our independent variables does not depend on whether California is included in the analysis.

Table 6.3. *Discretion in Nonsouthern States*

Independent Variables	(1)	(2)	(3)	(4)
Unified Legislature	−5.66	−24.85	32.39	−18.66
	(9.24)	(9.90)	(18.90)	(11.58)
Unified Legislature × Compensation	—	2.25	—	1.92
		(.91)		(1.00)
Unified Legislature × Professionalization Index	—	—	18.80	—
			(7.35)	
Divided Legislature	−9.18	−20.02	−9.64	−14.24
	(7.71)	(11.44)	(7.28)	(13.55)
Divided Legislature × Compensation	—	.51	—	.21
		(.39)		(.57)
Divided Legislature × Professionalization Index	—	—	2.51	—
			(1.70)	
Compensation	0.50	—	—	0.31
	(0.30)			(.38)
Legislative Veto × Unified Legislature	5.48	−25.52	−22.90	−25.32
	(13.66)	(11.25)	(12.40)	(11.44)
Medicaid Expenditures	29.67	36.15	30.83	35.17
	(16.89)	(20.70)	(22.45)	(21.86)
California dummy	248.22	248.88	250.49	248.29
	(9.45)	(12.98)	(10.46)	(13.69)
Constant	−3.88	2.35	5.20	−3.24
	(11.12)	(14.01)	(14.79)	(16.13)
Adjusted R^2	.76	.77	.79	.78
N	38	38	38	38

Note: The dependent variable is *Discretion* in Medicaid-related legislation in 1995–1996, measured in thousands of words (see text for details). Estimates are from OLS regression. Positive coefficients reflect less agency discretion. Numbers in parentheses are White standard errors. *Unified Legislature* takes the value 1 when the majorities of both chambers of the legislature are of a different party than that of the governor. *Divided Legislature* takes the value 1 if one of two chambers is controlled by a different party than that of the governor.

other. As we argued in Chapter 4, which of these approaches is correct depends on the distribution of capacity and conflict in the data.

We begin by looking at models that include only the direct effects of policy conflict and capacity on discretion in legislation. The results in column 1 of Table 6.3 are striking for their lack of significance. The divided government variables even have the wrong sign. *Compensation* does have the correct sign, but it falls short of the conventional $p < .05$

standard of significance, even with a one-tailed test. In fact, only the two control variables for Medicaid expenditures and California are significant.

In our view, these strong null results about policy conflict are not terribly surprising. Because legislative capacity in many of the states is very low, it would not be surprising in such states to find that legislation will remain reasonably vague even when policy conflict is high. Similarly, the level of policy conflict during unified government should create few incentives to adopt significant policy constraints, regardless of the level of capacity. Put differently, it seems entirely plausible that the distribution of legislative capacity with respect to policy conflict is something like Distribution 1 in Figure 4.4.

The problem we discussed in conjunction with Figure 4.4 is that we do not know where the relevant threshold might be. We do not know the level of capacity above which political conflict will lead to a decrease in discretion or the level of conflict above which increased capacity will produce decreased discretion. We can explore this issue empirically, however, by looking at the interactions of capacity and conflict variables. In particular, we can examine whether capacity matters on its own or, as is more likely given the wide range of capacities in the states, matters only when interacted with conflict. We explore these issues in the remaining columns of Table 6.3.

In column 2 of Table 6.3 we investigate whether capacity might matter not on its own, but rather in conjunction with policy conflict. To do this, we include the direct effect of policy conflict along with the interaction between *Compensation* and our two dichotomous conflict variables. Since we do not enter *Compensation* directly, this statistical model assumes that legislative capacity matters only when policy conflict is high. Thus, increases in capacity will decrease discretion only when the presence of policy conflict produces the incentive to limit discretion. This assumes, then, that the policy conflict threshold – above which capacity matters – is somewhere between unified and divided government. Viewed somewhat differently, in this model divided government, which provides the legislature with the incentive to constrain the agency, has an independent effect on the level of discretion; but to assess the overall effect of divided government, we also need to take into account its interaction with the level of capacity, which determines whether the legislature has the ability to act on this incentive.

Several aspects of the results are worth noting. First, the estimation allows us to uncover a *legislative capacity threshold* above which policy conflict has the expected effects. Note that the coefficients for both *Unified*

Legislature and *Unified Legislature* × *Compensation* are statistically significant ($p < .05$, one-tailed tests) and that the coefficient for the *Unified Legislature* is negative, while the coefficient for *Unified Legislature* × *Compensation* is positive. Considering the two coefficients together, discretion decreases during *Unified Legislature* government if legislative compensation in a state exceeds $11,040, a total exceeded by 24 of the 38 nonsouthern states in our sample.[18]

Second, the results provide some support for our theoretical expectations regarding *Divided Legislature*. Both *Divided Legislature* and *Divided Legislature* × *Compensation* are significant (at $p < .05$ and $p < .10$, respectively, one-tailed tests). In general, these results support our argument. For any given level of compensation, the effect of *Unified Legislature* exceeds that of *Divided Legislature*, which is consistent with our hypothesis about bicameralism and bargaining. However, the relatively small coefficient on *Divided Legislature* × *Compensation* means that a divided legislature results in an increase in words for only highly compensated legislatures.[19]

Third, there is strong support for our argument about the substitution effect: *Unified Legislature* × *Legislative Veto* is negative, large, and very precisely estimated. Thus, if states have the incentive and capacity to use legislation to micromanage agencies, they will be most likely to do so if they lack the institutionalized means for vetoing agency rules. Because the interacted terms can make these results somewhat difficult to interpret, in Figure 6.1 we have plotted the number of added words as a function of compensation for both types of divided government. In each case, we assume that we are looking at a nonsouthern state other than California, one with no legislative veto (which is the modal category) and with the mean level of Medicaid expenditures per capita (0.57). We also interpret all coefficients as being unbiased estimates.

[18] It is also exceeded by 29 of the 48 states in the full sample. This figure for compensation is obtained by dividing the absolute value of the coefficient for *Unified Legislature* by the coefficient for *Unified Legislature* × *Compensation*. Since 24.85 / 2.25 = 11.04, when *Compensation* equals $11,040, the effect of *Unified Legislature* × *Compensation* will be exactly equal to the effect of *Unified Legislature*. For levels of compensation greater than $11,040, the combined effect of *Unified Legislature* and *Unified Legislature* × *Compensation* will be positive.

[19] *Divided Legislature* produces more words for levels of *Compensation* above $39,250, a level exceeded by six of the states in our sample. It should be kept in mind, however, that the coefficient of the interactive term is estimated somewhat imprecisely. To the extent that the true value of this coefficient is higher than .51, the level of *Compensation* needed to produce a positive number of added words will decrease.

Figure 6.1 clearly demonstrates the ways in which our measures of conflict interact with the level of compensation. For legislatures in which members receive little compensation – in other words, for legislatures that have very low levels of capacity – there is almost no difference between divided legislatures and unified legislatures in terms of the amount of discretion in legislation. However, for all except those with the lowest levels of compensation, unified legislatures produce more low-discretion laws than divided legislatures. Furthermore, the difference between these two types of legislatures increases as the level of compensation increases.

In column 3 of Table 6.3, we replicate the results reported in column 2 using a different measure of capacity. Using this other measure, an index created from legislative compensation, the number of staff, and the number of committees, we obtain essentially identical results.[20] The coefficient for the legislative veto once again is significant ($p < .05$), with a value (–22.90) that is very similar to that shown in column 1. The coefficients for *Unified Legislature*, both on its own and interacted with *Compensation*, are significant at $p < .05$, and the corresponding coefficients when the legislature is divided are significant at $p < .10$. Finally, the effect of a *Unified Legislature* is greater for all levels of compensation than the effect of a *Divided Legislature*.[21]

As noted earlier, the models in columns 2 and 3 assume that legislative capacity has an effect only during divided government (i.e., that the policy conflict threshold, above which capacity matters, is between unified and divided government). It could also be the case that capacity matters when conflict is lower but that it has a smaller effect. It may be, for example, that during unified government, policy conflict is sufficiently high that capacity has a direct effect on compensation. Thus, in column 4 we include our measure of capacity as a separate variable. We find that the coefficient is very small and is estimated with considerable error. Thus, there is no evidence of a direct effect of capacity at low levels of conflict. Again, this

[20] To create this index, we created z-scores for each of these variables and added these z-scores together. We obtain similar results when we create an index that combines days in session, compensation, committees, and staff.

[21] Similarly, a *Unified Legislature* produces a positive number of words for more states than does a *Divided Legislature*. The former actually produces a positive number of words for all states, while the latter produces a positive number for states where the professionalism index exceeds 3.84. As pointed out in the text, this number has no intuitive meaning, which is why we choose to report the results using legislative compensation. What it implies, however, is that for only four states in our sample is the overall level of professionalization high enough to produce more low-discretion laws when the legislature itself is divided.

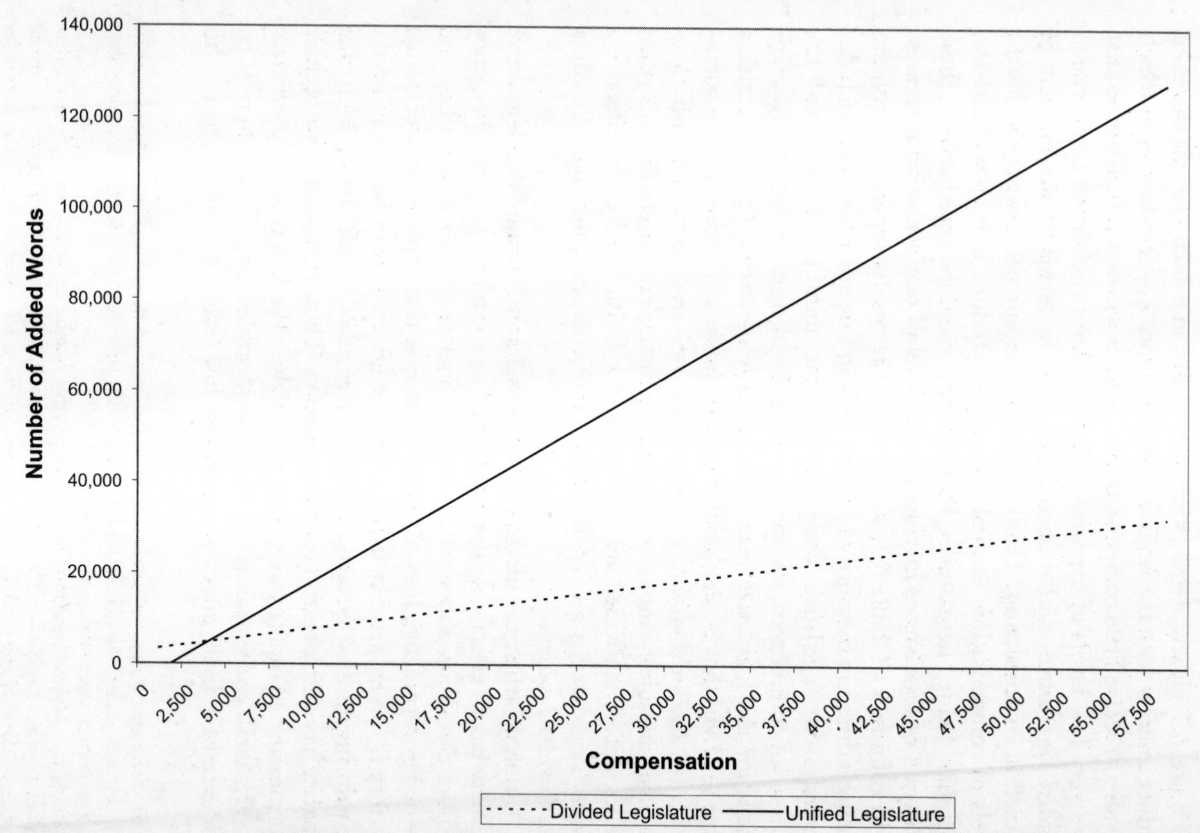

Figure 6.1 Discretion and legislative compensation

is not surprising. In the absence of conflict – which, in our data, means the presence of unified government – state legislatures have no incentive to write detailed laws that constrain the discretion of agencies. Thus, both logically and empirically, we see that the level of compensation has no independent effect on the level of discretion, and as a result we omit it from future equations.[22]

Before moving on, it is worth noting that in Column 4 we also find that our control variables – Medicaid expenditures per capita and the California dummy variable – take on almost exactly the same values as in the equation reported in column 1. More importantly from the standpoint of our theory, so does the interaction of the legislative veto with divided government. Most important, the coefficients for *Unified Legislature* and *Unified Legislature* × *Compensation* remain significant, with values similar to those reported in column 2. The only real change from column 2 occurs in the significance of the two *Divided Legislature* variables, which for the interacted term (*Divided Legislature* × *Compensation*) can be explained in large part by the high level of collinearity between this variable and *Compensation* ($r = .49$).[23]

The results from Table 6.3, then, show that divided government has both a direct effect on the level of discretion in statutes and an indirect effect through its interaction with legislative capacity. Thus, we do find the expected effects when we assume the existence of a policy conflict threshold (above unified government). And this allows us to estimate the location of capacity thresholds, using the interactive term, above which conflict has the expected effects. The results make a lot of sense given the political environments in the U.S. states. For divided government to produce a decrease in discretion, the legislature must have enough capacity to address the potential problems caused by policy conflict. Divided government produces the incentive to limit discretion, but to do so requires a sufficient level of capacity.

[22] Although political scientists often automatically include main effects as well as interactive effects – that is, X_1 and X_2, as well as $X_1 * X_2$ – there is no methodological requirement to do so. As a result, we believe that columns 2 and 3 present the most appropriate and accurate account of our model. For a good discussion of the use of interaction terms, see Friedrich (1982). For an example and early discussion within political science of the appropriateness of excluding main effects, see Lewis-Beck (1977).

[23] *Divided Legislature* and *Compensation* are also correlated ($r = .30$), which lessens the likelihood of finding significant results for the *Divided Legislature* variable. *Compensation* is not, however, highly correlated with either *Unified Legislature* or *Unified Legislature* × *Compensation* ($r = -.16$ and $r = .10$, respectively).

Testing Alternative Explanations

As discussed earlier, it is possible that the number of new words might be a function of changes in the political control of government, the level of electoral competition in a state, partisan control of government, the level of bureaucratic professionalism, or other factors. Although these features of the political landscape are not part of our theory, we need to control for them in order to gain more confidence that the results shown in Table 6.3, especially those in columns 2 and 3, are not spurious.

We begin by examining changes in the political environment in each state. *Unified-to-Divided* is a dummy variable that we set equal to 1 if the 1994 election resulted in a switch from unified to divided government. This variable is intended to capture the idea that political change in the 1994 elections could have led to the demand for new legislation independent of the need to control the bureaucracy. If the election resulted in divided government, then partisan control of at least one branch of government has changed, and it has done so in a way (toward divided control) that should lead to an increased number of new words. Thus, to the extent that *Discretion* might measure policy change independent of the need to control agencies, and to the extent that political change leads to policy change, the coefficient of this variable should be positive. Later, we discuss other variables that could also be used to measure relevant political changes in the 1994 elections.

Column 1 of Table 6.4 presents the results when we control for political change. *Unified-to-Divided* is measured very imprecisely, lending little support to the notion that the number of new words is a function of political change independent of the need to control the bureaucracy. More important, controlling for this variable does not substantially change the results reported in Column 2 of Table 6.3.

It is possible, of course, that *Unified-to-Divided* is simply a bad proxy for political change, so we reran the regression presented in column 1 using three other proxies for political change: (1) a dummy variable that took the value 1 if the government went from divided to unified; (2) a dummy variable that took the value 1 if any branch of government changed party in 1994; and (3) a dummy variable that took the value 1 if the legislature went from divided to unified. None of the estimates for these variables was remotely significant, and the inclusion of the various alternatives did not affect either the significant or insignificant results described for Table 6.3.

While these results provide little support for the possibility that political change influences the number of new words, we also need to investi-

Table 6.4. *Discretion in Nonsouthern States: Controlling for Additional Legislative Factors*

Independent Variables	(1)	(2)	(3)	(4)
Unified Legislature	–20.85	–31.70	–27.73	–25.86
	(9.82)	(13.22)	(13.41)	(9.97)
Unified Legislature × Compensation	2.23	2.29	2.28	2.19
	(.86)	(.92)	(.87)	(.98)
Divided Legislature	–18.00	–23.92	–21.91	–21.04
	(11.71)	(12.20)	(12.31)	(12.00)
Divided Legislature × Compensation	.49	.38	.36	.56
	(.37)	(.45)	(.44)	(.43)
Legislative Veto × Unified Legislature	–28.19	–27.41	–29.95	–23.68
	(10.85)	(11.91)	(11.92)	(12.36)
Unified-to-Divided	–7.95	—	–7.66	—
	(8.60)		(8.05)	
Ranney Index	—	60.85	59.96	—
		(61.27)	(62.28)	
Democratic Control	—	—	—	8.62
				(24.44)
Medicaid Expenditures	36.94	36.36	37.13	31.47
	(20.30)	(20.23)	(20.27)	(25.80)
California dummy	247.90	249.40	248.46	246.60
	(12.57)	(13.20)	(12.76)	(15.08)
Constant	1.92	–46.40	–46.10	1.13
	(13.94)	(52.96)	(53.91)	(14.64)
Adjusted R^2	.78	.78	.78	.77
N	38	38	38	38

Note: The dependent variable is *Discretion* in Medicaid-related legislation in 1995–1996, measured in thousands of words (see text for details). Estimates are from OLS regression. Positive coefficients reflect less agency discretion. Numbers in parentheses are White standard errors. *Unified Legislature* takes the value 1 when the majorities of both chambers of the legislature are of a different party than that of the governor. *Divided Legislature* takes the value 1 if one of two chambers is controlled by a different party than that of the governor.

gate another alternative hypothesis discussed earlier: that greater political uncertainty would lead those in power to write more detailed legislation. Thus, we include a variable called *Ranney Index*, which is a widely used proxy for the level of political competition in the U.S. states.[24] If political

[24] Our measure of the Ranney Index is for the 1995–1998 period (Bibby and Holbrook 1999). We use the Ranney Competition Index, which varies from 0 to 1, and where a higher

uncertainty increases with electoral competitiveness, then this variable should have a positive coefficient. As with our variable measuring political change, however, the results in column 2 show little support for the alternative hypothesis. Political uncertainty, as measured by the Ranney Index, has no effect on *Discretion*.[25]

Although the Ranney Index is a widely used proxy for political competitiveness, perhaps it is not a good proxy for political uncertainty. We therefore considered several other proxies for political uncertainty: (1) the size of the legislative majority (the idea being that smaller majorities should lead to more uncertainty about the future), (2) the sum of the number of changes in majority control of each branch of government over the last four elections (the idea being that a history of change should lead to greater uncertainty), and (3) term limits (the idea being that if legislators know they will not be around in the future, incentives to insulate are maximal). It turns out that there is only one state (Maine) where both chambers have members who were prevented by term limits from running in 1996, and only one other state (California) where term limits were in effect in one chamber in 1996 and in the other chamber in 1998. Thus, we cannot test the term limits idea in any systematic way; however, a dummy variable for these two states was not significant and did not change our other results. The other two variables similarly produced insignificant results. Neither the size of the majority nor the sum of partisan changes, entered alone or interacted with *Compensation*, has a significant effect, and the inclusion of these variables has no effect on our previous results.

Although neither *Ranney Index* nor *Unified-to-Divided* was significant in previous equations, it is possible that one (or both) will be significant when both are included. As column 3 demonstrates, however, neither variable is significant. The results presented in this column, like those in the previous columns, yield little support for the idea that either political uncertainty or political change has a significant influence on legislatures' design

number indicates a greater level of electoral competitiveness. The formula for this index is 1 – |(.5 – Ranney Party Control Index)|. The Party Control Index is calculated as a function of three variables: (1) the percentage of votes won in gubernatorial elections and sets won in state legislative elections, (2) the duration of partisan control of the state legislature and governorship, and (3) the frequency of divided control. See Ranney and Kendall (1954) and Ranney (1976).

[25] Interacting *Ranney Index* with *Compensation* leads to similar results. In addition, when *Unified-to-Divided* is interacted with *Compensation* and added to the regression reported in column 2, this interactive term is not significant, and inclusion of this variable has no impact on the other results presented in that column.

of statutes. At the same time, the results continue to show support for our theoretical argument.

Another possibility is that preferences concerning the amount of legislation are simply a function of partisanship. According to this scenario, Democrats would be more likely to write longer laws than Republicans because they favor a more activist role for government and because creating such a role for government requires more detailed statutes. If this is true, then Democratic governments should be associated with more legislative words, and this association might have much to do with general attitudes toward policy and little to do with attitudes toward discretion. The results in column 4, however, do not bear this out. When we include a variable, *Democratic Control*, that accounts for instances in which Democrats control government, we find results similar to those in the earlier columns of this table: *Democratic Control* is insignificant, and its inclusion does not affect our other results.

We turn next to factors that are outside of the legislature in order to see whether these factors might influence the level of discretion in legislation. First, we control for the level of bureaucratic professionalism, which we operationalize by using the annual salary of the head of the health agency in each state.[26] As column 1 of Table 6.5 shows, this variable is not significant. At the same time, all of our other variables remain significant. To check on the robustness of this result, we also tried two other measures for this variable: the average pay for all noneducational state employees and the average pay for state employees who work in the area of health. Once again, these variables were not significant, and their inclusion did not affect our other variables. In additional tests we also included measures specific to the governor that might influence the level of discretion, such as the percentage of legislators needed to override a veto, the governor's overall appointment powers, the governor's prospects for staying in power, a summary measure of the governor's veto powers, and a summary measure of the governor's institutional powers. None of these variables were significant, and none affected our results.[27]

[26] When control of health policy was split between two agencies, we used the average of the salaries paid to the officials in charge of both agencies.

[27] We obtained the various measures of bureaucratic professionalism from *The Book of the States* and obtained the measures of the governor's powers from *The Book of the States* and from Beyle (1999). We find it somewhat surprising that none of these measures are significant, and believe that the relationship between bureaucratic professionalism, the governor's powers, and delegation of discretion deserves further investigation. See Huber and McCarty (2001) for an initial theoretical investigation into this topic.

Table 6.5. *Discretion in Nonsouthern States: Controlling for Additional Nonlegislative Factors*

Independent Variables	(1)	(2)	(3)
Unified Legislature	–25.61	–25.84	–22.44
	(10.79)	(9.88)	(8.84)
Unified Legislature × Compensation	2.35	2.37	2.01
	(.95)	(.95)	(0.87)
Divided Legislature	–20.35	–20.91	–24.71
	(11.09)	(11.54)	(12.27)
Divided Legislature × Compensation	.47	.54	.67
	(.38)	(.36)	(0.39)
Legislative Veto × Unified Legislature	–27.80	–26.60	–20.85
	(13.43)	(11.89)	(12.24)
Bureaucratic Professionalism	.10	—	—
	(.40)		
Most Effective Interest Groups	—	–6.65	—
		(9.51)	
Individualistic State Political Culture	—	—	–10.99
			(8.68)
Medicaid Expenditures	36.08	39.97	39.83
	(22.245)	(19.72)	(19.10)
California dummy	248.73	251.21	24.08
	14.43	(12.66)	(13.63)
Constant	–6.10	3.78	4.56
	(30.36)	(14.42)	(13.76)
Adjusted R^2	.78	.78	.78
N	38	38	38

Note: The dependent variable is *Discretion* in Medicaid-related legislation in 1995–1996, measured in thousands of words (see text for details). Estimates are from OLS regression. Positive coefficients reflect less agency discretion. Numbers in parentheses are White standard errors. *Unified Legislature* takes the value 1 when the majorities of both chambers of the legislature are of a different party than that of the governor. *Divided Legislature* takes the value 1 if one of two chambers is controlled by a different party than that of the governor.

In column 2 of this table, we examine whether the interest group environment in the state influences the amount of discretion that legislatures give to agencies. If health interest groups are among the dominant interest groups in a state, we might find that these groups use this power to influence legislation by pressuring legislators to write more detailed laws, or that they provide the detail for legislators to put into the laws. Measuring interest group influence in each state is a difficult job; fortunately, we can draw on a state-level survey conducted in 1994 by Thomas and Hrebenar (1999) to determine which interest groups were seen as most effective in each state. We used the Thomas–Hrebenar rankings for each state to determine whether health-related interest groups – for example, hospital associations, medical insurance companies, or physician associations – were among the groups listed as most effective in each state.[28] If one or more of these health-related groups were listed among the primary groups in each state, we coded the state as 1; otherwise we coded it as 0. As we report in column 2, however, this variable has no effect.

Finally, it is possible that a state's culture leads its legislature to write bills that allow for more (or less) discretion. Perhaps the best statement of state political culture can be found in Elazar (1984), who explores the ways in which state cultures shape state politics. Some states are said to have *individualist* cultures in which government is relegated to a limited role. Other states are said to have *moralist* cultures, in which government's role is to provide for the common good. Between these two cultures is the *traditionalist* culture, which allows for more governmental activism than the individualist culture but less than the moralist culture.

To assess whether individualist states produce less legislation and non-individualist states produce more, we set a state political culture variable equal to 1 for individualist states and 0 for other states. If a dominant culture of individualism does lead to less (and less detailed) legislation, we should expect to see a negative coefficient for this variable. As we show in column 3, the coefficient for individualist state political cultures is negative, but it is not significant. Equally important, its inclusion does not affect any of our theoretical variables.

In addition to testing these alternative explanations, we attempted to examine the effect of several alternative nonstatutory mechanisms. One variable we used measured whether there existed a joint-oversight committee in the legislature. Since such committees have the power to suspend agency rules, we wanted to examine whether their presence diminished incentives to write detailed statutes. A second variable concerned state administrative procedures acts (APAs). We wanted to explore whether a presence of such acts created less incentive to write detailed legislation. A third variable concerned the judiciary. We wanted to learn whether states that had courts that were likely to be sympathetic to the legislative majority were also more likely to write shorter laws. We were able to construct

[28] We are grateful to Clive Thomas for providing us with these data.

variables in each of these three areas and the results generally supported our argument, though we do not report them here. The problem is that we can have little confidence in these results because, in each case, almost all of the states have the same values on these variables. For the administrative procedures variable, for example, all states have an APA, and only Nevada exempts health care from the APA statute. Thus our APA variable is actually just a dummy variable for Nevada. Similarly, for the judiciary variable, which is based on the way judges are elected, only two states have "sympathetic judiciaries" and unified legislatures. Thus, we found ourselves somewhat limited in our ability to test the impact of nonstatutory mechanisms in the U.S. states. When we turn to the parliamentary systems in the next chapter, we are able to explore a wider range of nonstatutory mechanism in testing this aspect of our theory.

Divided Government and the South

Scholars have found that differences between the South and the rest of the country remain but have narrowed in recent years (Hood, Kidd, and Morris 1999; Berard 2001). We therefore consider our arguments about divided government and the legislative veto with the southern states included in the analysis. As in Table 6.3, we begin with the most straightforward test of our model.[29]

Column 1 of Table 6.6 shows that when southern states are included, we again find the correct results for all of our theoretical variables. Both the dummy variables and the interacted variables for each type of divided government are significant. Furthermore, when we look at the combined effects, we find that a unified legislature produces positive values for levels of compensation above $10,640 and a divided legislature does the same whenever compensation exceeds $29,220. Thus, as our theoretical argument suggests, there is less of an effect with a *Divided Legislature* than with a *Unified Legislature*.

In column 2 we include a dummy variable for the southern states, as southern politics differs in ways other than ideology from the rest of the country (Black 1987). The southern dummy variable has the expected

[29] We also ran regressions with the political uncertainty and political change variables. We do not report these, as the results are identical to those in Table 6.4. There is no effect for the uncertainty and change variables, and inclusion of these variables does not affect the results for the other variables.

Table 6.6. *Discretion in 48 States*

Independent variables	(1)	(2)	(3)
Unified Legislature	−16.91	−16.23	—
	(8.28)	(8.17)	
Unified Legislature × Compensation	1.59	1.56	—
	(.70)	(.71)	
Divided Legislature	−17.24	−16.17	—
	(9.96)	(9.72)	
Divided Legislature × Compensation	.59	.56	—
	(.32)	(.34)	
Unified Legislature (South)	—	—	0.45
			(10.24)
Unified Legislature × Compensation (South)	—	—	.46
			(.72)
Divided Legislature (South)	—	—	−16.48
			(17.82)
Divided Legislature × Compensation (South)	—	—	.73
			(.95)
Unified Legislature (Non-South)	—	—	−23.04
			(9.79)
Unified Legislature × Compensation (Non-South)	—	—	2.00
			(.81)
Divided Legislature (Non-South)	—	—	−18.09
			(11.24)
Divided Legislature × Compensation (Non-South)	—	—	.52
			(.40)
Legislative Veto × Unified Legislature	−13.80	−13.51	−18.53
	(7.55)	(8.09)	(6.36)
South	—	−2.07	—
		(5.20)	
Medicaid Expenditures	28.30	28.27	35.56
	(17.53)	(18.05)	(21.19)
California dummy	244.04	243.97	248.52
	(10.93)	(11.25)	(13.31)
Constant	4.44	4.72	5.38
	(11.82)	(12.21)	(13.87)
Adjusted R^2	.72	.71	.70
N	48	48	48

Note: The dependent variable is *Discretion* in Medicaid-related legislation in 1995–1996, measured in thousands of words (see text for details). Estimates are from OLS regression. Positive coefficients reflect less agency discretion. Numbers in parentheses are White standard errors. *Unified Legislature* takes the value 1 when the majorities of both chambers of the legislature are of a different party than that of the governor. *Divided Legislature* takes the value 1 if one of two chambers is controlled by a different party than that of the governor.

negative sign, but it has a huge standard error. Inclusion of this variable does not affect the previous results.

Column 3 tests the idea that our theoretical argument applies to both southern and nonsouthern states, but with a weaker effect in the South (because partisan differences are weaker there). We therefore estimate a model that includes the various divided government variables interacted with region. The results provide no support for our theoretical arguments in the South, but strong support for our arguments regarding *Unified Legislature* government and legislative vetoes in nonsouthern states. This underscores the appropriateness of omitting the South from the analysis.

Conclusion

The results of our tests using state Medicaid policy are largely consistent with the theory. We find strong evidence, for example, of a substitution effect for *Legislative Veto*. When legislatures can rely on the existence of such a veto, they are less likely to pay the costs needed to write low-discretion laws and instead are more likely to write high-discretion laws. We also find that policy conflict, in the form of both unified and divided legislatures, increases the likelihood of low-discretion laws, all else equal.

Our results also demonstrate the importance of looking at the interaction between policy conflict and legislative capacity in state governments. As we argued in Chapter 4, it is not necessary to interact these terms in all political systems. In the U.S. states, however, many legislatures have very low levels of capacity, and thus we need to include capacity interacted with conflict. It is not until a state legislature has a level of legislative capacity that exceeds an unobservable threshold that policy conflict leads to less discretion in writing laws. During divided government our data show that, using our compensation measure of capacity, this threshold is approximately $11,000 for unified legislatures and $29,000 for divided legislatures. For legislatures with capacities above these levels, policy conflict and legislative capacity interact to produce low-discretion laws.

While this chapter provides evidence in support of our theory in a separation of powers environment, we claimed that our theory is a general comparative theory that can be applied in different political settings. The challenge now is to operationalize abstract concepts like conflict, capacity, and alternative mechanisms in settings other than separation of powers systems. We turn to this task in the next chapter.

7

The Design of Laws across Parliamentary Systems

In the previous chapter, we operationalized the abstract explanatory variables in our theory within the context of presidential systems. The important role of all the U.S. states in Medicaid policymaking, along with sudden changes in the Medicaid policymaking environment in the mid-1990s, allowed us to study how a large number of states legislated on the same basic issue. By measuring all relevant legislation on this specific topic, we found that the political and institutional contexts had a significant impact on how legislative majorities designed statutes. Factors like divided government, divided legislatures, legislative professionalism, and legislative vetoes influenced the level of policy details that states included in their legislative statutes.

We now evaluate our theory in parliamentary systems, where there is a melding of legislative and executive powers. Our parliamentary tests must differ from our tests in the U.S. states in two significant respects. The first concerns how we measure discretion. Since our theory concerns how the political context affects the way different political systems design legislation *on the same basic issue*, we must have a means to control for the nature of the issue. Across the 19 parliamentary democracies that we examine, there obviously does not exist the transnational equivalent of the Medicaid program. That is, there is no single issue that all of these different countries had to address at the same time. We therefore cannot proceed by collecting all legislation on the relevant issue, as we did for the U.S. states, and instead must find a different strategy to control for the nature of the policy issue.

The second difference from the U.S. states concerns our explanatory variables. Since parliamentary systems lack the separation of legislative and executive power, we cannot proceed by simply adopting the same variables used in our examination of the U.S. states. The concept of divided government, for example, is not meaningful in the parliamentary context. In addition, it is not clear that compensation or other indicators of legislative professionalism are the appropriate measures of legislative capacity. And since there is more general institutional variation across the parliamentary systems than across the U.S. states, there is a wider variety of relevant nonstatutory factors.

How, then, do we test our theory in parliamentary systems? More specifically, how do we measure our dependent variable, the amount of discretion in legislation, in a way that permits cross-national comparisons? What creates conflict between the agents who adopt statutes and those who implement them? What influences the capacity of the adopters to include legislative details? And what are the relevant nonstatutory factors that create incentives or disincentives to make policy in legislation itself? We address these questions in this chapter and use our answers to provide an empirical test of our argument.

Policy Constraints in Labor Legislation

We begin by defining how we use the length of legislative statutes to measure discretion. Before discussing how we operationalize this measure, however, it is useful to remind ourselves of how the length of statutes is related to the level of discretion by looking at several examples of labor legislation. As in Chapters 1 and 3, we consider several laws about gender equality in the workplace, focusing here on the language that statutes use to define gender discrimination.

The objective of professional equality laws is typically to ensure that women and men are treated equally in all aspects of employment, including the way job descriptions or job advertisements are written, the way hiring, retention, transfer, pay, and promotion decisions are made, and the way professional training and development opportunities are made available. A standard approach in legislation is to state that discrimination based on sex is prohibited in any of these areas of employment. Legislative majorities recognize, however, that there are problems with attempting to use legislation to make blanket prohibitions of discrimination, especially when sex unavoidably affects the circumstances under which employees can do certain jobs. It is difficult for men to model bikinis, for example, and it is difficult for a woman to play the role of Hamlet in a traditional production of Shakespeare's play. Thus, decisions must be made in legislation about where exceptions to prohibitions on discrimination can occur.

We see considerable variation across countries in how these exceptions are defined. In France, Article 1 of Law 83–635, enacted in 1983, is very brief. It simply states in one sentence that prohibitions on sex discrimination do not apply to positions in which one's sex is the "condition déterminante" for performing the job. The article also states that the Council of State ("Conseil d'Etat"), in conjunction with representatives of employers and workers, will determine by decree which specific jobs have the worker's sex as the "condition déterminante."

In France, the Council of State is in many respects at the apex of the French civil service, functioning in part as an agency that drafts administrative decrees and in part as an administrative court. Consequently, in delegating to the Council of State, the French statute effectively delegates to the French civil service. One therefore finds the definition of jobs for which gender discrimination is allowable not in legislation but in Article R123-1 of the French Code du Travail (Partie Réglementaire – Décrets en Conseil d'Etat). That article of the Code reveals that the Council of State adopted a decree on May 25, 1984, that states that sex is a determining condition for artists who must interpret a masculine or feminine role and for models. The French legislation, then, does nothing to define specific exceptions to prohibitions on discrimination, but rather only adopts the vague policy regarding the "condition déterminante." Filling in the main policy details is left to civil servants.

The Norwegian approach is similar to the French one. The relevant portions of the legislation can be found in Figure 7.1. As in France, the third clause of the article clearly delegates authority for defining which jobs are excluded from the prohibition on discrimination. But unlike the French law, which delegates a policymaking role to the civil service, the Norwegian clause delegates this power to the "King." The "King" here refers in practice to the cabinet, which meets formally on Friday mornings in the Royal Castle with the king (or crown prince). Although the king formally chairs the meetings, in reality the decisions are made in the governmental offices the day before.[1] Thus, rather than asking the civil service to make policy on exceptions to discrimination laws, the Norwegian legislation asks the government to make policy on these exceptions.

[1] We are grateful to Bjorn-Erik Rasch for clarifying the role of the Norwegian king in actual practice.

Article 2 Subject of the Act

This Act applies to discrimination between men and women in all areas, except for internal conditions within religious communities.

With regard to family life and purely personal matters, this Act is not to be enforced by the authorities mentioned in Art. 10.

In special cases the King may determine that the Act shall not apply, in whole or in part, to certain specific sectors. The opinion of the Board (cf. Art. 10) shall be obtained in such cases.

Article 3 General Clause

[. . .]

The King may issue regulations regarding the kinds of differential treatment which can be accepted pursuant to this Act, including provisions on positive special treatment of men in relation to care for and education of children.

Note: Act no. 45, June 9, 1978.

Figure 7.1. Norway's Gender Equality Act of 1978

We see quite a different approach in Ireland. The text of the relevant Irish legislation, shown in Figure 7.2, is quite lengthy. Article 25(1) is similar to the French and Norwegian legislation – discrimination on the basis of sex is permitted if sex is "an occupational qualification." But unlike the French and Norwegian laws, the Irish statute goes on to define directly, in subsections (2) through (4), circumstances under which sex is an occupational qualification. Subsection (2), for example, discusses the roles of physiology, strength, stamina, and entertainment in defining such circumstances. Subsection (3) discusses (among other things) the impact of laws or customs in other countries, and subsection (4) discusses (among other things) the decisions that must be made when there are special sleeping or sanitary issues. Article 27 is devoted to issues that arise in connection with the Irish National Guard and prison service. Nowhere in the legislation is there any explicit delegation to civil servants, and only in Article 27 is there any delegation at all, in this case to ministers who must make decisions when there are insufficient numbers of applicants, either male or female.

25. Exclusion of discrimination in certain employments

(1) Nothing in this Part or Part II applies to discrimination against A in respect of employment in a particular post if the discrimination results from preferring B on the ground that, by reference to one or more of subsections (2) to (4) the sex of B is or amounts to an occupational qualification for the post in question.

(2) For the purposes of this section, the sex of B shall be taken to be an occupational qualification for a post where, on grounds of physiology (excluding physical strength or stamina) or on grounds of authenticity for the purpose of entertainment, the nature of the post:

(a) requires a person of the same sex as B, and
(b) would be materially different if filled by a person of the same sex as A.

(3) For the purposes of this section, the sex of B shall be taken to be an occupational qualification for a post where it is necessary that the post should be held by B because it is likely to involve the performance of duties outside the State in a place where the laws or customs are such that those duties could not reasonably be performed by a person who is of the same sex as A.

(4) For the purposes of this section, the sex of B shall be taken to be an occupational qualification for a post:

(a) where the duties of the post involve personal services and it is necessary to have persons of both sexes engaged in such duties, or
(b) where, because of the nature of the employment it is necessary to provide sleeping and sanitary accommodation for employees on a communal basis and it would be unreasonable to expect the provision of separate accommodation of that nature or impracticable for an employer so to provide.

27. Garda Siochana and prison service

(1) With regard to employment in the Garda Siochana or the prison service, nothing in this Act:

(a) applies to the assignment of a man or, as the case may require, a woman to a particular post where this is essential:

(i) in the interests of privacy or decency,
(ii) in order to guard, escort or control violent individuals or quell riots or violent disturbances, or

Figure 7.2. Ireland's Employment Equality Act of 1998

(iii) in order, within the Garda Siochana, to disarm or arrest violent individuals, to control or disperse violent crowds or to effect the rescue of hostages or other persons held unlawfully, or

(b) prevents the application of one criterion as to height for men and another for women, if the criteria chosen are such that the proportion of women in the State likely to meet the criterion for women is approximately the same as the proportion of men in the State likely to meet the criterion for men.

(2) (a) If:

(i) in the opinion of the Minister there are insufficient numbers of either men or women serving in the Garda Siochana to be assigned to such posts as are for the time being referred to in subsection (1)(a), and
(ii) the Minister by order under this subsection so provides,

this Act shall not apply to such competitions for recruitment to the Garda Siochana as may be specified in the order.

(b) If:

(i) in the opinion of the Minister there are insufficient numbers of either men or women serving in the prison service to be assigned to such posts as are for the time being referred to in subsection (1)(a), and
(ii) the Minister by order under this subsection so provides,

this Act shall not apply to such competitions for recruitment to the prison service as may be specified in the order.

Figure 7.2. *(continued)*

These examples, then, confirm what we argued in Chapter 3. Longer statutes on the same topic typically have more detailed policy language that places greater constraints on the individuals who implement laws. The challenge that we face is to measure differences in the length of statutes on the same topic, and to do so with a relatively large amount of data.

Measuring Discretion

To test our theory across the 19 parliamentary systems, we created a large data set on labor legislation, using information from the International Labour Organization (ILO). Each year, states belonging to the ILO submit a list of labor-related laws that have been adopted in the previous

100	General provisions
200	Human rights
300	Conditions of employment
400	Conditions of work
500	Economic and social development
600	Employment
700	Industrial relations
800	Labour administration
900	Occupational safety and health
1000	Social security
1100	Training
1200	Special provisions by category of persons
1300	Special provisions by sector of economic activity

Figure 7.3. Natlex policy codes

year. The ILO data contain, among other pieces of information, the law's title, the date it was adopted, its subject matter, and its publication information (which gives the length of the law in pages). Specifically, our dependent variable measures the (standardized) length (in pages) of 4,102 statutes adopted in 19 countries between 1986 and 1998. These laws are included in the ILO's Natlex database.[2]

Since our general objective is to test the effects of political and institutional variables on statute design, holding the issue type constant, we need statutes that pertain to the same issue across countries. The ILO's coding of labor legislation makes this possible. Each piece of legislation affects labor interests, which means that we are not, for example, comparing legislation on agricultural price supports with legislation on defense spending with legislation on taxes. More importantly, each piece of labor legislation is coded by experts at the ILO into 13 issue categories, which are listed in Figure 7.3. Our tests treat the individual statute as the unit of analysis, and will include policy dummy variables based on these issue categories to control for issue effects. At the conclusion of this section, we discuss the advantages and disadvantages of this approach in comparison with the state data. Before doing so, however, it is important to

[2] The 19 countries include all advanced parliamentary democracies except Greece and Japan (where we could not accurately measure our dependent variable). The ILO data can be found at http://natlex.ilo.org/.

describe precisely how we use the Natlex data to measure our dependent variable.

To create our data set, we obtained a text file from the ILO in Geneva containing all their data through the end of 1998. Although there are many laws from the period before 1986, staff members at the ILO informed us that the data were not collected systematically until 1986, which is why our data set begins in that year. To turn the text file into usable data, we used a text recognition program to create a database entry for each law. We then obtained original documents for entries with relevant missing data, such as page length or date, and for entries that identified documents over 100 pages long (to check for accuracy). We also did random checks on documents that are one page long to check for systematic errors in the reporting from specific countries. We found no such errors.

Table 7.1 describes the data. There are two problems associated with comparing raw page lengths across countries. The first is that languages differ in their efficiency; that is, it takes longer to say the same thing in some languages than in others. To control for this problem, we created a variable that we call the *verbosity multiplier*, which measures the relative efficiency of different languages. To calculate it, we downloaded four different pieces of EU legislation from the European Union's (EU's) Web page. Each of the four laws was downloaded in each of the EU's official languages.[3] We then used Microsoft Word to count the number of characters (with spaces) for each law in each language. These character counts were used to calculate the verbosity of the different languages. We found English to be the most efficient, and thus it has the baseline value of 1. The verbosity multiplier for other variables measures how many pages in these languages it takes to say the same thing in 1 page of English. German, for example, is the least efficient language, with a verbosity multiplier of 1.22. Thus, it takes 1.22 pages in German to say exactly the same thing that it takes 1 page to say in English.

The second problem is that the amount of text on a page of the official journal varies across countries (and, in some cases, within countries over time). Canada, for instance, uses a relatively large font, and each page has separate columns for French and English. Portugal, on the other hand, uses a small font and puts a large amount of text in two columns on each page. Thus, 1 page in Portugal contains as much text as 4.69 pages in

[3] As noted in Table 7.1, this approach leaves us without estimates for Icelandic (for which we used Danish) and Norwegian (for which we used Swedish).

Table 7.1. *Length of Laws in Natlex Data*

Country	Number of Bills in Sample	Mean Unstandardized Page Length	Verbosity Multiplier	Page Length Multiplier	Mean Standardized Page Length (std. dev.)
Australia	269	44.2	1	1.47	65.0 (117.8)
Austria	215	10.3	1.22	2.79	23.5 (28.4)
Belgium	176	12.4	1.13 (French)	2.42	26.5 (65.0)
Canada	85	34.2	1 (English)	1	34.2 (66.8)
Denmark	373	6.3	1.06	2.73	16.3 (35.0)
Finland	558	2.2	1.04	2.19	4.5 (7.6)
France	178	6.3	1.13	3.87	21.6 (30.9)
Germany	159	14.3	1.22	3.42	40.0 (72.8)
Iceland	94	3.6	1.06 (Danish)	1.39	4.8 (5.9)
Ireland	63	33.6	1	1.6	53.8 (55.4)
Italy	155	12.9	1.14	3.67	41.4 (69.0)
Luxembourg	127	12.8	1.13 (French)	2.08	23.6 (57.5)
Netherlands	324	14.0	1.16	2.04	24.5 (37.9)
New Zealand	147	26.8	1	1.28	34.3 (60.4)
Norway	143	5.3	1.01 (Swedish)	1.27	6.6 (18.6)
Portugal	260	6.6	1.12	4.69	27.6 (128.4)
Spain	145	10.2	1.14	4.27	38.2 (61.7)
Sweden	551	3.0	1.01	1.54	4.5 (8.5)
United Kingdom	80	63.3	1	1986: 1.4 1987–98: 1.98	120.6 (179.1)
	Total bills: 4,102				Total sample: 24.6 (66.7)

Canada. Column 4 of Table 7.1 gives the *page length multiplier* for each country.[4] These numbers represent how many pages in Canada's official journal, which has the fewest words per page, would be needed to print one page in each of the other countries' official journals.

Together, the verbosity multiplier and the page length multiplier can be used to develop a standardized page length, which is given in column 5.[5] This is the measure of discretion that we use in the random effects regressions to be described. Two important features of the data are rather obvious. First, there is considerable cross-national variation, with countries like Finland and Iceland having, on average, much shorter bills than countries like the United Kingdom or Australia. Second, within each country, there also exists considerable variation, with all countries having a large standard deviation in their means. Our goal is to understand whether, when controlling for issue and country-specific effects, the variables suggested by our model help us to understand the variation in Table 7.1.

Before turning to this task, however, several comments are in order. The first concerns bias in our data that might be created by the membership of some of our countries in the EU. In particular, the Maastricht Treaty for European Union expanded the role of the EU in domestic labor policy through its Social Chapter. The Social Chapter allows the EU to issue directives in labor-related areas. It also revised enforcement policy within the EU, allowing the European Court of Justice to fine states for failure to comply with such directives. Thus, if a large collection of states are implementing the same text from a directive, then perhaps the text in the directive rather than the factors that we study are influencing the level of policy detail in legislation.[6]

In fact, this concern is unwarranted. Following the adoption of a directive in the EU, member states can write the implementation documents as they see fit. We saw this earlier in the considerable differences that exist in the French, German, and Irish statutes that have been adopted to

[4] To calculate the page length multiplier we collected a random sample of bills from the ILO data, and then counted the number of characters per line and the number of lines per page of these bills to determine how much text was on an average page.

[5] The standardized page length for a bill is the number of pages* (page length multiplier/verbosity multiplier). We did not standardize one-page bills.

[6] Although it is impossible to count the number of statutes in our database that implement EU directives, our impression is that they constitute a very minor proportion of our total statutes.

implement an EU directive on gender equality in the workplace. This is part of a more general pattern. We randomly collected information on the implementation of 34 directives and found references in the CELEX database of National Implementing Measures to 1,485 implementing measures.[7] Since there is far more than one national document per directive, it is obvious that countries do not simply incorporate the language of the directive verbatim into their own national law. Instead, the process is more piecemeal in each country, with some countries reporting numerous measures to implement directives and many countries reporting none. In addition, of 1,485 national measures, only 395 were statutes. The rest were some form of regulation issued in the cabinet. For any given directive, we also found considerable variation across and within countries with respect to the specific implementation instruments used. In particular, we found that in 201 cases, countries used only regulations to implement directives; in 61 cases, they used only statutes; and in the remaining 104 cases, they used a combination of the two instruments. Finally, it is worth noting that 256 of the national implementing measures were adopted *before* the directive was adopted. If the EU adopts a directive that forbids gender discrimination, for example, and member states already have legislation on the books to this effect, then no further action is needed.

One could hardly argue, then, that the issuance of directives influences the language of statutes that are adopted by EU member states. When faced with a directive on a specific issue, member states have a wide range of autonomy with respect to how they actually go about implementing it, and the exercise of this autonomy is evident in the enormous variation we see in implementation instruments. The limited legislation that does implement EU directives should therefore be subject to the same political forces as the legislation that is unrelated to EU activity.[8]

Our second observation concerns the differences that exist between our tests in the U.S. states and our tests in parliamentary democracies. In our state data, the state itself is the unit of analysis, and we are able to identify all relevant legislation on a specific policy during a specific time period. Since this is impossible in the parliamentary systems, we instead use the

[7] CELEX is a database operated by the EU, which was available to us through Lexis-Nexis.

[8] A future possibility for testing our theory would be to examine variation in the responses of the EU member states to the same directive. At this time, not enough data are available for this undertaking (because, for any directive, the CELEX data base typically identifies national legislation for only a handful of countries).

legislative statute as the unit of analysis, collect a large number of statutes across a variety of policy areas, and include dummy variables for each policy category.

The parliamentary data have several advantages. One is that they allow us to test our theory across a range of issues, whereas in the U.S. states data we focus narrowly on the health care issue. The parliamentary data thus allow us to gain confidence that the general argument is not one that is narrowly limited with respect to the types of issues to which it applies. A second advantage is that it allows us to bring more data to bear on our theory by allowing us to examine a longer time period. In the U.S. states, we were limited to a two-year cross section.

The parliamentary data also have some potential disadvantages in comparison with the U.S. state data. One is that although we can include the policy dummy variables to control for issue type in the parliamentary systems, we cannot, with such a large number of statutes and diversity of languages, be as certain as in the state data about the quality of our control for issue type. This would be of particular concern if the policy dummy variables were not estimated accurately (which, as we show, turns out not to be the case). A second concern is about the unit of analysis. By aggregating across all relevant statutes in the U.S. states, we need not worry whether different states have different tendencies with respect to the *bundling* of legislation. It does not matter in the state data whether a state writes 10 short bills or 1 long one. All the words count the same.

In the parliamentary data, we must treat the statute as the unit of analysis, and Table 7.1 suggests reasons to be concerned that some countries may write a few long bills and others may write a lot of short ones. Sweden and Finland are the most obvious examples that raise concern. Both countries have very short bills, on average, and they have a very large number of bills in our sample. Overall, the correlation across the 19 countries between standardized page length and the number of bills is –.44 ($p = .06$).

It is not clear to us, however, whether this is a significant problem. These patterns could be a function of legislative bundling patterns, or they could simply be a function of variation in the number of statutes adopted or of reporting patterns to the ILO.[9] After all, we see very long laws in all countries, even those with low average page length. Both Finland and Sweden, for example, have statutes that exceed 100 pages. And there are

[9] The staff at the ILO told us that the completeness of reporting varies both across countries and within countries over time.

other countries, such as Iceland, with small numbers of bills and low page length. In fact, the correlation between page length and number of bills is much smaller and insignificant when we exclude Finland and Sweden ($r = -.28$, $p = .28$). We therefore take this potential relationship between page length and bundling practices as an issue to be explored through the statistical tests that we perform. Later, we describe our approach in this regard.

Policy Conflict in Parliamentary Systems

We now turn to the task of operationalizing the variables in our theory. We begin by discussing the concept of policy conflict between the authors and implementers of legislation. As in the previous chapter, our tests are based on the assumption that there exists a political actor who enjoys a privileged position with respect to influencing bureaucrats during policy implementation. In the U.S. states, this privileged actor was obviously the governor, and we followed previous research in focusing on the importance of divided government.

Now consider this issue in parliamentary systems. We argued in Chapter 2 that parliamentary government is typically cabinet government with cohesive parties. There is no clear separation of power between the legislative and executive branches, and party leaders become cabinet ministers, with significant opportunities to influence policy. We therefore assume that individual cabinet ministers are the relevant privileged actors in the policy implementation process. In what follows, we discuss this assumption and its implications for the specific hypotheses that emerge from our theory.

The cabinet minister has a privileged position during policy formulation and implementation. The process of adopting new legislation begins with the individual ministers overseeing preparation of the initial drafts of bills. If a bill concerns reform of agricultural programs, for example, the agriculture minister will take a leading role. And whenever bills have strong financial implications, the minister of finance will be actively involved. Individual ministers are constrained at this stage of the policy-making process by other members of the cabinet. Usually there is considerable discussion of the bill at this time, both within and across parties that support the government. And usually, important legislative deals by members of the governing majority are struck before a bill comes to the floor of parliament. The collective cabinet must approve a minister's bill, sometimes by voting and sometimes by consensus. If a bill cannot achieve this approval, the bill and possibly even the government will die. Governments in fact often break up over the inability to agree on a particular policy. Ministers, then, play a strong role in shaping legislation, but they cannot ram unwanted policies down the throats of unwilling partners in the majority.

Cabinet ministers also play the central role during policy implementation. Ministers are the formal heads of the specific departments associated with their portfolios. The justice minister, for example, sits atop the ministry of justice and can often exercise great influence over actions taken in this department. As noted in Chapter 2, ministers exercise control over implementation in numerous ways. There are informal means, for example, such as the daily meetings that ministers have with senior civil servants or the assignment of tasks by ministers to specific individuals within a department. And there are more formal possibilities. Ministers in some countries, for example, can decide which individuals to hire or promote at the top of the administrative hierarchy. Sometimes ministers can even dismiss officials, as in France. And ministers generally play a central role in drafting regulations and departmental circulars, which tell departments how laws should be interpreted and implemented.

Laver and Shepsle (1990, 1994, 1996) consider the impact of cabinet ministers on policy to be so important that they have developed a formal theory of government formation that assumes that cabinet ministers unilaterally determine policy outcomes on the policies under their jurisdiction. This assumption is very strong, of course, and it is not intended as a precise description of reality, but rather as a simplification that facilitates theorizing about government formation. Although the assumption is extremely controversial, Laver and Shepsle use it to generate a set of predictions about government formation for which they find empirical support.[10]

We recognize that the powers of cabinet ministers over implementation are limited by their relations with civil servants and with other cabinet ministers. But we also feel that the formal and informal mechanisms described previously leave no doubt that individual cabinet ministers are much better positioned than other politicians to influence policy implementation in their departments. Since cabinet ministers can use their

[10] For an excellent recent analysis of government formation theories, see Martin and Stevenson (2001).

privileged position during implementation to shape policy outcomes, other members of the governing majority need to be concerned about whether the privileged ministers will use their autonomy to obtain unwanted outcomes. Incentives to micromanage the policymaking process through policy details in statutes will be greatest when members of the governing majority do not trust each other to implement desired policies. This fact has been recognized by scholars of government formation, who argue that coalition formation agreements are used as checks on individual ministerial authority (Andeweg 2000; Müller and Strøm 2000). We also believe it should apply to policymaking after government formation is complete.

The existence of policy conflict between the authors and implementers of statutes should therefore be related to government composition. All else equal, efforts to place policy details in laws should increase whenever there is *conflict among the parties* that together constitute the government's majority. This occurs during majority coalition government and minority government.

If parties are reasonably homogeneous and disciplined, then during single-party majority governments, the likelihood of substantial conflict between individual ministers and others in the governing majority is low. Single-party majority government is effectively the equivalent of unified government in presidential systems. If the members of the governing Labour Party in Britain have similar preferences, for example, then members of this majority can generally trust the cabinet members from their party to implement policies aimed at achieving desired outcomes, or at least they can do so to a greater degree than would be possible if policies were implemented by the Conservatives.

Coalition and minority governments, by contrast, are more like divided government in presidential systems. Suppose, for example, that the 1997 British election had resulted in a hung parliament, necessitating a coalition between the Liberal Democrats and Labour. If a Liberal Democrat was minister of employment, then, given policy differences between Labour and Liberal Democrats on policy outcomes for workers, Labour would have incentives to use policy details in legislation to limit the extent to which the Liberal minister could use his or her implementation prerogatives against the interests of Labour. Of course, Labour would also have ministers in charge of other portfolios, and Liberal Democrats would have the same interest in using legislation to curtail the Labour ministers in those areas. More generally, the party in the coalition that does not control a particular policy portfolio will have incentives to use legislation to constrain the minister who implements policies in the departments associated with this portfolio.

While legislation thus will be an important source of constraints, it should be kept in mind that during coalition majority government, the autonomy of individual ministers also can be constrained in the cabinet itself. The prime minister, for example, generally has to sign regulations, and major decisions will typically be approved by the cabinet, which often must stand collectively behind individual ministers. And Thies (2001) demonstrates that coalitions can use the strategic appointment of junior ministers to create checks on senior ones. If a minister of the Christian Democrats in Germany holds a specific portfolio, for example, then a coalition partner like the Free Democrats will often have a junior minister in this ministry.

During minority government, on the other hand, a party in the legislative majority will have no representation in the cabinet. This creates an even greater incentive to use legislation to constrain minister behavior. Thus, just as divided government affects the incentives of legislatures to spell out policy details in presidential systems, a government's coalition and majority status affect incentives in parliamentary systems. We should expect more policy details during coalition than during majority government, and we should particularly expect minority governments to include policy details in legislation.

Before concluding this discussion, it is useful to recognize that one could be tempted to make the opposite argument about coalition and minority governments. If parties are veto players during coalition and majority government, then perhaps the bicameral model could suggest that it will be more difficult during such governments to include details in legislation (because a party with the preferences of the relevant cabinet minister will block such details). This is a possibility we can explore empirically, but we feel that the veto players logic does not apply in this respect.

Bargaining in the bicameral model depends on the existence of *institutional veto players*. In the U.S. states, the Senate cannot decide to enact a policy without the House, and vice versa. In parliamentary systems, the parties in coalitions are *partisan veto players* (Tsebelis 1999, 2002), and these parties do not have the same privileged position as the institutional veto players because new coalitions can form at any time. That is, unlike in the case of the House and Senate in the U.S. states, which always must be in the winning coalition, if two parties cannot agree, then each can attempt to form alternative coalitions. Put differently, institutional veto players must choose by unanimity rule, whereas partisan veto players must choose by majority rule. In our view, this distinction has been underappreciated in the literature.

It is clear that the distinction between partisan and institutional veto players makes the bicameral model's logic inapplicable to the parliamentary context. The bicameral model focuses on comparing two different states of the world. In both states of the world, there is a pivotal member of the majority who conflicts with the politician who is privileged during policy implementation. In one state of the world – a unified legislature – the pivotal member does not have to bargain with anyone else, and in the other – a divided legislature – bargaining is necessary. The model shows that the need to bargain makes it more difficult to include legislative details.

In the parliamentary systems, however, one cannot compare these two states of the world because, depending on how we conceptualize the Politician, one of the two states of the world could never exist. If we think of the Politician in our model as the pivotal member of the coalition, then the second state can never exist (because, since it is pivotal, it can propose the policy it likes during coalition or minority government). And if we think of there being two Politicians, both pivotal, then the first state of the world never exists (because the only alternative to coalition and minority government is single-party majorities, where there is minimum policy conflict). In our view, then, although it is clearly conceivable that coalition and minority governments will affect the ability of governments to agree on policy change, there is no reason to suspect that this will affect the amount of discretion that they include in legislation if they do adopt new legislation.

The Capacity to Include Policy Details in Legislation

In our analysis of presidential systems, we argued that the cost of micromanaging the policymaking process by statute is affected by the professionalism of the legislature, in particular by the level of compensation paid to legislators. In parliamentary systems, on the other hand, cabinet governments with cohesive parties make the meaning and relevance of legislative professionalism less clear. Instead, we need to consider factors that influence the ability of cabinets to draft legislative details.

Cabinet ministers, unlike legislators in the U.S. states, always have substantial capacity to write detailed legislation. State legislators in some U.S. states are very poorly paid, and they spend little time on the job. Cabinet ministers, by contrast, are typically the most capable and well-paid politicians in their country. To become a minister, one has to have proven abilities and relevant experience. And upon becoming a minister, one has a significant staff, along with the entire department in the civil service, to assist in drafting legislative proposals. There should seldom be concern, then, that the cabinet in an advanced parliamentary democracy always lacks the capacity to formulate detailed proposals (as we found in some U.S. states). Returning to the logic of Figure 4.4 in Chapter 4, it seems that the distribution of capacity across cabinet ministers in our 19 parliamentary democracies should look much more like Distribution 2 than Distribution 1. That is, it seems very unlikely that there exist countries such that for any level of conflict, the capacity to write detailed legislation is *always* inadequate. Thus, the argument about direct effects seems more applicable than the argument about indirect effects.

This is not to say that the cabinets never face significant costs in formulating policy details in legislation. The biggest problem cabinets may face is time, which can be cut short by premature government terminations. Scholars have frequently argued that cabinet instability can diminish the capacity of politicians to achieve their policy goals. Observers of the French Fourth Republic, one of the parliamentary systems with a very high level of instability, have often argued that this instability made it very difficult for ministers to achieve their goals, transferring power to civil servants (e.g., LaPalombara 1958; Williams 1964; Scheinman 1965; Suleiman 1974). Scholars not focusing specifically on the Fourth Republic have often made similar arguments (e.g., Putnam 1973; Heady 1974; Dogan 1975; Warwick 1994, 139; Peters 1997). Lijphart (1999), for example, takes executive durability to be a measure of executive power in parliamentary systems. And the link between ministerial stability and capacity has even figured prominently in research on Britain (see, e.g., Heady 1974).

One theme in this research is that *expectations* of instability are crucial. Suleiman (1974, 169) writes that the "expectation of relatively long tenure" is "as important as the actual length of tenure." The expectation of a long ministerial tenure makes it less likely that bureaucrats will try to obstruct ministerial initiatives. Suleiman quotes a French senior civil servant (director) on this issue: "It is very difficult to hide something from a minister who expects to stay. When he proposes a project, we know he is likely to follow up." (p. 169).

Huber and Lupia (2001) use a formal model to develop an explicit theory of how the expectation of instability affects behavior. Their model suggests that if expected duration is short, ministers will have difficulty achieving their policy objectives. The logic, however, is interesting in that the cost of this instability exists even when the minister and his or her top civil servant agree on what policy to adopt. The reason is related to Suleiman's argument about obstruction: "friendly" civil servants will be hesitant to do what the minister wants because they will fear having to undo their actions later on, when the new minister takes over. They thus are more likely to delay and obstruct. This leads to the hypothesis that even when the level of conflict between ministers and civil servants is low, the expectation of cabinet instability should make it more difficult to micromanage policy implementation by writing detailed statutes. Thus, the most straightforward legislative capacity argument to test is that in our large cross section of statutes, countries that have higher expected turnover will on average place fewer policy details in legislation.

Although the legislative capacity of the cabinet should influence the design of legislation, the capacity of parliament could also be important, but only during minority government. We argued that since a pivotal party in the legislative majority does not have representation in the cabinet during minority government, writing legislative details should be a valuable tool allowing such outside support parties to achieve policy goals. Does the capacity of parliaments matter in these situations?

The answer depends on how bargaining occurs during minority government. One possibility is that the key issues between parties in government and opposition support parties are worked out by party leaders outside of the parliamentary domain. If this is the case, then the professionalism of parliament should not matter. Party leaders will know the policies that they want to adopt, and will negotiate for these policies independent of the institutional arrangements that affect capacity. This is in fact what Huber (1996, ch. 6) found in his case study of legislative activity during the Socialist minority government in France in the late 1980s. Since the Socialist Party had only minority support, it had to bargain with an opposition support party (either the Communists or the Centrists [UDC]). The leaders of these support parties had considerable expertise, and some of them had in fact served as cabinet ministers in the past. Although institutional arrangements make the French National Assembly one of the least powerful legislatures among advanced democracies, it was clearly possible for the opposition parties to obtain policy concessions. During the legislative debates, however, these opposition party leaders bargained with the government over policy details off the floor of parliament. In fact, many of the actual policy agreements found their way into legislation through government-sponsored amendments. Thus, there is clear evidence that the capacity of the parliament itself may not be relevant for the opposition parties to gain concessions.

Another possibility, however, is that the details are worked out on the floor of parliament through the normal legislative process. Consistent with this perspective, for example, is Strøm's (1984, 1990) argument about minority governments. Strøm argues that all else equal, minority governments are most likely to form if the institutions in parliament give opposition parties substantial influence over policy. In such cases, Strøm argues, parties can avoid the electoral penalty that often goes with joining the government without giving up a substantial ability to influence policy. He thus finds that all else equal, minority governments are most likely to form in situations where opposition influence in parliament is easiest to exercise.

This second possibility suggests that during minority government, the same sorts of variables used in our analysis of the U.S. state politics data might be relevant. In particular, we would expect that during minority government, where incentives to micromanage policy details in legislation are greatest, legislative detail should be greatest in the systems where the parliaments have the greatest capacity to influence policy.

Nonstatutory Factors That Affect the Design of Legislation

We now turn away from how inter- and intraparty dynamics affect the specificity of statutes to examine the role of factors that are external to parties, parliaments and cabinets. We have three arguments, which we consider in turn. Our first argument is specific to labor legislation, and concerns the influence of corporatist bargaining arrangements on incentives with respect to legislative design. Our next two arguments are not specific to labor legislation. We first discuss federalism and the role of subnational units in policy implementation. We then argue that the legal structure, and in particular the distinction between common and civil law, has an important influence on delegation incentives.

Corporatism

Labor policy, and economic policy more generally, is often influenced by extraparliamentary institutions. In highly corporatist systems, the major social partners – business and labor, along with the government – have significant autonomy in creating and implementing economic and social policies. Sometimes such policymaking requires legislation, and in corporatist systems the social partners play a central role in drafting it. At other times, no legislation is required. Such nonlegislative policymaking frequently occurs in secret, informal settings, where "gentlemen's agreements" are made out of the public eye (Gerlach 1992).[11]

A key feature of this policymaking from our theoretical perspective is that each of the major interests in society has an effective veto over policy outcomes. This leads to the common criticism that corporatist systems avoid conflictual issues, but it also means that the incentives to write detailed, constraining laws should be diminished in such systems. All major parties know that they have representation in the corporatist policymaking and implementation process, thereby decreasing incentives to specify particular types of policies in legislative statutes.

Federalism

In every large democracy, some form of delegation occurs from central to subnational units in the implementation of laws. Assessing the impact of decentralized implementation on incentives to write detailed laws is quite complicated because of the considerable variation that exists in how countries decentralize. This variation is multidimensional, with great differences in subnational jurisdictions, subnational fiscal autonomy, subnational legislative autonomy, and subnational regulatory autonomy, to name a few prominent examples.

How do these complicated and variable arrangements for delegating implementation authority to subnational actors affect the extent to which the authors of statutes share the same goals as those who implement them? Our answer focuses on a simple dichotomy between states that are constitutionally federal and those that are unitary. We hypothesize that incentives to fill laws with policy details should be greatest in federal states, where the national-level authors of statutes are most likely to have goals that diverge from those of the implementers of policy at the subnational level.

Of course, at times subnational units implement policy even in unitary states. In our view, however, the federal–unitary distinction is of central

[11] Recent studies of corporatist wage bargaining and policymaking include Iversen (1999) and the essays in Kitschelt, Lange, Marks, and Stephens (1999).

importance for several reasons. The most important one is that in federal systems, the constitution defines and protects the prerogatives of the subnational units, giving them a legal standing that is protected by the courts. When there are constitutional and judicial protections of subnational authority, disputes between national and subnational units – over jurisdiction and over policy – are the norm rather than the exception. We see such conflict frequently in federal systems where ethnic divisions also define the boundaries of states or provinces, such as in Canada or Belgium. But even Germany's cooperative federalism has been notorious for its conflicts over jurisdiction and authority.

In unitary systems, even if considerable delegation to subnational units occurs (as is often the case, for example, in Scandinavian countries), such delegation is done willfully by the national government using legislation. Since such delegation is not typically required by the constitution, and since legislative authority is never shared, subnational governments must anticipate that if they act against the wishes of the national government, then the national government has every right to change the nature of the delegation regime. Indeed, we should expect the national government in such systems to delegate to subnational units precisely on those issues where they are most likely to trust these subnational units. Moreover, unlike in federal systems, in unitary systems the subnational governments have no legal standing that can be protected by constitutional courts.

There are also differences between federal and unitary systems in the direct role of national government actors in subnational affairs. In all systems, various forms of cooperation and deconcentration exist. But in unitary states, where delegation to subnational units occurs, there is typically some form of institutionalized representation of the national government at the subnational level. Most typically this representation occurs through some form of prefect system, where national government officials take up residence in cities and towns to monitor and influence the policy implementation process. Such institutionalized representation of the central government in subnational politics is much rarer in federal systems. Thus, the risk that subnational policy implementers will behave opportunistically should be greater in federal than in unitary systems. Our expectation, then, is that all else equal, conflict between authors and implementers of legislation is likely to be higher in federal than in unitary systems. This argument, we should note, is not about parliamentary politics, but rather should apply across presidential systems as well. But for obvious reasons, the argument cannot be tested on our data from the U.S. states.

Legal Structure

Finally, the nature of the legal system should affect the incentives to micromanage policymaking in legislative statutes. We argue that in the absence of statutory detail, judges are less predictable allies of the legislative majority in common law than in civil law systems. Consequently, majorities in common law systems are more inclined to use policy details in legislation in efforts to tie the hands of judges.

In common law systems, law includes both statutes and judicial decisions, and there is a long history of competition and antagonism between judges and politicians. In England, for example, common law existed prior to statutory law, and English judges viewed statutes as intrusions on the common law. In 1909, Ilbert argued, "My Lady Common Law regards with jealousy the rival [statute] who arrests and distorts her development, who plants ugly and inartistic patches on her vesture, who trespasses gradually and irresistibly on her domain" (quoted in Bridge 1981, 353). Pollock, in 1882, was less poetic but more blunt: "Parliament generally changes the law for the worse, and . . . the business of the judge is to keep the mischief of its interference within the narrowest bounds" (quoted in Sauveplanne 1981, 23). Bridge (1981, 354) argues that this "judicial tendency to regard statutes as exceptions to the common law, and as such to interpret them restrictively, has also influenced their drafting. Highly detailed and specific language is employed in an attempt to ensure that the courts apply statutes in the way intended by Parliament."

In civil law systems, by contrast, the formal source of law does not include judicial decisions, but rather is based on a strict hierarchy of statutes, regulations, and customs (in that order) (Watson 1981, 168; Merryman 1985). The absence of judicial decisions from this list is not the accident of an idiosyncratic, evolutionary process of legal development, but rather was based on the eighteenth-century revolutionary ideology on the Continent that there should be a strict separation of powers between judicial and law-making processes (Merryman 1985). According to this ideology, legislation is the only legitimate and authoritative source of law, and the role of judges is simply to apply the law as specified in statutes and legal codes. Thus, differences in the source of law itself create a greater need to specify policy details in common law as opposed to civil law systems.

Legislative majorities must also worry more about the scope and effect of any specific decision in common law systems. In common law systems, the doctrine of *stare decisis* is central. This doctrine states that if a judge deems that a statute is silent on an issue before the court, then judges must search previous judicial decisions in an effort to make a decision. Thus, the court's decisions must be applied in the future whenever similar issues are before the courts. In civil law systems, decisions on particular cases have a much less enduring influence on policy. This is true because if a statute or code is silent on a particular issue, precedent plays a much smaller role than in common law systems. Courts are not bound to follow precedent (Dainow 1967, 430), and decisions from past cases often cannot even be cited as sources of law or superior authority (David and Brierly 1978, 123–124; Zweigert and Kötz 1998, 123). Thus, incentives to limit the possibility of adverse decisions are greater in common law systems.

Differences in judges themselves, and in how they are selected, also make courts a greater threat in common law than in civil law systems. In common law systems, judges are usually lawyers who are appointed or elected, typically after distinguished and influential careers. Appointment to the highest judicial levels is viewed as a crowning achievement, and the individuals at the top of the hierarchy are often household names. In civil law systems, judges are more akin to average bureaucrats. They have received standard training, have done well on a standardized exam, and have begun their careers receiving low pay in a lower court. The individuals at the top have worked their way up through the system in much the same way that any civil servant works his or her way up. They thus have a much lower status than judges in common law systems. Merryman (1985) argues that this difference in the way judges are selected and promoted, and in the way they make decisions, leads to much less activist judiciaries in civil law systems (see also Cappelletti 1981; Watson 1981, 176–177).

There exist, then, a variety of reasons that legislative majorities will typically face greater risks from not including details in statutes in common law as opposed to civil law countries. These include the origin of law itself, the role of precedent, and the selection of judges. We should therefore expect that all else equal, statutes will be more detailed in common law systems than in civil law ones.[12]

[12] There are, of course, interesting and noteworthy differences in how courts operate within the groups of common and civil law systems. These differences, however, are beyond the scope of this book.

Testing the Theory

Table 7.2 summarizes the hypotheses that emerged in the previous discussion. We now define the variables and estimation procedures used to conduct the empirical analysis. To measure coalition status, we used data on government composition provided to us by Paul Warwick that he collected for Warwick (1994). We supplemented this by consulting *Keesing's Contemporary Archive* and the *European Journal of Political Research*'s annual *Political Data Yearbook* to identify the coalition and majority status of the government in each of our democracies for the 1986–1998 period of our study. We then created two dummy variables: *Coalition Government* takes the value 1 if the government is a majority coalition, and *Minority Government* takes the value 1 if the parties in the government do not have a majority in parliament. The coefficients on these two dummy variables will reflect the differences in page length with single-party majority government, the suppressed category.

We use two measures of cabinet instability. The first is bill-specific: if cabinets have had little time to draft legislation, then they should be less able to write detailed statutes, and the opportunity costs of legislating details on a particular bill will be larger (in terms of forgone opportunities to consider other issues). *Elapsed Time* therefore measures how many days pass between the time a government forms and the time a bill is adopted. We expect this variable to have a positive coefficient.

The second variable measures politicians' expectations about cabinet stability. If a cabinet is not expected to last long, then politicians may have smaller incentives to work out detailed legislation, as they might expect their effort to go for naught. Scholars, however, point out that cabinets may fall frequently, with the same individuals resuming their posts once a new cabinet is formed (Williams 1964; Dogan 1989; Petry 1994). This would not create the same problems as frequent turnover in governments in which individuals control portfolios. We therefore use *Cabinet Turnover* as our measure of instability and base this measure on Huber's (1998) definition of individual portfolio volatility. For each year, we use *Keesing's Contemporary Archive* and the *European Journal of Political Research*'s annual data yearbook to identify each time (a) a portfolio is eliminated, (b) a portfolio is added, and (c) the individual controlling a portfolio changes. Each of these events creates a new relationship between ministers and civil servants, increasing the possibility of obstruction by civil servants. *Cabinet Turnover* is the average of these yearly scores for the period 1984–1998.

Table 7.2. *Summary of Parliamentary Variables and Measures*

Conceptual Variable	Measure
Policy Conflict	
Policy conflict between the legislative majority and individual cabinet ministers is:	
Likely to be greater during coalition majority government than during single-party majority government.	Dummy variables for coalition majority and minority governments
Likely to be greater during minority government than during any type of majority government.	
Legislative Capacity	
Policy details of legislation are typically worked out in the cabinet, and increases in cabinet instability diminish the capacity of cabinet ministers to draft detailed statutes.	*System level*: Mean level of turnover in individual control of portfolios
	Bill-specific: Elapsed time between government formation and bill adoption
During minority government, however, parliaments that give greater opportunities for opposition influence may include more legislative details that constrain ministers.	(a) Laver and Hunt (1992) Opposition Influence score (b) Salary premium
Nonstatutory Factors	
The legislative majority is less likely to need detailed legislation to achieve its policy objectives in nonfederal systems.	Dummy variable for federal system
The legislative majority is less likely to need detailed legislation to achieve its policy objectives in corporatist systems.	Dummy variable for corporatism
The legislative majority is less likely to need detailed legislation to achieve its policy objectives in civil law (as opposed to common law) systems.	Dummy variable for common law countries

This system-level variable, which is shown in Table 7.3, is intended to capture politicians' general expectations about how long a given government will last, and thus their expectations about how likely it is that a given minister's relationship with civil servants will be severed. The variable ranges from 5 portfolio changes per year in Luxembourg to more than 30 in Italy.

It is useful to note that cabinet turnover does not affect capacity only. It can also be considered an indicator of political uncertainty about future control of government. Viewed this way, as turnover increases, politicians' expectations that they will control policy in the future should decline. Thus, if we believe that political uncertainty encourages politicians to write detailed statutes that lock in policy in the future, this variable should have a positive rather than a negative coefficient.

We have also argued that during minority government, legislative arrangements *may* influence the ability of opposition support parties to obtain the legislative details that they desire (though we also pointed out that legislative institutions may in fact be irrelevant if party leaders negotiate policy details with the government off the floor of parliament). To measure the extent to which legislative arrangements permit members of parliament to influence policy, we utilize a survey conducted by Laver and Hunt (1992). They asked experts in each of the political systems in our data to rate the opportunities that members of the opposition have to influence policy from parliament. We prefer this variable, which we call *Opposition Influence*, to various other indices of parliamentary power mostly for practical reasons: this measure exists for all of our countries, whereas the other measures do not. Also, for reasons noted in the previous chapter, we avoid indices whenever possible. We should note, however, that *Opposition Influence* is highly correlated with these other indices (see the discussion in Powell 2000).

Legislative compensation has not received the same attention in the parliamentary context as it has in studies of U.S. state legislatures. Given the strong role of political parties and the fact that most elected deputies are motivated by the prospect of gaining leadership positions in the cabinet, we feel that ignoring this variable in the parliamentary context makes sense. Nonetheless, for purposes of comparison with the previous chapter, we create a compensation variable called *Salary Premium*. The salary premium is a ratio: the numerator is the deputies' salary, and the denominator is the average salary in the country. As can be seen in Table

Table 7.3. *Political Variables Affecting the Design of Statutes*

Country	Cabinet Turnover	Opposition Influence	Salary Premium	Elapsed Time	Federalism	Corporatism	Common Law
Australia	17.6	4.29	3.0	564	1	0	1
Austria	13.8	4.14	4.5	1,032	1	1	0
Belgium	13.1	2.60	2.5	755	1	1	0
Canada	29.7	3.46	2.1	1,082	1	0	1
Denmark	10.3	6.50	2.0	463	0	1	0
Finland	8.4	4.86	1.8	644	0	1	0
France	24.9	3.40	3.0	790	0	0	0
Germany	10.6	3.47	2.9	822	1	1	0
Iceland	5.8	4.80	2.6	655	0	1	0
Ireland	16.6	4.06	2.6	610	0	0	1
Italy	30.4	7.13	4.5	489	0	0	0
Luxembourg	5.0	4.00	1.8	1,002	0	1	0
Netherlands	6.8	3.60	2.8	793	0	1	0
New Zealand	29.7	3.29	4.7	600	0	0	1
Norway	14.0	6.76	2.2	593	0	1	0
Portugal	10.5	4.29	5.4	707	0	0	0
Spain	9.7	2.00	2.2	644	0	0	0
Sweden	17.6	5.16	2.0	615	0	1	0
United Kingdom	13.9	2.03	3.6	966	0	0	1

7.3, this premium ranges from a low of 1.8 in Finland to a high of 5.4 in Portugal.[13]

The remaining three dummy variables are used to test the impact of nonstatutory factors on the level of details in statutes. We create a *Federalism* dummy variable that takes the value 1 in countries where the constitutional arrangements require that subnational governments play a substantial role in policy implementation (Lijphart 1999). We create a *Corporatism* dummy variable to test the hypothesis regarding corporatism. To create this dummy, we draw on Siaroff (1999), who creates a 5-point variable based on averages of 13 different corporatism measures compiled by others (see his Tables 1 and 2). Our corporatism dummy variable takes the value 1 if a country's score in Siaroff (1999)'s 5-point index of corporatism is above the mean country score of 2.69. Finally, we test the hypothesis about common versus civil law by creating a dummy variable, *Common Law*, that takes the value 1 in Australia, Britain, Canada, Ireland, and New Zealand. These data are summarized in Table 7.3. It is useful to bear in mind that the institutional variables are often highly correlated. In particular, the correlation between *Common Law* and *Corporatism* is –.63.

In estimating the effects of these variables on discretion, it is important to control for idiosyncratic policy-specific and country-specific factors that affect the length of parliamentary statutes. It may well be, for example, that certain categories of legislation present more technical difficulties, making it more (or less) difficult to write detailed statutes. And it may be, as legal scholars have argued, that cultural factors lead to longer statutes in some countries than in others (see, e.g., Zweigert and Kötz 1998, 268).

To control for policy-specific effects, we simply include a dummy variable for the major policy categories in the Natlex classification (the 13 categories in Figure 7.3). To address concerns about country-specific effects, one approach is to simply include country fixed effects. The problem with this approach, however, is that inclusion of all the country dummy variables, along with so many institutional variables that are fixed across countries, makes it impossible to estimate the actual effects of the institutional

[13] We obtained data on deputies' salaries from country reports that are posted on the Inter-Parliamentary Union's Internet site (www.ipu.org). For countries that do not report salary information there, we relied on the national parliaments directly (and on individuals with contacts at these parliaments). Data on average national salaries were taken from the Organization for Economic Cooperation and Development (OECD) (1996; "Labour Force, Wage and Salaried Employment, Average Earnings, Current Prices, National Currency Units," which is taken from the OECD's Quarterly Labour Force Statistics, Paris).

variables.[14] To address this problem, rather than estimating a model with fixed effects, we estimate random effects regressions.[15] The random effects approach is attractive because it allows us to control for country fixed effects while also estimating the impact of variables that are country-specific, varying only across countries. The specific approach involves estimating the following equation:

$$(y_{it} - \theta \bar{y}_i) = (1-\theta)\alpha + (\mathbf{x}_{it} - \theta \bar{\mathbf{x}}_i)\beta + [(1-\theta)\nu_i + (\varepsilon_{it} - \theta \bar{\varepsilon}_i)]$$

where i indexes countries; ν_i is a country-specific error; ε_{it} is an ordinary error; and θ is a function of σ_ν^2 and σ_ε^2 (and moves toward 0 (1) as σ_ν^2 (σ_ε^2) moves to 0).

The main idea, then, is to create a dependent variable that accounts for the deviation in the number of pages from a country-specific mean number of pages. The country-specific mean, however, is weighted by the covariance matrixes, σ_ν^2 and σ_ε^2. The strong assumption we must make to justify this approach is that ν_i and $\bar{\mathbf{x}}_i$ are uncorrelated. This means, for example, that controlling for the other independent variables in the model, we must assume that the influence of a variable like *Elapsed Time* on discretion is the same across countries. Although it is always conceivable in cross-sectional research that particular variables, such as government status, work differently in different countries, we have no specific hypotheses about what country-specific biases might exist for any of our explanatory variables, and thus we accept this "no correlation" assumption. It is also important to bear in mind that the only variables that we examine that vary within countries are the (unreported) policy dummies, the government status variables (which do not vary within all countries), and elapsed time. Thus, the major variation we can explain is across the 19 countries rather than within them.

Empirical Results

Tables 7.4 through 7.6 present our empirical results. In Table 7.4, we explore whether policy and legislative capacity have direct effects on policy details or whether they work in interaction with each other. Table 7.5 presents tests of several alternative hypotheses about the length of statutes.

[14] Because the coefficient matrix is not full rank, this would lead to the arbitrary dropping of one or more variables during estimation.

[15] We used Stata 6.0's xtgls procedure with the "mle" option.

Table 7.4. *The Effect of Political Context on Laws in Parliamentary Systems*

	Dependent Variable: Standardized Page Length					
Independent Variables	(1)	(2)	(3)	(4)	(5)	(6)
Cabinet Turnover	−1.68	−1.43	−1.79	−1.71	−1.65	—
	(0.671)	(0.754)	(0.645)	(0.688)	(0.675)	
Elapsed Time	0.003	0.003	0.003	0.003	0.003	0.003
	(0.002)	(0.002)	(0.002)	(0.002)	(0.002)	(0.002)
Minority Government	26.52	26.77	26.85	24.52	23.14	27.86
	(5.56)	(5.57)	(5.54)	(12.74)	(14.68)	(10.79)
Coalition Government	13.91	13.64	13.44	14.27	13.49	12.17
	(6.04)	(6.04)	(6.00)	(6.37)	(6.26)	(6.83)
Corporatism	−37.60	−33.69	−30.05	−38.43	−36.65	−21.83
	(12.51)	(13.60)	(13.03)	(13.38)	(13.00)	(12.51)
Common Law	34.16	32.63	38.43	34.13	34.29	30.98
	(12.51)	(12.60)	(12.31)	(12.51)	(12.43)	(14.49)
Federalism	17.74	15.15	16.18	18.08	17.22	12.89
	(9.89)	(10.48)	(9.50)	(10.08)	(10.05)	(11.23)
Opposition Influence	—	−2.50	—	—	—	—
		(3.58)				
Salary Premium	—	—	6.01	—	—	—
			(4.18)			
Minority Government × Opposition Influence	—	—	—	0.520	—	—
				(2.97)		
Minority Government × Salary Premium	—	—	—	—	0.878	—
					(3.53)	
Minority Government × Cabinet Turnover	—	—	—	—	—	−0.141
						(0.635)
Policy-specific dummy variables	Yes	Yes	Yes	Yes	Yes	Yes
Constant	75.48	81.25	54.90	75.86	75.18	44.89
	(16.01)	(17.93)	(20.90)	(16.16)	(15.95)	(11.66)
N	4,102	4,102	4,102	4,102	4,102	4,102
Log likelihood	−22,799	−22,799	−22,798	−22,799	−22,799	−22,802
σ_v	16.52	16.37	15.68	16.53	16.39	19.45
	(3.16)	(3.12)	(3.00)	(3.17)	(3.18)	(3.59)
σ_e	62.37	62.37	62.37	62.37	62.37	62.37
	(0.690)	(0.690)	(0.690)	(0.690)	(0.691)	(0.690)

Note: Estimates are from random effects regression using maximum likelihood estimation. Standard errors are given in parentheses.

And Table 7.6 presents several additional robustness tests. All of the results are from models that also include dummy variables for the policy categories listed in Figure 7.1. Since we are interested in controlling for policy effects rather than understanding or explaining them, we do not report or discuss the results for the policy dummies.[16]

Column 1 of Table 7.4 presents what we view as the model most directly implied by our theory. Consistent with the preceding discussions, this model assumes that institutional arrangements in the parliament itself do not affect capacity, and that cabinet instability and policy conflict have direct rather than interactive effects on the design of statutes. The results are highly consistent with our expectations. All of these variables, with the exception of *Elapsed Time*, are estimated rather precisely, and all have the expected sign. For the policy conflict hypotheses, we find that both *Minority Government* and *Coalition Government* increase the amount of policy detail, with the coefficient of *Minority Government* quite large and roughly double the size of the coefficient for *Coalition Government*. The results also indicate that as *Cabinet Turnover* increases, the level of policy detail in statutes decreases, and the result is substantively large. A country like France, which has a large average level of individual turnover, would write statutes that are roughly 25 standardized pages shorter than a country like Germany, which has a relative by low average level of individual turnover. This indicates that the legislative capacity aspect of cabinet turnover is more important than any incentives to lock in policy details that are created by political uncertainty. Finally, we see strong support for the arguments about nonstatutory factors. Corporatism reduces the length of statutes by over 37 pages, common law legal structures increase the length by around 34 pages, and federalism increases the length by almost 18 pages.

We have argued against interacting our cabinet capacity variables with policy conflict, and against including variables that measure the capacity of parliament itself, although we pointed out that one could argue that such capacity variables will be relevant during minority government. The remaining regressions in Table 7.4 test these claims. In columns 2 and 3,

[16] As we have mentioned on several occasions, this is not to argue that we do not believe issue-specific effects are important. Indeed, the regressions confirm that they exist. In our statistical models, we exclude the "General" policy category. In our baseline model (Table 7.3, column 1), all but one policy category has a coefficient that is statistically significant, and the coefficients range from –6 to –43 standardized pages.

we include the two legislative capacity variables directly. Neither *Opposition Influence* nor *Salary Premium* is significant, and *Opposition Influence* has the wrong sign. In columns 4 and 5, we include the interaction effects with minority government. We should point out a practical problem associated with interpreting these results. The minority government observations are rather concentrated, with only 9 countries out of 19 ever having a minority government, and 78% of the minority government observations are in 3 Scandinavian countries. This gives us a rather small amount of data with which to compare the effect of any variable interacted with *Minority Government*. We nonetheless can run the models and consider the results. Again, they do not support including the parliamentary capacity variables. Finally, in column 6, we interact *Minority Government* with *Cabinet Turnover* and find the interacted variable to be insignificant.[17] We therefore feel that both the arguments and the evidence point toward including only the cabinet instability variables for legislative capacity, and doing so by focusing on direct effects.

The results in Table 7.4 are relatively robust: across columns 2–6, the results for the core variables in our theory remain strong, although the standard error for *Federalism* often increases. We further explore the robustness of our results in Tables 7.5 and 7.6. In Table 7.5, we test several alternative arguments about the factors affecting our dependent variable. One concern readers might have, here as in Chapter 6, is that our dependent variable is not really measuring discretion, but rather "more policy." We have tried to address this issue as best we can through our discussion of the examples of gender discrimination legislation and through the analysis in Chapter 3. An alternative way to make the point is to think about the types of factors that might lead to the demand for more policy and to include independent variables that measure this demand.

In some respects, we have already done this. If we think of labor organizations as being strongest in corporatist countries, then the demand for labor policy should be greatest in such countries. Thus, if our dependent variable measures the amount of policy, we should find *Corporatism* to be positive. Instead, we find that the coefficient for *Corporatism* is consistently large and negative. It should not be controversial to interpret this result not as representing less labor policy in corporatist countries, but rather as indicating that nonlegislative arenas are central for such policymaking.

[17] We also interacted *Minority Government* with *Elapsed Time*, with identical null results.

Similarly, Tsebelis (1999, 2002) presents evidence that coalition and minority governments find it more difficult than single-party majorities to adopt new policies. Thus, if our dependent variable is a measure of more policy rather than less discretion, we should find that *Coalition Government* and *Minority Government* should be negative. Instead, we find that they are positive. Thus, the regressions in Table 7.4 provide some assurance that our results are related to discretion levels rather than to the demand for policy.

In columns 1–3 of Table 7.5, we present two additional tests of the "more policy" argument. Column 1 includes a variable measuring the ideological location of the government (measured on a 10-point left–right scale).[18] It seems reasonable to think that governments on the left might be more inclined to pursue labor legislation than governments on the right, and if our dependent variable measures the demand for labor policy, then we should pick up this effect of government ideology. If our dependent variable measures discretion, by contrast, then we have no reason to believe that left or right governments will be more inclined to include policy details in statutes. The results in column 1 show that the left–right location of the government in fact has no effect. The variable actually has the wrong sign and is estimated with considerable error.

It may also be the case that it is not the ideological location of the government that determines the demand for legislation, but rather changes in this location. If new governments are most likely to change labor policy, and if our dependent variable measures the amount of policy adopted rather than the level of discretion in the policies that are adopted, then changes in government ideology should affect page length. To test this, we include a *Government Change* variable. This variable is the absolute value of change in the left–right location of the government during the year preceding the adoption of the statute. Consistent with our argument about page length, this variable is not significant, and its inclusion does not affect our other results.

A third variable we consider is changes in unionization rates. The period that we study is characterized by considerable changes in some countries in the percentage of workers who belong to unions, and one might expect that the demand for labor legislation will increase in

[18] This variable is created using data on party positions from expert surveys in Huber and Inglehart (1995). We weight each party in government according to the percentage of seats that they hold in parliament.

Table 7.5. *Controlling for Alternative Factors Affecting Laws in Parliamentary Systems*

	Dependent Variable: Standardized Page Length				
Independent Variable	(1)	(2)	(3)	(4)	(5)
Cabinet Turnover	–1.93	–1.68	–1.75	–1.63	–1.42
	(0.634)	(0.670)	(0.672)	(0.667)	(0.638)
Elapsed Time	0.004	0.003	0.003	0.003	0.003
	(0.002)	(0.002)	(0.002)	(0.002)	(0.002)
Minority Government	27.97	26.64	26.55	26.37	26.40
	(5.630)	(5.57)	(5.56)	(5.57)	(5.54)
Coalition Government	25.33	14.13	13.57	13.47	11.69
	(6.422)	(6.06)	(6.05)	(6.07)	(6.13)
Corporatism	–40.24	–37.61	–37.31	–34.84	–20.43
	(11.84)	(12.49)	(12.41)	(13.13)	(15.21)
Common Law	41.97	34.16	32.42	33.37	37.31
	(11.98)	(12.49)	(12.67)	(12.43)	(11.75)
Federalism	15.76	17.66	17.74	16.53	7.34
	(9.38)	(9.88)	(9.81)	(9.96)	(10.91)
Government Left–Right Position	–1.05	—	—	—	—
	(1.05)				
Change in Government Left–Right Position	—	–0.548	—	—	—
		(1.38)			
Change in Unionization	—	—	–0.113	—	—
			(0.168)		
Total Number of Laws Adopted	—	—	—	–0.020	—
				(0.032)	
Scandinavia	—	—	—	—	–21.91
					(12.63)
Policy-specific dummy variables	Yes	Yes	Yes	Yes	Yes
Constant	78.09	75.69	75.87	78.38	71.24
	(16.00)	(15.99)	(15.89)	(16.51)	(15.10)
N	4,102	4,102	4,102	4,102	4,102
Log likelihood	–22,535	–22,799	–22,799	–22,799	–22,798
σ_v	15.50	16.49	16.36	16.31	15.16
	(3.05)	(3.16)	(3.12)	(3.14)	(2.97)
σ_e	61.49	62.37	62.37	62.37	62.37
	(0.684)	(0.690)	(0.690)	(0.690)	(0.690)

Note: Estimates are from random effects regression using maximum likelihood estimation. Standard errors are given in parentheses.

countries where the labor force is going through the greatest changes. *Change in Unionization* is therefore a variable that measures changes in trade union density.[19] The results are presented in column 3. Again, we find no effect of this variable on standardized page length.

In column 4, we explore the bundling issue discussed earlier in this chapter. As we noted in the discussion of Table 7.1, there are reasons to be concerned that some countries may have a tradition of writing a large number of short legislative statutes rather than bundling the same number of policy details into a single larger statute. Our estimation technique alleviates this concern to a certain extent because the measure of our dependent variable is not the standardized number of pages in a statute, but rather the difference between this number and a weighted, country-specific mean. However, we can also simply include a variable for the total number of statutes in a country. If the number of statutes in Table 7.1 is a function of bundling, rather than of simple differences in the number of statutes adopted or reported, then the variable for the total number of statutes should be negative and significant. Instead, we find that this variable is estimated with substantial error and that its inclusion does not affect our other results.

Finally, we explore the possibility that Scandinavian countries have a different approach to legislating than other countries. In Table 7.1, it is hard not to be struck by how short the statutes in Scandinavia are on average, and to wonder whether in fact there is some sort of cultural or other factor at work in these countries that affects the drafting of statutes. Getting at this issue is difficult, however, because Scandinavian countries are all highly corporatist, and thus a Scandinavian dummy variable is highly correlated with *Corporatism*. This correlation, of course, will inflate the standard errors. Column 5 nonetheless presents the results when a dummy variable for Scandinavia is included. The variable is negative and significant at $p = .08$, and not surprisingly, the estimate for *Corporatism* decreases somewhat in magnitude and increases in its standard error. The results for the remaining variables, however, are unaffected. Given the correlation of Scandinavian countries with corporatism, we would not be inclined to dismiss the general effects of corporatism based on column 5,

[19] The variable is the percentage of wage and salary earners who were union members in 1995 minus this percentage in 1985. It is taken from the ILO's Task Force on Industrial Relations (GT/RP) report "World Labour Report 1997–98." The data are at http://www.ilo.org/public/english/dialgue/govlab/publ/wlr/97/annex/tab13.htm.

Table 7.6. *The Effect of Political Context on Laws in Parliamentary Systems: Additional Robustness Tests*

	Dependent Variable				
	$\sqrt{SPL}$[a]	$\sqrt{SPL}$[b]	SPL[b]	$\sqrt{SPL}$[c]	SPL[c]
Independent Variable	(1)	(2)	(3)	(4)	(5)
Cabinet Turnover	–0.091	–0.103	–1.89	–0.085	–1.40
	(0.039)	(0.037)	(0.719)	(0.039)	(0.642)
Elapsed Time	0.000	0.000	0.003	0.000	0.001
	(0.000)	(0.000)	(0.003)	(0.000)	(0.002)
Minority Government	0.938	1.17	31.38	0.708	16.06
	(0.254)	(0.294)	(6.86)	(0.243)	(4.31)
Coalition Government	0.399	0.530	16.76	0.254	7.18
	(0.286)	(0.316)	(7.11)	(0.274)	(4.78)
Corporatism	–2.64	–2.81	–42.36	–2.48	–30.18
	(0.718)	(0.692)	(13.49)	(0.721)	(11.94)
Common Law	1.52	1.26	32.78	1.40	29.88
	(0.716)	(0.687)	(13.39)	(0.720)	(11.92)
Federalism	1.346	1.373	19.59	1.24	13.31
	(0.568)	(0.546)	(10.62)	(0.57)	(9.45)
Policy-specific dummy variables	Yes	Yes	Yes	Yes	Yes
Constant	7.11	7.93	84.90	7.06	73.44
	(0.908)	(0.881)	(17.36)	(0.911)	(15.12)
N	4,102	3,167	3,167	4,098	4,098
Log likelihood	–10,138	–8,016	–17,977	–9,921	–21,707
σ_v	0.970	0.917	17.43	0.980	16.13
	(0.171)	(0.168)	(3.48)	(0.171)	(2.89)
σ_e	2.85	3.02	70.14	2.70	47.99
	(.032)	(.038)	(.885)	(.030)	(.531)

Note: Estimates are from random effects regression using maximum likelihood estimation. Standard errors are given in parentheses.

[a] $\sqrt{SPL}$ is the square root of standardized page length.

[b] Omits one-page laws.

[c] Omits laws of over 400 pages.

but we do feel that the role of statutes in policymaking in Scandinavia is clearly worth additional study.

Table 7.6 presents some further specifications to assess the robustness of our results. To this end, we assess our baseline model from column 1 of Table 7.4 and explore some issues related to functional form and the nature of our sample. Recall that in Table 7.1, we found considerable differences in the mean standardized page length across countries, as well as in the variance of these means. This raises the concern of heteroskedasticity. In column 1 of Table 7.6, we reestimate our model where the dependent variable is the square root of the standardized page length, which diminishes the cross-national variance in our dependent variable. All of the variables are in the expected direction, and all but *Coalition* are estimated very precisely, some much more so than in Table 7.4. *Coalition Government* has a *p*-value of .16 and a 95% confidence interval of −.16 to −.95.

Columns 2–5 present further tests of the robustness of our results. In our data, 22.4% of our statutes have an unstandardized page length of one. We are not significantly concerned that these data values are due to errors by the ILO because we obtained a random sample of approximate 40 of these statutes and found that they were indeed one page long. Still, it is worth checking whether the inclusion of such short bills in our data set affects our results, in particular because there is considerable variation in the percentage of one-page statutes across countries. Columns 2 and 3 therefore reestimate the models without the one-page laws, using the square root in column 2 and the untransformed dependent variable in column 3. The support for our theoretical argument, including coalition government, is strong when the one-pagers are excluded, regardless of whether we use the standardized page length or the square root of this length.

Finally, we also need to consider whether our results are driven by the undue influence of some of the very long statutes that are included in our data. In particular, there are four statutes that are over 400 unstandardized pages long, one of which is 504 pages and one of which is 994 pages. In columns 4 and 5, we estimate the model without these outlying observations. The results again support our theory, although in column 5 the standard error on *Coalition Government* has increased substantially.

Conclusion

As in our study of policymaking in the U.S. states, our cross-national analysis of parliamentary democracies provides substantial support for our general argument that the strategies politicians use to delegate to bureaucrats are shaped in clear and systematic ways by broad features of the political and institutional environments. Specifically, we find that the language of legislation is an important tool that parties within governing coalitions use *to control each other*. In other words, coalition governments, and especially minority governments, write more policy details than single-party majority governments. We also find that legislative capacity has an important effect, but unlike in the U.S. states, it is not the capacity of parliament itself that matters. Instead, high average levels of cabinet turnover make it more difficult for some countries to write policy details into statutes. Furthermore, as we would expect for a group of high-capacity political systems, capacity has a direct effect on discretion rather than the interactive one with policy conflict that we found in the U.S. states, many of which did not have a sufficient level of capacity for policy conflict to matter. Nonstatutory factors also play an important role. In particular, federalism and common law legal structures encourage parties to write more detailed legislation, while corporatism encourages less detailed legislation.

These results regarding the impact of political context on the role of legislation in policymaking processes stand in sharp contrast to the traditional view about the language of statutes in parliamentary systems. As noted in Chapter 2, to the limited extent that legislation has received attention, parliamentary statutes are typically viewed as being consistently vague, providing only general outlines to guide policymaking processes. In contrast, we find not only considerable variation in the level of details in statutes, but also that this variation can be explained in large part by the political and institutional incentives that exist to use legislative statutes to influence policy outcomes. We discuss the significance of these findings in more detail in the next chapter.

8

Laws, Institutions, and Policymaking Processes

Legislators in modern democracies perform a wide variety of tasks, ranging from constituency service to the confirmation of political appointees. While these are significant activities in democracies, the most important function that legislators perform is making public policy. Citizens in representative democracies elect legislators to make laws, after all, and democratic theory holds that citizens will reelect those politicians who support policies they like and turn out of office those politicians who support policies they do not like.

In Chapter 1, we set out some examples of how politicians have taken different approaches to policymaking in different areas and in different political contexts. In the area of health care in the U.S. states, for example, we saw that Idaho and Texas took very diverse approaches to setting up a managed care system for Medicaid, with Idaho writing a very short, general, and vague law that authorized an agency to implement managed care and Texas writing a longer, more specific law that set out in greater detail what such a system should look like. Similarly, we saw differences between Germany and Ireland in the area of sexual harassment. While both countries passed laws designed to combat instances of sexual harassment, Ireland passed a precise, explicit law, while Germany wrote one that was much more ambiguous and open to interpretation.

As the rest of the book has demonstrated, such differences are not unusual but rather are systematic and even predictable. Some legislative majorities at some times choose to write detailed and specific laws that limit the ability of other political actors, particularly bureaucrats, to make policy. Other legislative majorities, however, grant broad policymaking discretion to these other actors. The goal of this book has been to describe carefully the nature and extent of these differences in legislative statutes, to provide a theoretical explanation for why such differences occur, and to test our argument using data from different political contexts. In this concluding chapter, we review the distinguishing features of our study, summarize our findings, discuss their normative implications, and suggest avenues for future research.

The Distinguishing Features of Our Study

As we have noted, many other scholars have studied and written about the nature of legislative delegation to bureaucrats. Through their analyses, we have gained significant knowledge and understanding about the ways in which features of politics and policies influence the decision to delegate. In what ways has this book advanced beyond what these previous studies already have accomplished?

A Comparative Theory of Delegation

Most importantly, in contrast to previous research, our study is explicitly comparative. Of course, the term *comparative* means different things to different people. For some, it simply means to study "someplace else." Our analysis is certainly comparative in this expansive (and not especially useful) sense of the word. For others, *comparative politics* involves exploring whether a theory that is developed to understand behavior in one particular political system can also help us to understand behavior in another system. Such studies are very valuable because they establish the robustness of particular theories – the ability of theories to explain behavior across different political systems. Again, our theory is comparative in this sense because we draw on insights that have been developed in studies of the U.S. Congress.

Developing theories within a fixed institutional context, however, places limits on the nature of the theories because it precludes us from considering how the institutional context itself affects behavior. If we look only at the post–World War II U.S. Congress, for example, we cannot understand how the high level of capacity in that assembly affects delegation strategies because this level is invariant. Similarly, we cannot understand how the structure of the legal system affects delegation strategies because this, too, is fixed.

A third notion of *comparative*, then, is central to our approach. Rather than examining the "cross-national traveling capacity" of arguments that have been developed in studies of one country, we build a theory that has as its foundation *differences that exist primarily across political systems*. With such an approach, the institutional context plays a central role in explaining delegation strategies and is not a constant that merely lurks in the background, playing an unobservable role. In particular, we examine how institutional factors like legislative professionalism, judicial structure, party system fragmentation, legislative oversight, and corporatism affect the design of legislation. The comparative nature of the argument and evidence – in this specific sense of the word – is the most significant distinguishing feature of this book.

Distinguishing Features and Parliamentary Systems

This is not the only way, however, that our study differs from previous research. When compared with previous studies of parliamentary systems, one difference is our focus on the design of legislation as a strategic instrument in the policymaking process. Previously, scholars either ignored the role of legislative statutes in parliamentary policymaking processes or argued that these statutes are characterized by their vague, sweeping design. We find that both within and across countries, there is considerable variation in the level of policy detail that is placed in legislation, and we have endeavored to show that this variation is related in systematic ways to the political and institutional contexts.

A second difference from other parliamentary studies is our development of an explicit and testable theory. Previous research, we noted in Chapter 2, typically focused either on claims about the quality of control of bureaucrats or on describing (nonlegislative) instruments for control. Very little effort has been made to develop theories of delegation processes that could be tested cross-nationally. We have attempted to construct such a theory.

A final difference is that we have subjected our theory to systematic empirical tests. Given the lack of explicit theories of delegation in parliamentary contexts, it is not surprising that little quantitative empirical testing has existed in the parliamentary literature. We hope that our efforts to do so highlight the feasibility of large-*n*, quantitative research on delegation across parliamentary democracies.

Distinguishing Features and Presidential Systems

When compared with previous studies in the U.S. politics literature, we also find differences in the nature of our study, but they are of a different, subtler sort. Unlike the parliamentary literature, the recent U.S. politics literature has focused on legislative statutes, the development of explicit theories, and the carrying out of rigorous empirical tests. This body of research has added enormously to our understanding of delegation processes, and its imprint on what we have done in this volume is considerable. Nonetheless, our points of departure are worth highlighting.

First, many studies of the 1980s and 1990s focused heavily on the role of procedural provisions in legislation. Such a focus was understandable, as these insightful studies were identifying a feature of politics that previously had been seen almost exclusively in an apolitical, legalistic light. But at the same time, this focus led to a belief that procedural provisions were the main tools available to politicians who wanted to constrain agencies. By focusing on actual legislation, we have been able to determine the relative extent to which states and countries rely on specific policy instructions and not just broad, general procedural instructions. As Chapter 3 demonstrates, policy instructions – specific statements in legislation that tell bureaucracies not only how to implement policies, but exactly which policies should be implemented – are common in legislation both in the U.S. states and in parliamentary democracies. In fact, while we find important examples of procedural provisions, we also find that policy instructions are much more common than procedural instructions in U.S. state legislation. We also argue that the level of policy detail varies enormously across statutes but the level of procedural detail does not. We thus attempt to reorient the literature away from its predominant focus on procedures and toward a consideration of how politicians use policy details in statutes as an instrument for controlling policy implementation.

We hasten to add that this does not mean that procedural instructions are unimportant. Instead, it shows that legislatures have another tool – specific policy instructions – that they frequently use to constrain agency behavior. Furthermore, we have argued that procedural instructions actually gain more teeth when paired with specific policy instructions.[1]

[1] This is consistent with the evidence that Spence (1999a) presents in his analysis of the Federal Energy Regulatory Commission.

After all, a law that tells an agency to do X using procedure Y is far more constraining than a law that tells an agency to do "something" using procedure Y.

In all of the legislation we examined, we found a much smaller role for administrative procedures than we had expected given the emphasis placed on these instruments in the literature on the U.S. Congress. In addition, while we cannot directly compare the relative importance of procedural provisions in state-level statutes and parliamentary statutes, for reasons we discussed in detail in Chapter 3, our analysis does seem to indicate that administrative procedures are more prevalent in the former than in the latter. We argued that the general thrust of this finding is consistent with what one should expect. When there is a clear separation between legislative and executive power, legislation provides the most direct and consequential tool with which to speak to bureaucrats, and once legislation is adopted, the balance of policymaking power shifts decidedly to an executive that is partly insulated from legislative interference. When executive and legislative powers are fused, as in parliamentary systems, the legislative majority relinquishes much less control over bureaucratic decision making because of the central role that cabinet ministers play atop departments. Thus, the need for administrative procedures is smaller.

A second set of differences from the existing U.S. literature concerns some specific assumptions in our theory. We assume, for example, that bureaucrats are fully strategic and that they must therefore choose whether or not to comply with legislative statutes. This contrasts with some previous formal models that assume that bureaucrats *must* comply with statutes. We also study the effect of bicameral conflict on legislative design, whereas previous (formal) studies typically assume that a single legislative actor drafts the details of legislation. And we focus on noninformational costs of designing detailed statutes, which refocuses attention on legislative capacity.

Our most important departure from the U.S. literature, however, is the comparative nature of our theory and evidence. By pushing the theoretical debates in this direction, we have brought to light new, largely institutional explanatory factors that affect the role of legislation in policymaking processes. By so doing, we have refined our understanding of how factors that are central to the U.S. politics literature – like divided government – apply in contexts outside the U.S. Congress.

Our Theory and Empirical Findings

We will now summarize our argument and empirical findings. The four main variables in our theory are policy conflict, legislative capacity, the bargaining environment, and nonstatutory factors. We argue that legislative statutes will most clearly define the nature of public policy when (a) a pivotal member of the legislative majority has different policy goals than the political actor who has the most control over the policy implementation process (e.g., *policy conflict* is high), (b) the legislative majority is able to afford the costs of writing policy details into statutes (e.g., *legislative capacity* is high), (c) the majorities of the two chambers in a bicameral system share similar policy goals (*bicameral conflict* is absent), and (d) the political system does not allow the legislative majority to rely on nonstatutory factors to influence policy implementation (*nonstatutory factors* are unreliable).

Importantly, our analysis demonstrates that these explanatory factors play different roles in different political systems. A clear example is the effect of policy conflict between the authors and implementers of legislation. As we have noted, the literature on the U.S. Congress, a legislature with very high capacity, pays considerable attention to how divided government affects delegation strategies. Our comparative theory argues that divided government does not work the same way everywhere, but rather depends on other factors. State legislators, for example, may have incentives to include detailed legislation during divided government, but they must have the ability to do so. Thus, if we went to a state like New Mexico, which has low legislative capacity, and found that divided government does not work as predicted by the theories of Congress, we should not conclude that the logic of these theories is flawed, but rather that, as general theories of delegation, they are incomplete. For divided government to have the effects that are predicted in the Congress literature, the legislature must have sufficient capacity to pay the costs of writing detailed laws. Similarly, the impact of divided government on the design of legislation in two states with similar levels of legislative capacity will not always be the same. Instead it will be affected by the extent to which the legislative majority can expect to achieve its policy goals by nonstatutory means, such as direct legislative influence over agency decisions.

We also gain a new perspective on the role of bureaucratic expertise in delegation strategies. Our theory, for example, assumes that bureaucrats may have more expertise than politicians, and all of our arguments about delegation emerge under this assumption. It is also possible, however, that there is no uncertainty about policy, and that both the legislature and the bureaucracy know the relationship between policies and outcomes with certainty. Somewhat surprisingly, all of our central hypotheses remain unchanged under such a scenario, as long as there remain any costs associated with writing policy details. Thus, taking the costs of writing policy details into account allows us to deemphasize somewhat the role of asymmetries in expertise and to learn that policy conflict, bicameral conflict, legislative capacity, and nonstatutory factors all should affect delegation strategies across different types of policy and informational environments.

Our study, then, is intentionally not about delegation on a particular type of policy issue. We do not set out to develop and test a theory of health care policymaking or labor policymaking, for example. Instead, our goal is to examine how different political systems, when faced with the same basic policy issue, approach the task of defining policy details in legislation, and in particular to examine how the political context affects the choices that are made. We emphasize that we are not arguing that the nature of the issue has no effect on policymaking. Instead, by controlling for idiosyncrasies inherent in different policy environments, we show that it is possible to uncover systematic institutional effects of the type we have described.

Similarly, we obviously have not focused on understanding policymaking processes *within* specific countries or states. Such an approach would preclude us from understanding the comparative issues that are central to our analysis. This is not to say, however, that our analysis applies equally across all countries, and we have been careful to point out that inherent in our study is the assumption that bureaucrats have a high level of professionalism, and that in principle, politicians could draw on these professionalized bureaucrats to achieve their goals. We contend later that relaxing this assumption is an important avenue for future research.

Empirical Results

Many studies have examined the effect of policy conflict on delegation, and we follow these studies by including this variable in our study. Because our theoretical approach is comparative, however, we need to think about what policy conflict means in different political systems. In presidential systems, for example, we follow existing work in arguing that policy conflict is greatest during divided government, when the executive and legislative branches are controlled by different parties. While the concept of divided government serves as a useful proxy for policy conflict in separation of powers systems, it makes no sense in parliamentary systems, where legislative and executive powers are fused. Thus, we identified coalition majority governments and minority governments as the parliamentary analogs to divided government.

Similarly, legislative capacity plays a different role in presidential and parliamentary systems. In presidential systems, a great number of legislative decisions are made in the legislature itself, particularly when its majority opposes the executive. In parliamentary systems, by contrast, the fusion of executive and legislative powers implies that most important legislative decisions are made in the cabinet. Consequently, the capacity of legislators themselves to micromanage policymaking in statutes is important in presidential systems, whereas this capacity is largely irrelevant in parliamentary systems. Instead, in parliamentary systems, factors internal to the cabinet, such as ministerial turnover, affect the capacity to write laws that are specific and detailed.

To take a final example, we see considerable differences with respect to measuring nonstatutory factors, most of which are *not* inherent in whether executive and legislative powers are fused, but rather in the national versus state distinction that exists in our data. Thus, in the national parliamentary data, to take one example, federalism is an important variable, but one that is obviously irrelevant when we look at our state data. And legal structure varies considerably across our parliamentary countries but much less so across the U.S. states.

The bottom line, then, is that we need to take care in operationalizing our theoretical concepts in different political systems. There is no single measure of conflict that we can use across all political systems. Rather, we need to take into account the workings of each political system in order to find appropriate measures of conflict. Similarly, we cannot assume that each factor works the same way in each system. Instead, we need to consider what sorts of nonstatutory factors might exist in one system but not in another. And we need to acknowledge that other factors, such as capacity, will have differential effects across systems.

When we take such concerns into account and conduct the empirical tests of our theory, we find substantial support for the main arguments that we have advanced. First, policy conflict increases the amount of policy detail in laws. In the cross-national context, we found that coalition governments and minority governments were more likely to write policy details into statutes. Similarly, in the U.S. states, divided government produced more policy details in states with a sufficient level of capacity. Second, legislative capacity acts to increase the level of detail in laws in the U.S. states, where we found that, given the presence of policy conflict, higher-capacity legislatures write more detailed and constraining statutes. In parliamentary democracies, on the other hand, the capacity of parliament does not affect the design of legislation. As we noted in Chapter 7, this finding is consistent with the standard view of how party governments operate in parliamentary systems. At the same time, we find that another measure of capacity, cabinet turnover, does influence the design of legislation and decreases the amount of details in policy. Third, in the U.S. states, we find that when different parties control the two chambers in a legislature, legislation is less detailed than when the legislature is unified against the executive. And finally, we find strong support for the notion that nonstatutory factors influence the design of legislation. In parliamentary democracies, higher levels of corporatism, centralized (as opposed to federal) systems, and civil law legal systems all lead to legislative statutes that impose fewer policy constraints. Similarly, legislatures in U.S. states with legislative vetoes are likely to write less detailed statutes than those without such vetoes.

Thus, our variables have a strong and systematic impact on the design of legislation in quite different policy arenas and in both the U.S. states and the parliamentary systems. We feel that this evidence strongly rejects any claims to the effect that the design of statutes in a given country (or U.S. state) is determined primarily by cultural or other idiosyncratic features in that country (or state). While such factors certainly are at work, there also exists a coherent and systematic relationship between the political and institutional contexts in which politicians find themselves and the ways in which they use legislation to delegate authority to bureaucrats.

The Normative Implications of Our Study

The evidence we present about the level of discretion in statutes provides compelling support for our comparative theory of delegation, both across the U.S. states and across parliamentary systems. In light of these results, an important question arises. If in fact these institutional factors affect the design of laws in the ways that we argue they do, what are the normative implications? That is, what does our study teach us about the normative trade-offs associated with choosing particular institutions for democratic governance? We focus on four issues: transparency in policymaking processes, compliance by bureaucrats with the language of legislation, the distributive implications of legislative discretion, and the ability of politicians to make efficient policy changes.

Before undertaking this discussion, however, we offer two general observations. First, normative institutional inquiries often involve something akin to a search for the holy grail, with scholars often trying to determine what's "best." In the context of previous studies of delegation, for example, scholars might worry about which institutional arrangements are most conducive to effective control over bureaucrats, or about the optimal inclusion of policy expertise in policy formulation. In our view, this approach misses an important point: the consequences of particular institutional choices inevitably entail trade-offs. It may not be the case, for example, that institutions that encourage transparency also encourage compliance, or that institutions that lead to low bureaucratic autonomy allow politicians to respond efficiently to the need for policy change. Thus, discussions of the effects of institutions should bear in mind that there is no holy grail. It may well be possible to choose institutions that have positive effects in some respects, but they will typically have negative ones in others.

Second, scholars of delegation often seem driven to make absolute normative claims. This is most obvious in the ongoing debates about whether citizens in advanced democracies live in *administrative states* and whether political control of bureaucrats is inadequate. We will not push such absolute normative claims with respect to any of the issues we discuss. The simple reason is that we would have no confidence in any such claims. This does not imply that we throw our hands up at contributing to normative debates. Instead, our contribution follows the method of comparative statics. That is, we do not make claims about the level of transparency, or control, or responsiveness, but we can make claims about the factors that should influence these levels. This, we believe, provides important food for thought when scholars contemplate the normative implications associated with particular institutional choices.

Transparency in Policymaking Processes

We begin with the issue of transparency. A central justification of democracy is that it allows citizens to use ballots to sanction and reward policymakers. Voters can punish politicians who have performed poorly by not supporting them at election time. And they can reward politicians who have performed well. In order to make such judgments, voters benefit from understanding which politicians have pursued which policies. To this end, voters benefit from transparency in policymaking, which ensures that political actors reveal their policy positions and their policy choices in a forum that is visible to voters.

In our view, policymaking processes that occur in the public forum of legislatures are likely to be more open and transparent than policymaking processes that occur behind the oft-closed doors of executives and bureaucrats. In the modern democracies that we consider, legislative debates are open for all to see. If politicians consider detailed policy provisions in an open legislative assembly – as the Irish politicians did on their gender discrimination bill – voters will be in a position to learn far more about the policy positions of various political actors than if vague legislative statutes push the actual details of policy choice into the less open forum of the executive. We acknowledge, of course, that not all legislation is written in full view of the public and that not all bureaucratic actions take place in private. But as limited as citizens' knowledge of legislative activity might be, their knowledge of bureaucratic activities is undoubtedly lower. Thus, to the extent that the political and institutional contexts encourage the inclusion of policy details in statutes, they allow voters to have a better sense of the preferences and actions of their elected political representatives.

Our theory and evidence outline the instances in which policy is most likely to be debated in the relatively open forum of the legislative assembly. In both presidential and parliamentary systems, some form of distrust, or conflict, among politicians leads to more policy details in legislation. In parliamentary systems, coalition and minority governments lead to such distrust, and the existence of such governments is largely determined by electoral institutions. Countries that choose forms of proportional representation that result in highly fractionalized party systems will create such distrust, and thus, all else equal, will push the debate over policy details into the more open arena of assemblies. In addition, in parliamentary systems, the policymaking process will be more likely to occur in elected assemblies than behind closed executive doors in federal systems, common law systems, noncorporatist systems, and systems with low levels of cabinet turnover.

In presidential systems, distrust occurs during divided government. But we find that legislatures will be more engaged in setting the actual details of policy when such distrust exists *and* legislative capacity is high. This result is striking in light of the complaints that often are leveled against divided government in the United States, on the one hand, and the support that is often expressed for *citizen legislatures* (as opposed to more professionalized ones), on the other. To the extent that the public values transparency in policymaking, it is better off with divided government than with unified government, but only if it empowers legislatures with the institutional resources necessary to get involved in crafting policy details. In addition, giving legislatures strong powers of oversight, such as the legislative veto, will diminish transparency.

Transparency, it should be kept in mind, is one potential goal for policymaking in a democratic system. But it is not the only one, nor is it necessarily the dominant one. Its normative appeal comes from the idea that citizens will be more likely to be able to observe the debates about policymaking, as the legislature attempts to figure out a priori the exact form that policy should take. At the same time, there are potential drawbacks to having legislatures sink specific details into legislative concrete. These drawbacks are precisely the benefits of administration that scholars and practitioners have noted since the 1800s: bureaucracies have more expertise, are more flexible, are potentially less politicized, and are more able to respond quickly and to act incrementally than legislatures. Thus, while transparency has some normative appeal, we make no claim that it is clearly the best approach to policymaking.

Compliance by Bureaucrats with Legislative Statutes

Bureaucrats must choose whether or not to comply with laws; such compliance does not occur automatically. Even in advanced democracies, courts or politicians at times find that bureaucrats haven taken actions that were determined to be inconsistent with statutes, such as when the U.S. Supreme Court ruled in the summer of 2000 that the Food and Drug Administration did not have the legislative authority to regulate tobacco. And, of course, other such noncompliant actions certainly might pass undetected. Theories of delegation should therefore help us to understand the factors that lead to more or less compliant behavior by bureaucrats.

In our theory, noncompliance with legislation is caused by a noteworthy interaction between legislative capacity and technical uncertainty. If politicians adopt a vague statute that allows bureaucrats to implement their most preferred policy, then noncompliant behavior can never occur. Thus, noncompliance occurs only when politicians attempt to put policy constraints on bureaucrats. In our theory, this happens when politicians mistakenly overrestrict the autonomy of bureaucrats.

Recall that in our theory, there always exists some statute that could be written to yield compliant behavior *and* the politician's preferred outcome. If politicians had perfect information about the relationships between policies and outcomes, they would always adopt such a statute (if they could). The problem is that politicians do not always know this policy. Noncompliant behavior therefore occurs only when the politician's policy uncertainty leads to a mistake – to a statute that highly restricts policymaking discretion, but does so by requiring a policy that the bureaucrat will refuse to implement. One insight from our model, then, is that policy uncertainty by the politician is necessary for noncompliant behavior by bureaucrats.

Furthermore, since noncompliance can occur only when the politician writes a low-discretion statute, the factors that lead to low-discretion statutes also create the risk of noncompliant behavior. In this regard, the models provide several arguments about noncompliance that are unsurprising: noncompliance by bureaucrats with statutes is most likely when policy conflict with politicians is high (because such conflict triggers restrictions), nonstatutory factors are ineffective (because this leads not only to statutory restrictions, but also to a lower risk of getting caught), and sanctions are low (because this lowers the risk of getting caught).

The model, however, also suggests less obvious arguments about compliance. Noncompliant behavior occurs only when the politician overrestricts the bureaucrat. Since legislative capacity is necessary for such overrestriction, noncompliant behavior by bureaucrats is most likely to occur when the legislative capacity of politicians is high. This finding reminds us of a trade-off that politicians face when they attempt to micromanage policymaking by statute. By putting a large number of restrictions on bureaucratic behavior into a statute, politicians raise the burden to the bureaucrats of compliance. If this burden becomes too large because statutes are too detailed, the strategy will backfire for the politicians because the bureaucrats may simply ignore the law.

Of course, even compliant behavior does not imply that the policymaking process leads to outcomes that the politician desires. Politicians may give bureaucrats the discretion that allows these bureaucrats to adopt policies that they prefer and that do little to serve the interests of politicians. The focus on compliance with statutes thus ignores the question of whether politicians will be able to obtain desired policy outcomes, a question to which we now turn.

Political Control of Bureaucrats and the Consequences of Discretion

As we argued in Chapter 2, issues of political control over bureaucrats, and fears of an administrative state, have motivated a tremendous amount of research on delegation. Scholars want to understand the extent to which bureaucrats run the show, and arguments about the quality of political control over policy outcomes characterize much of the debate. In this study, we have intentionally sidestepped thorny debates about the absolute quality of political control over bureaucrats (see Chapter 2). In this concluding chapter, however, we would like to make three points that are related to this general debate.

The first point, a rather minor one, emerges from our discussion of compliance. In particular, the issues of compliance and political control are only indirectly related. Depending on how statutes are designed, bureaucrats can comply with the law while running the show. Indeed, rather than being mutually exclusive, the two can coexist. Similarly, bureaucrats could receive a vague mandate in legislation because this leads to optimal outcomes for politicians or because politicians lack the legislative capacity to do otherwise. Discussions of control therefore cannot unfold without careful consideration of politicians' ex ante abilities and intentions.

Second, our study suggests that politicians have in fact a nontrivial ability to control bureaucrats. Recall that the operationalization of our theory is predicated on the assumption that there always exists a political actor – the governor in the U.S. states and the cabinet minister in the parliamentary democracies – who enjoys a privileged position with respect to policy implementation. We argue (and assume in our model) that these actors have significant opportunities to control bureaucratic behavior, and we then derive hypotheses about how, given this ability, other political actors should want to design legislation. We then find considerable evidence supporting these hypotheses.

Thus, although we never offer any evidence about the quality of control, it would be difficult to explain why the empirical patterns we find would exist if the privileged actor did not in fact enjoy meaningful control over the policy implementation activities of bureaucrats. Of course, we end up in this regard where so many other studies of delegation have as well

– somewhere in the gray area. We can only infer that the ability of the privileged actor to control bureaucrats is sufficient to warrant a purposeful legislative response. At the same time, although we cannot understand why we would see the patterns in the data that we do if the privileged actor did not exercise significant control over bureaucrats, and although we cannot understand why legislative majorities would respond to policy conflict with detailed statutes if this response had no effect on policy outcomes, we also must admit that we cannot say anything about the absolute quality of control over bureaucrats or about what, in fact, bureaucrats do after legislation is adopted.

Third, we can ask when authors of statutes can use the law-making process to obtain outcomes that they like and when this possibility is likely to break down, with policymaking authority shifting to the politician, such as the governor or cabinet minister, with the most direct control over bureaucrats. Two insights about such questions emerge from our model. One insight, consistent with many arguments that precede ours, is that our model suggests that a low level of policy detail in laws does *not* imply that the legislative majorities do not obtain desired policy outcomes. In many situations, these policy details are absent from statutes because they are unnecessary. For example, there may be little policy conflict between the legislature and the agency, in which case the legislature has no need to tell the agency exactly what to do. Similarly, if the legislative majority can rely on nonstatutory means – such as friendly judges – to help ensure the policy outcomes it favors, then it has little need to write detailed statutes. In such cases, then, the absence of detailed language in legislation does not indicate that policy outcomes will differ from those the majority prefers.

Another insight concerns the ability of the authors of statutes to use legislation to obtain desired outcomes. Our theory shows that this ability is weakened only by a very specific set of circumstances: (a) the legislative capacity of the politicians who propose policy must be low; (b) there must be a high level of conflict between these politicians and bureaucrats; and (c) the politician's possibility of relying on nonstatutory means to achieve policy objectives must be low. Only when these three conditions are met simultaneously does a low level of policy detail imply unwilling abdication by legislative majorities to the executive. Thus, vague statutes are not necessarily – or even usually – equivalent to abdication by legislative majorities. This is not to say, however, that such abdication does not occur.

Policy Responsiveness

Finally, our theory suggests that the issues of policy responsiveness and political control are interwoven in fundamental respects. Normatively, if all politicians can agree on Pareto-improving policy change, then such change should occur. But our theory suggests that the risks inherent in adopting new statutes can cause politicians to forgo such mutually beneficial policy gains.

Politicians always have a choice between implementing a new policy and maintaining the status quo. Many scholars have pointed out that when there exist no policies that all relevant veto players prefer to the status quo, no policy change can occur. This same veto players logic also emerges from our analysis of the bicameral and veto models, where no policy change can occur when the status quo lies between the ideal points of the two politicians who must agree on a new statute.

But in our theory, there also exist circumstances under which politicians do not change policy, even though Pareto-improving gains *are* available. The logic involves the impact of nonstatutory factors. In adopting a new law, politicians run the risk that nonstatutory factors will affect policy outcomes in unintended ways. Most obviously, judges may interpret the language of new statutes in ways that are unintended and unwanted by politicians. In parliamentary systems, cabinet ministers may issue undesirable regulations. In federal systems, actions by state bureaucrats may usurp the intentions of national policymakers. Adopting new laws therefore exposes politicians to the risks of unwanted actions by others.

The danger, then, arises when the preferences of these other actors are more aligned with those of bureaucrats than with those of the legislature. If a new statute opens the door to new judicial action, then a judge sympathetic to the agency may move policy to the agency's ideal point. If this risk becomes sufficiently large, the legislature will be better off adopting no new statute, preserving the status quo in order to avoid an outcome it dislikes.

Our theory, then, points to an avenue by which the institutional context affects the ability of elected majorities to respond to the need for policy change. As the institutional environment diminishes the role of legislators and bureaucrats for policymaking, the risk of undertaking new policy initiatives increases because of the unintended consequences that ensue. The result will be increased stasis.

Institutions and Normative Trade-offs

The preceding discussion describes how our model and evidence speak to a variety of normative issues in the study of policymaking. We conclude this section by briefly summarizing the specific implications of particular institutional arrangements. In particular, we consider the implications suggested by our study for strong and independent judicial systems, strong powers of legislative oversight, professionalized legislatures, and fractionalized party systems.

First, consider the courts. Empirically, we have found that in civil law systems, where politicians view judges as more reliable allies, statutes contain far fewer legislative details than in common law systems, where judges are less reliable allies and the absence of legislative details can come back to haunt legislators. Thus, our evidence shows that strong courts elicit a clear response from legislators. More specifically, the existence of strong courts pushes legislators to include specific policy details in laws in order to tie the hands of justices.

This legislative response to the anticipated role of judicial policymaking is noteworthy in several respects. First, if strong judicial institutions make legislative details a more salient aspect of the policymaking process, then such institutions may have the benefit of pushing the legislative process into the open and transparent legislative arena. Second, the extent to which politicians can respond to this sort of judicial threat by using specific legislation depends, of course, on the capacity of legislative actors to write policy details into statutes. And third, strong judiciaries may affect policy responsiveness, particularly in separation of powers systems. In such systems, there may be efficient bargains that can be struck between a legislature and a president, but if one of these actors has particular concerns about the likely response of the courts, it will be more difficult for them to agree on a policy change.

Next, consider legislative institutions. We have found that when legislative and executive powers are separate, as in the U.S. states, the capacity of the legislature has a significant effect on the ability of politicians to include policy details in statutes. In parliamentary systems, by contrast, we found no such relationship between the nature of legislation and parliamentary capacity. We have provided ample arguments about why this distinction should be unsurprising. In our view, these arguments should be kept in mind when comparative legislative scholars bemoan the "decline of parliament" and seek to augment the legislative role that assemblies play.

When legislative and executive powers are fused in systems with disciplined parties, it makes little sense to advocate strengthening legislative institutions. In fact, the relative capacity of parliaments has little bearing on the types of laws parliaments adopt. In presidential systems, by contrast, legislative capacity is crucial to the ability of legislative majorities to use legislation to influence policy outcomes. When legislative capacity is low and conflict with the executive is high, the distributional consequences are very real: power is unequivocally transferred from the legislative majority to the executive, and policymaking is moved out of the more open legislative arena and into the smoke-filled rooms of executive politics.

Our study is also suggestive with respect to the influence of institutions that allow effective legislative oversight of policy implementation. In particular, we have found a strong substitution effect in our analysis of the U.S. states: when legislative majorities have a strong veto over agency decisions, they are less likely to rely on policy details in legislative statutes. Such oversight institutions, then, not only assist legislatures in obtaining their policy goals, they also shape *how* policy is made, with the effect being to move the policymaking process out of the legislative arena and into the administrative one.

Finally, it is useful to think about how the party system affects policymaking processes. Scholars often worry that fractionalized party systems make it more difficult for voters to assess responsibility for policy outcomes, though they often have a difficult time finding this effect.[2] We find that fractionalized party systems, which lead to coalition and minority governments, lead to more detailed statutes. Since policy conflict among members of the majority is an inherent feature of fractionalized party systems, such systems can have the effect of elevating the role of legislative debates and legislative statutes in the policymaking process. It is important to bear in mind, however, that this is an "all else equal" claim. Many fractionalized party systems, for example, also adopt corporatist bargaining arrangements, which mitigate the effect just described. Similarly, some (though not all) fractionalized party systems are also very unstable, which makes it more difficult to include policy details.

In concluding this discussion, we would like to highlight what is largely absent from our study: claims about the relative trade-offs of presidential and parliamentary systems. This is intentional. Although the discussion of

[2] See Powell and Whitten (1993); Anderson (2000); Goodhart (2001); Stevenson (2001); and Tucker (2001).

trade-offs between these two types of regime frames many institutional debates in comparative politics, we feel that the distinction between presidentialism and parliamentarism is typically too noisy to be useful. This is not to say that the distinction is irrelevant. We find, for example, that legislative capacity plays a different role in the two types of systems. We also argue that strong court systems should have a different effect on policy responsiveness in the two types of systems.

Our purpose, however, has been to demonstrate that abstract variables like policy conflict, legislative capacity, and nonstatutory factors operate in the same fashion in both parliamentary and presidential systems. Consequently, some presidential systems (such as those with a high incidence of divided government and low levels of legislative capacity) may operate much more like parliamentary systems (such as those with fractionalized party systems and considerable cabinet instability) than like other presidential systems. We therefore feel that an important way forward in comparative institutional research lies not in focusing on broad typological categories such as presidentialism or parliamentarism. Instead, scholars need to develop causal arguments about how specific institutional forms, like professionalized legislatures or strong courts, affect behavior. Whether these institutional forms operate similarly across broad typological categories can be assessed only by stepping back from the categories themselves and treating the institutional forms as the objects of research.

Directions for Future Research

The main goal of this book has been to explain why legislatures sometimes use legislation to delegate broadly and at other times do not. Every study builds on previous work, and this one is no exception. And every study is incomplete, in the sense of containing gaps and identifying questions that future studies can address. In concluding this study, we propose a number of topics, both theoretical and empirical, for future research.

Theoretical Extensions

There are three important ways in which the basic comparative theory presented here should be extended. First, our model is presented in a highly reduced form. It includes variables that are intended to capture a wide range of institutional arrangements. Our variable for nonstatutory factors, for example, is applied to court systems, legislative oversight, and corporatism, among other concrete variables. While our approach has the advantage of leading to a theory that can be tested in a range of political settings, we also think it is important to theorize more explicitly about some specific institutions that we discuss in our empirical work, as well as others that we do not consider. In a comparative framework, for example, we could model the direct role of legislative vetoes, the strategic behavior of courts, or implementation by agents (such as subnational governments) that do not share the preferences of any of the actors in our model. We could also explore the effects of other institutional arrangements that we do not discuss. In presidential systems, for example, by issuing executive orders, executives can implement policy changes without needing to resort to legislative action. It would be useful to consider how the existence of this procedural prerogative, and the variation in its design and use, affect the legislature's calculations about whether to write detailed laws.

Second, the theory we present is static, whereas policymaking processes are clearly dynamic. Politicians adopt new programs over time, and they adjust to new information that becomes available, as well as new political realities (such as when elections change the preferences of particular actors). It would be useful to embed our comparative approach in a dynamic setting in an effort to explore directly how expectations about the future affect actions in the present.

Finally, an important assumption in our theory – and in all formal theories of legislative–bureaucratic interactions – is that the bureaucracy possesses a large informational advantage over the legislature. As we noted earlier in this chapter, this is an uncontroversial assumption to make in the context of advanced industrial democracies. However, it is not so clear that we should make the same assumption in other contexts. In newly emerging democratic states, for example, it is quite possible that bureaucracies have not built up the needed level of expertise to sustain such an assumption. Similarly, in the United States in the 1800s and early 1900s, bureaucracies were taking on a new, bigger role in governance, and had not yet had much of a chance to build up a reservoir of expertise similar to that found in agencies today. Clearly, then, examples exist in which the assumption that bureaucrats have an informational advantage might not hold; and we need to know more about how a legislature would choose to delegate in contexts where bureaucratic capacity is suspect.

Future Empirical Work

There are a variety of straightforward ways in which our empirical research could be extended. Future work could develop more fine-grained measures of discretion in statutes. It could explore the relationships we analyze in new policy areas. It could develop more direct measures of bureaucratic preferences. It could explore other variables that affect legislative capacity or nonstatutory factors. It could study the relationship between discretion in statutes and efforts at oversight. It could more carefully assess the use of procedural tools in statutes. Considerable additional empirical research of the sort we have undertaken is therefore crucial to understanding the value of our theory and the ways that it should be amended.

Our study also suggests the need for additional empirical research of a different sort. In this chapter, we have described a variety of normative issues that arise in thinking about the consequences of our theory. Two general points emerge from the discussion. The first is that issues of delegation and discretion touch many issues other than whether politicians control bureaucrats. Issues of transparency, responsiveness, and the distributive consequences of policymaking across elected officials are all affected by the inherent link between legislation and the delegation process. The second point is that it is often very difficult to think about delegation outcomes in absolute terms. Instead, it is often more practical (and thus useful) to take a comparative static approach, where the goal is to understand how particular variables influence particular types of outcomes, rather than to judge the absolute quality of these outcomes.

Of course, the empirical focus of this book has been on legislation as an instrument in the delegation process. Though we feel that our theory and evidence in this regard have interesting implications for the normative issues that we raise, we have offered no empirical evidence to this effect. We feel that a clear item on the agenda for future work is thus to explore some of the normative claims that we have sketched.

Appendix A

MMC Laws Used in Chapter 3

The following is information about the MMC statutes we coded, including the number of statutes from each state, the years in which the laws were written, and the total number of text blocks coded from each state. As discussed in the text, in this sample we included all laws that were identified as key bills and also included at least one statute from each state that passed an MMC statute. The rest of the statutes were chosen randomly from the full set of MMC laws that we identified.

State	Number of Statutes	Years	Number of Text Blocks
Alaska	1	1996	12
California	3	1992–96	54
Colorado	3	1995–97	278
Connecticut	4	1994–97	49
Delaware	1	1990	5
Florida	2	1995–96	310
Georgia	1	1996	4
Idaho	2	1993	28
Illinois	2	1993–94	97
Iowa	2	1989–93	53
Kansas	2	1993–94	11
Kentucky	2	1994–98	15
Louisiana	2	1995–97	28
Maine	1	1994	30
Maryland	1	1989	16
Massachusetts	2	1996–97	59
Michigan	1	1996	110

(continued)

State	Number of Statutes	Years	Number of Text Blocks
Minnesota	3	1989–97	526
Mississippi	1	1995	127
Montana	2	1993–95	92
Nevada	2	1995–97	145
New Jersey	1	1991	49
New Mexico	2	1994–96	26
New York	3	1991–96	388
Oklahoma	6	1993–98	292
Oregon	1	1989	115
Pennsylvania	1	1996	344
Rhode Island	2	1993	40
Texas	3	1995–97	386
Utah	2	1993–94	64
Vermont	1	1995	55
Washington	3	1993–95	163
West Virginia	1	1993	7
Wisconsin	1	1993	6

Appendix B

Policy Categories Used for MMC Laws in Chapter 3

Listed here are additional examples of policy instructions written into MMC legislation.

General Policy Language

Washington, 1993 – SB5304: The legislature establishes the rationale for the MMC program.

BASIC HEALTH PLAN – FINDINGS. (1) The legislature finds that:

(a) A significant percentage of the population of this state does not have reasonably available insurance or other coverage of the costs of necessary basic health care services;

(b) This lack of basic health care coverage is detrimental to the health of the individuals lacking coverage and to the public welfare, and results in substantial expenditures for emergency and remedial health care, often at the expense of health care providers, health care facilities, and all purchasers of health care, including the state; and

(c) The use of managed health care systems has significant potential to reduce the growth of health care costs incurred by the people of this state generally, and by low-income pregnant women, and at-risk children and adolescents who need greater access to managed health care.

Provider Responsibilities and Rights

Florida's SB321 (1989): Provides a good example of how legislatures provide specific reporting requirements for participating HMOs:

6.4. Any HMO participating in the state group insurance program shall, upon the request of the department, submit to the department standardized data for the purpose of comparison of the appropriateness, quality, and efficiency of care provided by the HMO. Such standardized data shall include: membership profiles; inpatient and outpatient utilization by age and sex, type of service, provider type, and facility; and emergency care experience. Requirements and timetables for submission of such standardized data and such other data as the department deems necessary to evaluate the performance of participating HMOs shall be promulgated by rule.

Nature of Coverage

Mississippi, 1997 – SB427: The legislature provides for the health condition of certain clients who must be covered.

(6) Agreements by providers of health care who contract to provide services to recipients of Medicaid to presume that certain persons are eligible for Medicaid, including, without limitation, certain pregnant women and persons with physical disabilities.

Massachusetts' Chapter 203 (1996): Focus on copayments
Consistent with the provisions of Title XIX and any waiver authority therein, the division shall establish premium and copayment amounts for beneficiaries of MassHealth. Said premiums and copayments may be established on a sliding scale commensurate with beneficiary income levels. The division may waive premiums and copayments upon a finding of substantial financial or medical hardship.

Definitions

Louisiana, 1995 – HB2146: The legislature defines the term *enrollee* for the purposes of the bill.

(2) "Enrollee" means any Medicaid recipient or indigent, uninsured, or underinsured person enrolled in a qualified plan for the provision of health care services whose enrollment costs are paid wholly or in part by the state under a federal waiver to the Medicaid program.

Minnesota, 1997 – Chapter 203: The legislature defines the concept *limitation of choice*.

(d) "Limitation of choice" means suspending freedom of choice while allowing eligible individuals to choose among the demonstration providers.

Selection of Providers

Illinois, 1993 – HB1852: The legislature establishes criteria for participating providers.

(c) Providers eligible to participate in the program shall be physicians licensed to practice medicine in all its branches, and the Illinois Department may terminate a provider's participation if the provider is determined to have failed to comply with any applicable program standard or procedure established by the Illinois Department.

Oklahoma's HB 1573 (1993): The legislature mandates that MMC contracts will be awarded on the basis of a bidding process:

The administrator shall establish a contract bidding process that encourages competition among entities contracting with the Authority for state-purchased and state-subsidized health care, is timely to the state budgetary process, and sets conditions for awarding contracts.

Client Participation

Vermont, 1995 – H159: The legislature includes stipulations for the establishment of an appeals process for clients.

(2) Grievance procedures for consumers and providers. A health plan shall provide grievance procedures that insure timely resolution of disputes relating to the denial of services or denial of payment for benefits by a health care facility, health care provider, or health insurance carrier and that afford patients, carriers, facilities, and providers a timely opportunity to contest decisions made by the plan. Managed care enrollees shall have access to the general Medicaid fair hearing grievance procedures available to the fee-for-service consumers.

Texas, 1995 – SB601: The legislature mandates an education program be established for MMC clients.

(B) In adopting rules implementing a managed care Medicaid program, the commission shall establish guidelines for and require managed care organizations to provide education programs for providers and clients using a variety of techniques and mediums.

Paying Providers

Illinois, 1993 – HB1852: The legislature describes the manner in which providers will be paid.

(b) Providers participating in the program may be paid an amount per patient per month, to be set by the Illinois Department, for managing each recipient's medical care.

Minnesota, Chapter 203, 1997: The legislatures specifies how the agency should determine the amount to be paid:

Payments to providers participating in the project are exempt from the requirements of sections 256.966 and 256B.03, subdivision 2. The commissioner shall complete development of capitation rates for payments before delivery of services under this section is begun. For payments made during calendar year 1990 and later years, the commissioner shall contract with an independent actuary to establish prepayment rates.

Quality Assurance

California, 1996 – SB1664: The legislature establishes an independent review of HMOs/MCOs in the MMC program.

(d) The department shall periodically evaluate each fee-for-service managed care program through an independent assessment as required under the department's approved federal waiver request to determine if the program is successfully providing quality health care while not placing the Medi-Cal program or counties at additional financial risk. The assessment shall evaluate quality of care, access, the provision of preventive health care, and costs. The department shall terminate a contract when the department finds that the fee-for-service managed care program is unsuccessful.

Financial

Colorado, 1995 – sb78: The legislature provides for the usage of savings accrued from the MMC program.

(3) (a) The general assembly declares that it is in the state's best interest to use savings in Medicaid per capita costs from the implementation of this subpart 2 and from the implementation of section 26-4-404 (1) (b) to cover the administrative costs of implementing managed care pursuant to the provisions of this subpart 2. (b) remaining savings in Medicaid per capita costs from the implementation of this subpart 2 shall be used to establish programs to insure additional low-income Coloradans and to support essential community providers as long as such new programs do not create an entitlement to services and minimize any substitution of subsidized coverage for employer-based coverage. (c) remaining savings in Medicaid per capita costs from the implementation of section 26-4-404 (1) (b) may be used for the expansion of the incentive program to providers of dental services for children under the early periodic screening, diagnosis, and treatment program.

Defining Participants

Maryland, 1989 – SB794: The legislature defines a certain demographic group that must be covered by the MMC program.

(III) Shall provide, subject to the limitations of the state budget and the availability of federal funds, comprehensive medical and other health care for all children from the age of 1 year up through and including the age of 2 years whose family income falls below 100 percent of the poverty level, as permitted by the federal law.

Other Providers

Maryland, 1996 – Chapter 705: The legislature provides for referrals outside of the MMC network.

6. (A) If a health maintenance organization determines that it does not have a health care provider with appropriate training and experience in its panel or network to meet the particular health care needs of an enrollee, the health maintenance organization shall make a referral to an appropriate provider, pursuant to a treatment plan approved by the health maintenance organization in consultation with the primary care provider, the nonparticipating provider and the enrollee or enrollee's designee, at no additional cost to the enrollee beyond what the enrollee would otherwise pay for services received within the network.

Privatization of Portions of the Managed Care System

Colorado, 1995 – SB78: The legislature provides for the privatization of portions of the MMC program.

(2) To that end, pursuant to section 24-50-504 (2) (a), C.R.S., the state department shall enter into personal services contracts that create an independent contractor relationship for the administration of not less than twenty percent of the statewide managed care system. The state department shall enter into personal service contracts for the administration of the managed care system according to the implementation of the statewide managed care system in accordance with section 26-4-113 (2).

Appendix C

Procedural Categories Used for MMC Laws in Chapter 3

Listed below are examples of procedural instructions written into MMC legislation.

Time Constraints

New York, 1995 – SB5280: The legislature sets a sunset clause on the MMC authorization.

§2. This act shall take effect immediately and shall remain in full force and effect through December 31, 1996.

New Mexico, 1995 (HB 702): The legislature directs an agency to implement a program by a specific date.

Section 23. HEALTH CARE DELIVERY AND PAYMENT PLANS. – A. The health care task force and the New Mexico health policy commission and its staff, including the health care initiative, shall develop health care delivery and payment initiatives to support and provide universal health care for all New Mexicans by October 1, 1997. The proposals shall include, to the maximum extent possible, preventive, primary, acute, chronic and long-term care.

Information Requirements

Oregon SB 27 (1989): The legislature made sure that the agency would consult all relevant groups and in particular ensured that advocates for Medicaid clients would be given a seat at the policymaking table.

SECTION 4a. (1) The Health Services Commission shall consult with the Joint Legislative Committee on Health Care and conduct public hearings prior to making the report described in subsection (3) of this section. The commission shall solicit testimony and information from advocates for seniors; handicapped persons; mental health services consumers; low-income Oregonians; and providers of health care, including but not limited to physicians licensed to practice medicine, dentists, oral surgeons, chiropractors, naturopaths, hospitals, clinics, pharmacists, nurses and allied health professionals.

Reporting Requirements to the Legislature

Pennsylvania, 1996 – SB91: The legislature provides for the annual report of the bureaucratic agency regarding the MMC program.

(F) The department in cooperation with the insurance department shall submit an annual report to the general assembly regarding the implementation, operation and enforcement of this article.

Texas SB 10 (1995): The legislature codifies a deadline for specific reports.

(d) Not later than February 1, 1997, the commission shall report to the 75th Legislature concerning the efficiency and cost-effectiveness of the pilot program.

Study Requirements

Alaska, 1996 – HB393: The legislature mandates the use of a pilot program.

Sec. 2. MANAGED CARE PROGRAM. (a) The Department of Health and Social Services shall begin development of a managed care system for recipients of medical assistance under AS 47.07 by designing and implementing no fewer than two innovative managed care pilot projects by June 30, 1997. The projects must be in one or more predominantly urban areas of the state that take into account the unique features of the project areas and include a rural element, if feasible. The department shall involve the public and affected consumers and providers of health care services in the selected project areas in the development of the managed care system that will be used in the projects.

Proposal Requirements to the Legislature

Massachusetts, 1997 – Chapter 47: The legislature requires that the agency must report before implementation of the program.

(14) Ninety days prior to implementing one or more of the programs under this section, the division shall provide a plan or plans for implementing said programs to the committee on health care and to the house and senate committee on ways and means. Said programs may be offered separately and implemented at different times, and a plan relative to each program may be submitted separately.

Establishment of a Legislative Committee

Vermont, 1995 – H159: The legislature creates a committee to oversee the MMC program.

HEALTH ACCESS OVERSIGHT COMMITTEE; CREATION: (A) A legislative health access oversight committee is created to monitor the development, implementation, and ongoing operation of the health access program. The committee shall consist of ten members, five representatives, who shall not all be from the same party, and five senators, who shall not all be from the same party. The speaker of the house shall appoint the chair and two other members from the committee on health and welfare; one member from the committee on ways and means; and one member from the committee on appropriations. The committee on committees shall appoint the chair and two other members from the committee on health and welfare; one member from the committee on finance; and one member from the committee on appropriations.

Establishment of a Nonlegislative Committee or Task Force

California, 1996 – SB1664: The legislature provides for the creation of a nonlegislative committee to be established in an advisory role.

(i) The board of supervisors of each county participating in the project authorized by this section shall establish or cause to be established an advisory committee comprised of county, physician, hospital, clinic, and beneficiary representatives to advise the county on the implementation and operation of the project provided for under this section.

Staffing Requirements

Delaware, 1990: The legislature provides staffing for the MMC agency.

Section 3. A total of eighteen (18.0) full time equivalent positions are authorized to the Department of Health and Social Services (35-00-00); Social Services (35-07-00); Social Services (35-07-01). These positions shall be used to implement the Medicaid program expansions and the Health Care Coverage Program for General Assistance Clients.

Appeals Process

In 1990, Minnesota established just such a procedure in Chapter 568, which mandated that providers must have an internal appeals process made available to them.

A vendor aggrieved by the commissioner's determination that services provided were not reasonable or necessary may appeal pursuant to the contested case procedures of chapter 14. To appeal, the vendor shall notify the commissioner in writing within 30 days of receiving the commissioner's notice. The appeal request shall specify each disputed item, the reason for the dispute, an estimate of the dollar amount involved for each disputed item, the computation that the vendor believes is correct, the authority in statute or rule upon which the vendor relies for each disputed item, the name and address of the person or firm with whom contacts may be made regarding the appeal, and other information required by the commissioner.

Creation of a New Agency/Department

Delaware, 1990: Creates the Health Care Commission within the Department of Health and Human Services.

Section 4. The sums appropriated in Section 1 of this Act to the Department of Health and Social Services (35-00-00); Administration (35-01-00); Delaware Health Care Commission (35-01-50) shall be used to establish the Delaware Health Care Commission (35-01-50) pursuant to the provisions of the Delaware Health Care Commission Act ("The Act"), Title 16, Del. C., Chapter 98. The Commission shall employ a Director and one additional staff person selected by the Commission to aid in performing the Commission's duties and responsibilities.

Appendix D

The Formal Model of Discretion

In this appendix, we provide the details of the formal models that provide the foundation for the main theoretical arguments described in Chapter 4.

The Parliamentary Model

The parliamentary model assumes that a Politician, L (for Legislative actor – we introduce P, for President, later), can unilaterally adopt a bill, and a Bureaucratic agent, B, can implement it. The interaction between these two players involves arriving at an outcome on the real line. Without loss of generality, we assume that L's ideal point is $x_L = 0$ and B's ideal point is $x_B \in [0,1]$. The ideal points are common knowledge, and each player's utility from the final policy outcome is a linear loss function.

In the first stage, the Politician either does nothing, which retains a status quo, $Q \in \mathbb{R}$, or adopts a new law, $x \in [0,\bar{I}]$. The policy $x = \bar{I}$ is the maximal discretion law, and to simplify the number of parameters in the model, we set $\bar{I} = x_B + 1$ (which, as will become clear, always allows the Bureaucrat to implement the policy that will yield his most preferred outcome). The law, x, defines the upper bound on policies that the Bureaucrat can implement that are in compliance with the statute. We've parameterized the model so that the Politician never has an incentive to set a lower bound that is less than 0. Thus, as x increases, the Bureaucrat's discretion increases.

The Politician must pay a cost, k, for limiting the Bureaucrat's discretion. These costs are decreasing in x (so that more discretion is less costly). We let $k = \left(a - \frac{ax}{\bar{I}}\right)$. Thus, the proposal that grants the most discretion,

$x = \bar{I}$ has zero cost, and the proposal that grants no discretion, $x = 0$, has a cost, a. The Politician's legislative capacity is captured by a: as a increases (decreases), the cost of any x also increases (decreases). Capacity therefore decreases with increases in a. When $a \geq \bar{I}$, the Politician's gains in policy utility from limiting discretion cannot exceed the costs. Thus, we constrain our analysis to $a < \bar{I}$.

In the second stage, Nature determines the consequence of policy choice (the shock that will occur for any policy that is implemented). Let $\varepsilon \in \{0,1\}$. The outcome of implementing any policy, y, is given by $y - \varepsilon$. Thus, the Politician's preferred policy is ε, and the Bureaucrat's preferred policy is $x_B + \varepsilon$. As with previous models, we assume that the Bureaucrat has policy expertise that the Politician lacks. To capture this informational asymmetry, we assume that the Bureaucrat observes the value of ε but the Politician does not. The Politician believes that $\varepsilon = 1$ with probability p and $\varepsilon = 0$ with probability $1 - p$. Since the shock can never move policy to the right, the Politician never has an incentive to adopt a lower bound on policy that is to the left of the Politician's ideal point. This is why we anchor the lower bound of the Politician's policy at 0; if we did not do this, the Politician would obviously have an incentive to adopt a lower bound that is as low as possible – to keep costs down – which makes her optimal bill undefined. We thus focus on the strategically relevant range of discretion (to the right of the Politician's ideal point).[1]

Third, the Bureaucrat implements a policy. Let $y_1 \in \Re^+$ be the policy B implements if $\varepsilon = 1$, and let $y_0 \in \Re^+$ be the policy B implements if $\varepsilon = 0$. Note that we do *not* assume that the Bureaucrat must comply with the law, although as we note later, he may be punished for failing to do so. It is also useful to note that although the Bureaucrat's action is conditional on ε, ε plays no signaling role because the Politician will not act after the Bureaucrat implements a policy.

Finally, the Bureaucrat's implementation strategy, along with nonstatutory factors, determines the final outcome. To model the nonstatutory factors, we define $\gamma \in (0,1)$ as the probability that *nonstatutory* mechanisms force the Bureaucrat to implement ε, the Politician's preferred policy. Thus, with probability $1 - \gamma$, the Bureaucrat's policy action and ε determine the

[1] For a generalization of the model presented here, see Huber and McCarty (2001). Their model, which focuses on the impact of bureaucratic capacity on delegation, makes less restrictive assumptions about the distribution of policy shock and about the ideal points of the actors, with the main intuitions presented here carrying through.

outcome. If the Bureaucrat implements a policy that does not comply with the statute (i.e., chooses $y_\varepsilon > x$), then γ also defines the probability that the Bureaucrat will be punished for noncompliance. We thus assume that with probability γ the Bureaucrat must pay a sanction, $d > 0$, whenever $y_\varepsilon > x$. The parameter γ thus plays a dual role, defining the probability that the Politician gets her ideal outcome and the probability that the Bureaucrat is punished for noncompliance. We make this assumption only to simplify the number of parameters in the model; the basic intuitions would remain if we assumed that these probabilities could differ.

We focus on pure strategy, subgame perfect Nash equilibria. To simplify the exposition, we assume that if the Politician is indifferent between any two laws, she adopts the one that limits discretion the most. We also assume that if the Bureaucrat is indifferent between implementing any two policies, he implements the one most favorable to the Politician. These indifference assumptions in no way alter the substantive results of our model.

The Bureaucrat's Best Response to x

We begin by defining the Bureaucrat's optimal response to the law passed by the Politician. In choosing an optimal policy to implement, the Bureaucrat must choose between the optimal policy in compliance with the statute ($y \leq x$) and the optimal policy that is not in compliance ($y > x$). If $x \geq x_B + \varepsilon$, then B's optimal policy is always in compliance. If $x < x_B + \varepsilon$, then the optimal policy that complies with x is x, while the optimal policy that does not comply with x is $x_B + \varepsilon$.

If $y_\varepsilon = x$, then $EU_B(y_\varepsilon) = -[\gamma x_B + (1 - \gamma)(x_B - (x - \varepsilon))]$. That is, with probability γ, nonstatutory factors force the policy to that preferred by the Politician (but the Bureaucrat pays no sanction), and with probability $1 - \gamma$, the Bureaucrat's implemented policy sticks, yielding an outcome of $x - \varepsilon$. If $y_\varepsilon = x_B + \varepsilon > x$, $EU_B(y_\varepsilon) = -\gamma(x_B + d)$. This is true because the Bureaucrat receives his ideal point with probability $1 - \gamma$ but is "caught" in noncompliance with probability γ, which forces the Bureaucrat to implement the policy preferred by the Politician and to pay a sanction, d, for noncompliance.

The Bureaucrat prefers to comply with the statute when

$$-[\gamma x_B + (1-\gamma)(x_B - (x-\varepsilon))] \geq -\gamma(x_B + d) \quad \text{or} \quad x \geq x_B + \varepsilon - \frac{d\gamma}{(1-\gamma)}.$$

Thus, we can define the compliance boundary as $x_\varepsilon = x_B + \varepsilon - \frac{d\gamma}{(1-\gamma)}$. Note that $x_0 = x_B - \frac{d\gamma}{1-\gamma}$ and $x_1 = x_B + 1 - \frac{d\gamma}{1-\gamma}$, so that $x_0 < x_1$. The Bureaucrat's best response to any x given ε depends on the relation between x and this compliance boundary. It is given by

$$BR_B(\varepsilon) = \begin{cases} x_B + \varepsilon & \text{if} \quad x \geq x_B + \varepsilon \quad \text{or} \quad x < x_\varepsilon. \\ x & \text{if} \quad x_\varepsilon \leq x < x_B + \varepsilon \end{cases}$$

The Politician's Optimal Statute

We focus on the Politician's decision of whether to adopt the optimal low-discretion law or the optimal high-discretion law. A low-discretion law is any law that could constrain the Bureaucrat's action in equilibrium. Thus, it is any $x \in [0, x_B + \varepsilon)$. A high-discretion law could not constrain the Bureaucrat's action in equilibrium (i.e., any $x \geq x_B + \varepsilon$, which we limit to $x = x_B + 1$).

Focusing on the Politician's choice between a low- or high-discretion law is more substantively meaningful than focusing on which low-discretion law is optimal. For example, if the Politician knows that the Bureaucrat will comply with any law and that $\varepsilon = 1$, the optimal policy for the Politician would be $y = 1$, whereas if the Politician knows that $\varepsilon = 0$ the optimal policy would be $y = 0$. Suppose that x_B, a, d, and γ are such that in the first case the optimal low-discretion law is $x = 1$, whereas in the second it is $x = 0$. It would not, in this case, be appropriate to examine the reasons for the variation in levels of discretion between these two laws because the variation is solely a function of the arbitrary assumptions we make about how policies map onto outcomes. Suppose, however, that there exist circumstances under which the Politician prefers some very-high-discretion law over adopting either $x = 0$ or $x = 1$. Identifying these circumstances is substantively interesting because this choice of a high-discretion law will be driven by the exogenous parameters rather than the stylized assumptions about the mapping from policies to outcomes.

The Optimal High-Discretion Law

Since a high-discretion law allows the Bureaucrat to implement the policy that yields his most preferred outcome, the optimal high-discretion law for the Politician is $\bar{I} = x_B + 1$, as it has the lowest cost $\left(k = a - \frac{a\bar{I}}{\bar{I}} = 0\right)$. This policy yields the Politician

$$EU_L(\bar{I}) = -(1-\gamma)x_B.$$

The Possible Low-Discretion Laws

As noted in Chapter 4, we focus on a special case of the model that applies to the modern democracies that we examine empirically. In this special case, there always exists some statute that, if adopted by the Politician, would yield the Politician's preferred outcome (though the nature of this policy is unknown to the Politician). Formally, this means that we examine only the case where $x_0 \leq 0$ (which implies that $x_1 \leq 1$). It is straightforward – though as per our discussion in Chapter 4, irrelevant in our view to the political systems we examine empirically – to examine the case where $x_0 > 0$ (see Huber and McCarty 2001).

Lemma 1 shows that when $x_0 < 0$, the only possible low-discretion laws are $x = 0$ and $x = 1$.

Lemma 1. If $x_0 < 0$, then $x^* \in \{0, 1, \bar{I}\}$.

Proof. Since $x_0 < 0$ implies that $x_1 < 1$, two distinct cases exist: $x_B \leq x_1$ and $x_1 < x_B$.

Case 1: $x_B \leq x_1$.

First, we show that the optimal law can never be $x \in [x_B, 1)$. If $x \in [x_B, x_1)$, then the only way that the outcome will differ from the Bureaucrat's ideal point is if nonstatutory factors move policy to the Politician's ideal point (because if $\varepsilon = 0$, the Bureaucrat can implement his ideal point and if $\varepsilon = 1$, then $x < x_1$ implies that the Bureaucrat will not comply with the statute and will instead implement his ideal policy). Thus, he always prefers adopting $x = \bar{I}$ to adopting $x \in [x_B, x_1)$. If $x \in [x_1, 1]$, then whenever $\varepsilon = 0$, the Bureaucrat will implement $y = x_B$ and whenever $\varepsilon = 1$ the Bureaucrat will implement x. In this interval, then, the optimal statute is always $x = 1$. Thus, the Politician always prefers $x = \bar{I}$ to $x \in [x_B, x_1)$, and she prefers $x = 1$ to $x \in [x_1, 1)$. She must therefore choose between $x < x_B$, 1 and $\bar{I}$.

Next, we show that the optimal law can never be $x \in (0, x_B]$. For any $x \in [0, x_B]$, if $\varepsilon = 0$, the Bureaucrat will implement x, and if $\varepsilon = 1$, the

Bureaucrat will implement a policy that yields his ideal point (because $x < x_1$). Thus, $EU_L(x) = -(1-\gamma)(px_B + (1-p)x) - \left(a - \frac{ax}{\bar{I}}\right)$. Note that $\frac{\partial EU_L(x)}{\partial x} = -(1-\gamma)(1-p) + \frac{a}{\bar{I}}$. Thus, the Politician's expected utility is decreasing in x if a is sufficiently small ($a \leq \bar{I}(1-\gamma)(1-p)$), implying that $x = 0$ is preferred to $x \in (0,x_B)$. Similarly, the Politician's expected utility is increasing in x if a is sufficiently large ($a > \bar{I}(1-\gamma)(1-p)$). In the first case (i.e., small a), $x = 0$ is preferred to $x \in (0,x_B]$ and $x = 1$ or $x = \bar{I}$ is preferred to any $x \in [x_B,1)$, leaving $x \in \{0,1,\bar{I}\}$ as the only possible equilibrium laws. In the second case (a large), $x = x_B$ is preferred to $x < x_B$, and since $x = 1$ or $x = \bar{I}$ is preferred to any $x \in [x_B,1)$, the only possible equilibrium laws are again $x \in \{0,1,\bar{I}\}$.

Case 2: $x_B > x_1$.

For $x \in [x_B,1]$, the Bureaucrat will comply with the statute regardless of ε, yielding the Politician $-(1-\gamma)[p(1-x)+(1-p)x_B] - \left(a - \frac{ax}{\bar{I}}\right)$, which is strictly increasing in x. So the Politician prefers $x = 1$ to $x \in [x_B,1)$. For $x \in [0,x_1)$, the outcome will be x if $\varepsilon = 0$ and will be x_B if $\varepsilon = 1$. Since expected utility is strictly decreasing with x in this interval, $x \in (0,x_1)$ can never occur in equilibrium. Finally, note that for $x \in [x_1,x_B]$, the Bureaucrat will implement x for any ε, which yields $EU_p(x \in [x_1,x_B]) = -(1-\gamma)(p(1-x) + (1-p)x) - \left(a - \frac{ax}{\bar{I}}\right)$. In this case, $\frac{\partial}{\partial x} EU_L(x \in [x_1,x_B]) = -(1-\gamma)(1-2p) + \frac{a}{\bar{I}}$. If $\frac{\partial}{\partial x} > 0$, then $x = 1$ is preferred to $x \in [x_1,1)$. If $\frac{\partial}{\partial x} \leq 0$, then $x = x_1$ is preferred to $x \in (x_1,x_B]$. Thus, the only possible equilibrium statutes are $x \in \{x_1,0,1,\bar{I}\}$. It only remains to show that x_1 cannot be an equilibrium proposal.

We show this by demonstrating that L can never simultaneously prefer x_1 to $x = 0$, $x = 1$, and $x = \bar{I}$. The Politician prefers $x = x_1$ to $x = 1$ only if $a < (1-\gamma)(1-2p)\bar{I}$, and the Politician prefers x_1 to 0 only if $a > (1-\gamma)(1-p)\bar{I}$. Both of these conditions can be satisfied only when $2 < 1$, a contradiction. Thus, the only possible equilibrium statutes are $x \in \{0,1,\bar{I}\}$. *QED*

Lemma 1 makes it straightforward to establish the main theoretical results from the Parliamentary model.

Proposition 1

In the Parliamentary model

(a) a high-discretion law will always be adopted if there is no policy conflict (i.e., if $x_B = x_L = 0$);
(b) a low-discretion law ($x < \bar{I}$) is adopted in equilibrium only when legislative capacity is sufficiently high (a is sufficiently small); and
(c) increases in policy conflict (increases in x_B) and decreases in the reliability of nonstatutory factors (decreases in γ) always make it easier to satisfy the conditions under which the Politician adopts a low-discretion law as opposed to a high-discretion law ($x = \bar{I}$).

Proof.
Part (a). Note that $EU_L(\bar{I}) = -(1 - \gamma)x_B = 0$ when $x_B = 0$, which is the best that the Politician can do in the game – she obtains her ideal point at no cost. Thus, adopting $\bar{I}$ dominates adopting any other x when $x_B = 0$.

Part (b). By Lemma 1, the only possible low-discretion laws are 0 and 1. We establish that for all possible locations of x_1, regardless of whether L prefers $x = 0$ or $x = 1$, the optimal low-discretion law will be preferred to $x = \bar{I}$ only when a is sufficiently small (i.e., legislative capacity is sufficiently high).

Assume that L prefers adopting $x = 1$ to $x = 0$. Then, since $x_0 < 0 \Rightarrow x_1 < 1$, the Bureaucrat, confronted with $x = 1$, will implement $y = 1$ if $\varepsilon = 1$ (yielding an outcome of 0) and will implement $y = x_B$ if $\varepsilon = 0$. Thus,

$EU_L(1) = -(1 - \gamma)(1 - p)x_B - (a - \frac{a}{\bar{I}}) \geq EU_L(\bar{I}) = -(1 - \gamma)x_B$ only if

$$a < (x_B + 1)p(1 - \gamma) \qquad \text{(A1.1)}$$

Assume that L prefers adopting $x = 0$ to $x = 1$. Then, if $x_1 < 0$, the Bureaucrat, when confronted with $x = 0$, will implement $y = 0$ for any ε. Thus, $EU_L(0) = -(1 - \gamma)p - a \geq EU_L(\bar{I})$ only if

$$a \leq (p - x_B)(\gamma - 1). \qquad \text{(A1.2)}$$

If $x_1 > 0$, then the outcome will be x_B whenever $\varepsilon = 1$ (because the Bureaucrat will not comply). In this case, $EU_L(0) = -(1 - \gamma)px_B - a \geq EU_L(\bar{I})$ only if

$$a \leq x_B(p - 1)(\gamma - 1). \qquad \text{(A1.3)}$$

Thus, regardless of whether the optimal low-discretion law is 0 or 1, this law will not be adopted unless a is sufficiently small.

Part (c). Let Z be the upper bound on a that satisfies

$$EU_L(x^*) \geq EU_L(\bar{I}). \tag{A2.0}$$

We show that for all values of the parameters in the model, and for any x^*, it becomes easier to satisfy (A2.0) as x_B increases and γ decreases. That is, we show that for (A1.1) through (A1.3), $\frac{\partial Z}{\partial \gamma} < 0$ and $\frac{\partial Z}{\partial x_B} > 0$.

Consider (A1.1):

$$\frac{\partial}{\partial x_B}[(x_B + 1)p(1-\gamma)] = p(1-\gamma) > 0$$

$$\frac{\partial}{\partial \gamma}[(x_B + 1)p(1-\gamma)] = p(x_B - 1) < 0.$$

Consider (A1.2):

$$\frac{\partial}{\partial x_B}[(p - x_B)(\gamma - 1)] = (1-\gamma) > 0$$

$$\frac{\partial}{\partial \gamma}[(p - x_B)(\gamma - 1)] = p - x_B < 0$$ given that [A1.2] can be satisfied only when $x_B > p$.

Consider (A1.3):

$$\frac{\partial}{\partial x_B}[x_B(p-1)(\gamma - 1)] = (1-p)(1-\gamma) > 0$$

$$\frac{\partial}{\partial \gamma}[x_B(p-1)(\gamma - 1)] = (p-1)x_B < 0.$$

Thus, it becomes easier to satisfy the conditions that lead to low-discretion laws when policy conflict increases and nonstatutory factors become more reliable. *QED*

The Veto Model

As in the Parliamentary model, we will focus on the case where $x_0 < 0$, which implies that absent a veto constraint, the Politician would choose among $x \in \{0, 1, \bar{I}\}$. In the Veto model, we introduce a President, P, and assume that P has an ideal point of x_B. As before, the Politician can choose whether to propose a policy. If she does, the President can accept or veto the policy, where a veto retains the status quo. If no veto occurs, nonstatutory factors operate as before.

For $Q < 0$, any bill that makes the Politician better off must also make the President better off, leaving the Politician unconstrained by the threat of the veto (so that all the results from the Parliamentary model remain unaffected). If $Q \in [x_L, x_B]$, then no law the Politician adopts could make both the Politician and the President better off, and thus no policy change can occur. If $Q > x_B$, then the best bill for the President, $x = \bar{I}$, yields an expected utility of $-\gamma x_B$ (because the President, by accepting a bill, exposes herself to the risk of nonstatutory factors that favor the legislature during implementation). Vetoing a bill yields $-(Q - x_B)$. The President will therefore veto any bill proposed by the Politician, including $x = \bar{I}$, if $Q \in [0, x_B(1 + \gamma)]$. Since the threat of the veto does not affect the nature of the statute when $Q < x_L$ and no law can be adopted when $Q \in [0, x_B(1 + \gamma)]$, to understand how the veto affects the *nature* of laws that are adopted, we need focus only on cases where $Q > x_B(1 + \gamma)$.

Proposition 2

For $Q > x_B(1 + \gamma)$, the theoretical results regarding legislative capacity, policy conflict between Politician and Bureaucrat, and nonstatutory factors are the same in the Veto model as in the Parliamentary model. That is, legislative capacity must be sufficient to allow the Politician to adopt the optimal constrained bill, and the likelihood that the Politician can adopt this bill in equilibrium increases as conflict between Politician and Bureaucrat increases, and decreases as nonstatutory factors become more reliable for the Politician.

Proof. The general logic of the proof is the same as in Proposition 1. We first identify the nature of the optimal constrained proposal in the Veto model. Then we show that (a) this proposal can be adopted only if capacity is sufficient and (b) the level of capacity necessary to adopt the constrained proposal declines as conflict increases, and increases as nonstatutory factors become more reliable for the Politician.

$x = 1$ *Optimal in the Parliamentary Model*

We begin by considering the case where the optimal constrained bill for the Politician, in the absence of a veto, is $x = 1$ (which is greater than x_1 by the assumption that $x_0 < 0$). What will be the Politician's optimal constrained bill when the veto constraint is added? It obviously cannot be the case that with a veto constraint, the Politician prefers a *more* constrained bill (e.g., $x < 1$), because if this were true, $x = 1$ could not have been the optimal constrained bill in the Parliamentary model. The Politician, however, may not be able to adopt $x = 1$ if the President can veto a bill. For any $x \geq x_1$, if the President signs the bill, she receives an expected utility of $-\gamma x_B - (1 - \gamma)p(x_B - x + 1)$ (because if $\varepsilon = 1$, the Bureaucrat will adopt x, yielding $x_B - x + 1$, and if $\varepsilon = 0$ the Bureaucrat will adopt x_B). If the President vetoes the bill, she receives an expected utility of $-(Q - x_B)$. Thus,

$$EU_P(accept;\, x \geq x_1) \geq EU_P(veto;\, x \geq x_1) \Rightarrow x \geq x_B + 1 + \frac{Q - x_B(1+\gamma)}{p(\gamma - 1)}.$$

Since $Q > x_B(1 + \gamma) \Rightarrow x_B + 1 + \dfrac{Q - x_B(1+\gamma)}{p(\gamma - 1)} < x_B + 1 = \bar{I}$, there always exists a constrained bill that the President will accept. If $Q \geq x_B(1 + \gamma - p(\gamma - 1))$, $x_B + 1 + \dfrac{Q - x_B(1+\gamma)}{p(\gamma - 1)} < 1$, which implies that the President will accept $x = 1$. In this case, the veto does not pose a constraint on the Politician, who can adopt the same optimal constrained bill in the Veto model that she would in the Parliamentary model. Consequently, the theoretical results from the Parliamentary model regarding legislative capacity, conflict of interest, and nonstatutory factors will be identical in the Veto and Parliamentary models.

Consider the case where $Q < x_B(1 + \gamma - p(\gamma - 1))$, which implies that $x_B + 1 + \dfrac{Q - x_B(1+\gamma)}{p(\gamma - 1)} > 1$, and thus that if the Politician adopts the optimal constrained bill from the Parliamentary model ($x = 1$), it will be vetoed. In this case, the optimal constrained bill is $\bar{v} = x_B + 1 + \dfrac{Q - x_B(1+\gamma)}{p(\gamma - 1)}$, which is chosen as the bill that minimizes the Bureaucrat's discretion without provoking a veto.

It remains to be shown that if the Politician's optimal constrained bill is $\bar{v}$, our comparative statics regarding legislative capacity, conflict of interest, and nonstatutory factors will be identical in the Veto and Parliamentary models. Since $EU_L(\bar{v}) = -(1 - \gamma)(p(\bar{v} - 1) + (1 - p)x_B) - \left(a - \dfrac{a\bar{v}}{\bar{I}}\right)$, and $EU_L(\bar{I}) = -(1 - \gamma)x_B$, we have $EU_L(\bar{v}) \geq EU_L(\bar{I})$ only if

$$a \leq (x_B + 1)p(1+\gamma). \qquad \text{(A1.4)}$$

Thus, as in all other cases, the Politician must have a minimal level of capacity in order to adopt the constrained bill. Moreoever, this is exactly the same condition that must be satisfied in the Parliamentary model when $x = 1$ is the optimal constrained proposal. Thus, the comparative statics regarding conflict of interest and nonstatutory factors are unaffected by the presence of the veto.

It is worth noting that whenever $\bar{v}$ is the optimal constrained proposal in the Veto model, the statute gives more discretion to the Bureaucrat than does the optimal constrained proposal in the Parliamentary model.

$x = 0$ *Is Optimal in the Parliamentary Model*

Next, assume that $x = 0$ is optimal in the Parliamentary model. There are two cases to consider, and we show that in both, the main theoretical predictions from the Parliamentary model (regarding legislative capacity, conflict of interest, and nonstatutory factors) carry over to the Veto model.

Case 1: $x_1 < 0$.

By assumption, the optimal unconstrained proposal by L is $x = 0$. But when a veto exists, this statute may not be acceptable to P. Consider $x \in [0, x_B]$:

$$EU_P(accept; x \in [0, x_B]) = -\gamma x_B - (1-\gamma)(p(x_B - x + 1) + (1-p)(x_B - x))$$

and

$$EU_P(veto; x \in [0, x_B]) = -(Q - x_B).$$

Thus, $EU_P(accept;\ x) \geq EU_P(veto) \Rightarrow x \geq \dfrac{Q + x_B(\gamma - 2) + p(\gamma - 1)}{(\gamma - 1)}$. Let $\bar{z} = \dfrac{Q + x_B(\gamma - 2) + p(\gamma - 1)}{(\gamma - 1)}$. We consider three possible locations of $\bar{z}$ and show that for each, the main theoretical relationships regarding capacity, conflict, and nonstatutory factors are unaffected.

(a) If $Q \geq x_B(2 - \gamma) + p(1 - \gamma)$, then $\bar{z} \leq 0$. In this case, the Politician can adopt exactly the same proposal that she would in the Parliamentary model, and the comparative static results from that model carry over to the Veto model.

(b) If $Q < x_B(2 - \gamma) + p(1 - \gamma)$, then $\bar{z} > 0$ is the best bill that the Politician can adopt that will not be vetoed. There are three subcases to consider.

Subcase (i). If $\bar{z} \in (0, x_B)$, then $EU_L(x = \bar{z}) = -(1 - \gamma)(p(1 - x) + (1 - p)x) - \left(a - \frac{ax}{\bar{I}}\right) \geq EU_L(\bar{I})$ only if

$$a \leq -\frac{(x_B + 1)(x_B - x + p(2x-1))(\gamma - 1)}{x_B + 1 - x}. \tag{A1.5}$$

Thus, an optimal constrained proposal will be adopted only when legislative capacity is sufficiently high. Note that $a \geq 0$ requires the right-hand side of the preceding expression to be positive, it must be true that $(x_B - x + p(2x - 1)) \geq 0$ or that $x \leq \frac{p - x_B}{2p - 1}$ (which can be satisfied only if $p < x_B$ given $p < \frac{1}{2}$ is necessary for L to prefer $x = \bar{z}$ to $x = 1$).

To see the effect of nonstatutory factors on incentives to adopt the constrained bill, note that $\frac{\partial}{\partial \gamma}\left[-\frac{(x_B + 1)(x_B - x + p(2x-1))(\gamma - 1)}{x_B + 1 - x}\right] = -\frac{(x_B + 1)(x_B - x + p(2x-1))}{x_B + 1 - x} < 0$ only if $(x_B - x + p(2x - 1)) > 0$. This expression is satisfied whenever $x \leq \frac{p - x_B}{2p - 1}$, which (as noted previously) must be true for $\bar{z}$ to be preferred by L to $\bar{I}$.

To see the effect of conflict between the Legislature and the President (or Bureaucrat) on incentives to adopt the constrained bill, note that

$$\frac{\partial}{\partial x_B}\left[-\frac{(x_B + 1)(x_B - x + p(2x-1))(\gamma - 1)}{x_B + 1 - x}\right] = -\frac{\left(1 + x_B^2 - 2x_B(x - 1) + x(p - 1) + x^2(1 - 2p)\right)(\gamma - 1)}{(x_B + 1 - x)^2}.$$

This derivative is positive only if $1 + x_B^2 - 2x_B(x - 1) + x(p - 1) + x^2(1 - 2p) > 0$, which is always true. (One easy way to see this is to expand this expression, which yields $1 + x_B^2 - 2x_Bx + 2x_B + xp - x + x^2 - 2px$. Since $1 - x > 0$ and $2x_B - 2x_Bx > 0$, the entire expression is positive if $x_B^2 + px + x^2 > 2px^2$, or if $x_B^2x^2 > 2px^2 - px$. Since $2px^2 - px = px(2px - 1) < 0$, it is always true that $x_B^2 + px + x^2 > 2px^2$, and thus that $\frac{\partial}{\partial x_B} > 0$.)

Subcase (ii). If $\bar{z} \in [x_B,1]$, then $EU_L(x \in [x_B,1] = -(1-\gamma)(p(1-x)+(1-p)x_B) - \left(a - \frac{ax}{\bar{I}}\right) > EU_L(\bar{I})$ only if

$$a < -\frac{p(x_B+1)(x_B+x-1)(\gamma-1)}{x_B+1-x}. \tag{A1.6}$$

Note that the right-hand side of this expression is positive only if $x_B + x - 1 > 0$.

For the comparative statics, we have

$$\frac{\partial}{\partial x_B}\left[-\frac{p(x_B+1)(x_B+x-1)(\gamma-1)}{x_B+1-x}\right] = \frac{-p\left((x_B+x-1)^2+2x(1-x)\right)(\gamma-1)}{(x_B+1-x)^2} > 0$$

and $\frac{\partial}{\partial \gamma}\left[-\frac{p(x_B+1)(x_B+x-1)(\gamma-1)}{x_B+1-x}\right] = -\frac{p(x_B+1)(x_B+x-1)}{x_B+1-x} < 0$ Thus, it becomes easier to satisfy the necessary condition for a constrained statute as professionalism increases, and becomes more difficult as nonstatutory factors become more reliable.

Subcase (iii). If $Q < x_B + p(1 - \gamma)$, then $\bar{z} > 1$ and the comparative statics are identical to those in equation (A1.4).

Case 2: $x_1 > 0$.

There are two subcases to consider.

Subcase (i): $x_B < x_1$.

Assume that Q is located such that $x \in [0,x_B]$ could be adopted without a veto. Then $EU_L(x \in [0,x_B]) = -(1 - \gamma)(px_B + (1 - p)x) - \left(a - \frac{ax}{\bar{I}}\right) > EU_L(\bar{I})$ only if

$$a < \frac{(p-1)(x_B+1)(x_B-x)(\gamma-1)}{x_B+1-x}. \tag{A1.7}$$

For the comparative statics, we have $\frac{\partial}{\partial x_B}\left[\frac{(p-1)(x_B+1)(x_B-x)(\gamma-1)}{x_B+1-x}\right]$
$=\frac{(p-1)\left((x_B-x)^2+(2x_B-x+1)\right)(\gamma-1)}{(x_B+1-x)^2}>0$ and
$\frac{\partial}{\partial\gamma}\left[\frac{(p-1)(x_B+1)(x_B-x)(\gamma-1)}{x_B+1-x}\right]=\frac{(x_B+1)(p-1)(x_B-x)}{x_B+1-x}<0$, as needed.

Assume that Q is located such that the best proposal that can avoid a veto is $x\in[x_B,x_1)$. Then the outcome will be x_B for any ε (because if $\varepsilon = 1$ the Bureaucrat will not comply with the law, and if $\varepsilon = 0$ the Bureaucrat can adopt his ideal policy). Such bills therefore cannot be adopted in equilibrium.

Assume that Q is located such that the best proposal that can avoid a veto is $x\in[x_1,1]$. Then $EU_L(x) = -(1-\gamma)(p(1-x)+(1-p)x_B) - \left(a-\frac{ax}{\bar{I}}\right)$. This case has already been analyzed (see equation A1.6).

Similarly, we have covered the case where Q is located such that the best proposal that can avoid a veto is $x > 1$ (equation A1.4).

Subcase (ii): $x_1 < x_B$.

This case has been covered for all possible values of Q. If Q implies that $x\in[0,x_1)$ is the best feasible bill that avoids a veto, then when nonstatutory factors do not alter the Bureaucrat's policy, the expected policy outcome is $px_B + (1-p)x$ (which is covered by equation A1.7). If Q implies that $x\in[x_1,x_B]$, the expected policy outcome is $p(1-x) + (1-p)x$ (which is covered by equation A1.5). If Q implies that $x\in[x_B,1]$ is the best feasible bill that avoids a veto, then when nonstatutory factors do not alter the Bureaucrat's policy, the expected policy outcome is $p(1-x) + (1-p)x_B$ (which is covered by equation A1.6). Finally, if Q implies that $x > 1$ is the best feasible bill that avoids a veto, then when nonstatutory factors do not alter the Bureaucrat's policy, the expected policy outcome is $p(x-1) + (1-p)x_B$ (which is covered by equation A1.7). *QED*

Corollary to Propositions 1 and 2

The existence of a veto can increase the amount of discretion in a bill, but cannot decrease it.

The Bicameral Model

We now extend the model to a case where two chambers of the legislature, each with different preferences (i.e., a different median voter), must agree in order for a law to be adopted. We assume that one of these chambers shares the preferences of the executive, and thus of the Bureaucrat. We call this chamber L_B and assume that its ideal point is x_B. L_B therefore has a most preferred policy of $\bar{I}$. We might think of L_B as a legislative chamber that shares the preferences of the executive (e.g., the governor) when a divided legislature exists. Since this chamber has to agree for any policy to be adopted, we do not include a formal veto stage. We assume that the other chamber has the same preferences as the Politician in our previous analyses. We call this chamber L_0, and assume that it has an ideal point at zero (as before) and thus an optimal law of ε. We assume that neither of these chambers knows ε when making a proposal; rather, they share the prior belief p that $\varepsilon = 1$.

One player is exogenously chosen to propose a bill. If he does so, he pays the standard costs associated with this proposal. The other Politician then either accepts the bill or makes a counterproposal. If she accepts the bill, then it becomes law and the Bureaucrat acts as in the unilateral game. If a counterproposal is made, the initial proposer can either accept or reject it. If she accepts, the Bureaucrat then implements a policy as before. If she rejects the bill, we assume that action on this issue ends and the status quo prevails.

As is standard in such bargaining models, we assume that delay in reaching an agreement is costly to the two chambers. For consistency with the Veto model, we assume that the first proposal is "free." If a counterproposal is made, then the value of the game is discounted. To capture this formally, we assume that there exist finite legislative resources, normalized to equal 1. If a second legislative proposal is made, the value of these legislative resources is discounted by $\delta \in (0,1)$. We assume that the two players have a common discount factor. Thus, if both Politicians make policy proposals that are rejected, then each player's utility is given by

$$\delta + u_i(Q) - k_i,$$

where k_i is the cost associated with player i's own proposal (and is defined the same way as before) and $u_i(Q)$ is the utility to player i of Q. Finally, if a policy is adopted, the Bureaucrat implements a policy and nonstatutory factors operate in the same fashion as previously described.

The main intuition from this model is that interinstitutional conflict can never lead to less discretion than we find in the Veto model and can lead to more discretion.

Proposition 3

When bicameral bargaining is necessary, the level of discretion in statutes that are adopted is never less than we find in the Veto model and often is more.

The logic of proposition 3 is very straightforward, and we do not offer a detailed proof. In the model, both players can exercise a veto by refusing to accept a policy that the other chamber has offered. Thus, in equilibrium L_B cannot accept any bill that gives less discretion than in the Veto model. And since L_B always prefers more discretion than L_0, L_B will never propose a statute that gives less discretion than what is optimal for L_0 in the Veto model.

There exist numerous situations, however, where the costs of bargaining can be extracted by L_B from L_0 in the form of greater discretion in statutes, leading to an equilibrium level of discretion that is larger in the Bicameral model than with a simple veto. We provide an example under the assumption that L_0 makes the first policy proposal. An identical logic is at work when L_B makes the first policy proposal.

When L_0 makes the first policy proposal, L_B must decide whether to make a counterproposal, which requires paying the cost of a proposal (k_B) and which consumes $1 - \delta$ of the legislative resources. To make the example simple, assume that both players know that $\varepsilon = 0$, that a is sufficiently small so that L could adopt $x = 0$ in the Veto model, and that $x_B^* = x_B$ is the best counterproposal that L_B can make that is accepted. (L_B obviously cannot prefer making a rejected proposal, which creates costs but no benefits.) Then $EU_{L_B}(x^*;x^0) = \delta - \gamma x_B - k_B$.

Similarly, accepting L_0's original proposal, $x^0 < x_B$, yields $EU_{L_B}(accept; x^B) = 1 - \gamma x_B - (1 - \gamma)(x_B - x^0)$. In this case, L_B will accept any $x^0 \geq x_B + \dfrac{\delta - k_B - 1}{(1-\gamma)}$. Note that if $x_B \leq \dfrac{k_B + 1 - \delta}{1-\gamma}$, then bicameral bargaining has no effect on the outcome because $x_B + \dfrac{\delta - k_B - 1}{1-\gamma} \leq 0$, implying that L_0 can obtain her preferred statute, $x = 0$. But if conflict between the two chambers is sufficiently large, so that $x_B > \dfrac{k_B + 1 - \delta}{1-\gamma}$, then the best proposal that L_0 can make is $x^0 > 0$ (implying more discretion than we find in the Veto model). Since the optimal bill that L_0 can adopt increases with x_B, there will reach a point where L_0's best strategy is simply to propose $x = \bar{I}$. Thus, as this example illustrates, there are many cases where the bargaining costs of delay allow the privileged chamber (which shares the preferences of the Bureaucrat) to extract concessions from the other chamber (in the form of increased discretion).

References

Aberbach, Joel D. 1990. *Keeping a Watchful Eye: The Politics of Congressional Oversight*. Washington, DC: Brookings Institution.

Aberbach, Joel D., Robert D. Putnam, and Bert A. Rockman. 1981. *Bureaucrats and Politicians in Western Democracies*. Cambridge, MA: Harvard University Press.

Anderson, Christopher J. 2000. "Economic Voting and Political Context: A Comparative Perspective." *Electoral Studies* 19(2–3): 151–170.

Andeweg, Rudy B. 2000. "Ministers as Double Agents? The Delegation Process Between Cabinet and Ministers." *European Journal of Political Research* 37(3): 377–395.

Aranson, Peter, Ernest Gellhorn, and Glen Robinson. 1982. "A Theory of Legislative Delegation." *Cornell Law Review* 68: 55–63.

Arnold, R. Douglas. 1979. *Congress and the Bureaucracy*. New Haven, CT: Yale University Press.

1987. "Political Control of Administrative Officials." *Journal of Law, Economics, and Organization* 3: 279–286.

1990. *The Logic of Congressional Action*. New Haven, CT: Yale University Press.

Balla, Steven J. 1998. "Administrative Procedures and Political Control of the Bureaucracy." *American Political Science Review* 92(3): 663–673.

2000. "Legislative Organization and Congressional Review of Agency Regulations." *Journal of Law, Economics, and Organization* 16(2): 424–448.

Balla, Steven J., and John R. Wright. 2001. "Interest Groups, Advisory Committees, and Congressional Control of the Bureaucracy." *American Journal of Political Science* 45(4): 799–812.

Barker, Anthony, and Graham K. Wilson. 1997. "Whitehall's Disobedient Servants? Senior Officials' Potential Resistance to Ministers in British Government Departments." *British Journal of Political Science* 27(12): 223–246.

Baron, David P., and John A. Ferejohn. 1989. "Bargaining in Legislatures." *American Political Science Review* 83(4): 1181–1206.

Barzelay, Michael. 1997. "Central Audit Institutions and Performance Auditing: A Comparative Analysis of Organizational Strategies in the OECD." *Governance* 10: 235–260.

Bawn, Kathleen. 1995. "Political Control versus Expertise: Congressional Choices about Administrative Procedures." *American Political Science Review* 89: 62–73.
1997. "Choosing Strategies to Control the Bureaucracy: Statutory Constraints, Oversight, and the Committee System." *Journal of Law, Economics, and Organization* 13: 101–126.
1999. "Money and Majorities in the Federal Republic of Germany: Evidence for a Veto Player's Model of Government Spending." *American Journal of Political Science* 43(3): 707–736.
Bendor, Jonathan. 1988. "Review Article: Formal Models of Bureaucracy." *British Journal of Political Science* 18: 353–395.
1990. "Formal Models of Bureaucracy: A Review" in Naomi B. Lynn and Aaron Wildavsky (eds.), *Public Administration: The State of the Discipline*. Chatham, NJ: Chatham House Publishers (pp. 373–417).
Bendor, Jonathan, Ami Glazer, and Thomas Hammond. 2000. "Theories of Delegation." *Annual Review of Political Science* 4: 235–269.
Bendor, Jonathan, Serge Taylor, and Roland Van Gaalen. 1987. "Politicians, Bureaucrats, and Asymmetric Information." *American Journal of Political Science* 31: 796–828.
Benn, Anthony. 1990. *Conflicts of Interest: Diaries 1977–80*. Edited by R. Winstone. London: Hutchinson.
Bennett, Colin J. 1997. "Understanding Ripple Effects: The Cross-National Adoption of Policy Instruments for Bureaucratic Accountability." *Governance* 10(3): 213–228.
Berard, Stanley P. 2001. *Southern Democrats in the U.S. House of Representatives*. Norman: University of Oklahoma Press.
Bernhard, William. 1998. "A Political Explanation of Variations in Central Bank Independence." *American Political Science Review* 92(2): 311–327.
Beyle, Thad. 1999. "The Governors." In Virginia Gray, Russell L. Hanson, and Herbert Jacob (eds.), *Politics in the American States: A Comparative Analysis*, 7th ed. Washington, DC: CQ Press (pp. 191–231).
Bibby, John F., and Thomas M. Holbrook. 1999. "Parties and Elections." In Virginia Gray, Russell L. Hanson, and Herbert Jacob, (eds.), *Politics in the American States: A Comparative Analysis*, 7th ed. Washington, DC: CQ Press (pp. 66–112).
Black, Earl. 1987. *Politics and Society in the South*. Cambridge, MA: Harvard University Press.
Borcherding, T. E. (ed.). 1977. *Budgets and Bureaucrats: The Sources of Governmental Growth*. Durham, NC: Duke University Press.
Boylan, Delia. 2000. "Bureaucratic Delegation in Comparative Perspective: Constitutional Structure and Reform Timing." Manuscript, University of Chicago.
Bridge, John. 1981. "National Legal Tradition and Community Law: Legislative Drafting and Judicial Interpretation in England and the European Community." *Journal of Common Market Studies* 19(4): 351–376.
Budge, Ian, Richard I. Hofferbert, and Hans-Dieter Klingemann. 1994. *Parties, Policies, and Democracy*. Boulder, CO: Westview Press.

References

Canes-Wrone, Brandice. 2000. "Bureaucratic Decisions and the Composition of the Lower Courts." Manuscript, MIT.

Cappelletti, Mauro. 1981. "The Doctrine of Stare Decisis and the Civil Law: A Fundamental Difference – or No Difference at All?" In Herbert Bernstein, Ulrich Drobning, and Hein Kötz (eds.), *Festschrift für Konrad Zweigert*. Tübingen: J. C. B. Mohr (pp. 381–393).

Carey, John M., Richard G. Niemi, and Lynda Powell. 2000. *Term Limits in the State Legislatures*. Ann Arbor: University of Michigan Press.

Carey, John M., and Matthew Soberg Shugart. 1998a. "Calling Out the Tanks or Filling in the Forms?" In John M. Carey and Matthew Soberg Shugart (eds.), *Executive Decree Authority*. Cambridge: Cambridge University Press (pp. 1–29).

1998b. "Institutional Design and Executive Decree." In John M. Carey and Matthew Soberg Shugart (eds.), *Executive Decree Authority*. Cambridge: Cambridge University Press (pp. 274–298).

Carter, Larry E., and James T. LaPlant. 1998. "Diffusion of Health Care Policy Innovation in the United States." *State and Local Government Review* 29: 17–26.

Carter, Neil, and Patricia Greer. 1993. "Evaluating Agencies: Next Steps and Performance Indicators." *Public Administration* 71 (Autumn): 407–416.

Chang, Kelly H., Rui J. P. de Figueiredo, Jr., and Barry R. Weingast. 2000. "Rational Choice Theories of Bureaucratic Control and Performance." In William F. Shughart II and Laura Razzolini, *The Elgar Companion to Public Choice*. Cheltenham: Edward Elgar Press (pp. 271–292).

Clark, W. 1998. "The Modernization of the French Civil Service: Crisis, Change, and Continuity." *Public Administration* 76: 96–115.

Clarke, Wes. 1998. "Divided Government and Budgetary Conflict." *Legislative Studies Quarterly* 23: 5–23.

Congressional Research Service. 1993. *Medicaid Source Book: Background Data and Analysis*. Washington, DC: Government Printing Office.

Cox, Gary. 1987. *The Efficient Secret*. New York: Cambridge University Press.

Crozier, Michael. 1964. *The Bureaucratic Phenomenon*. Chicago: University of Chicago Press.

Crozier, Michael, S. P. Huntington, and J. Watanuk. 1975. *The Crisis of Democracy*. New York: New York University Press.

Dainow, Joseph. 1967. "The Civil and the Common Law: Some Points of Comparison." *American Journal of Comparative Law* 15: 419–435.

David, R., and J. E. C. Brierley. 1978. *Major Legal Systems of the World Today*, 2nd ed. London: Stevens.

de Figueiredo, Rui J. 1997. "Political Uncertainty and Policy Insulation: Testing the Formal Theory with State Line-Item Veto Adoption." Manuscript, University of California at Berkeley.

1998. "Electoral Competition, Political Uncertainty, and Policy Insulation." Manuscript, University of California at Berkeley.

Debbasch, Charles. 1969. *L'administration au pouvoir: fonctionnaires et politiques sous la Ve Republique*. Paris: Calmann-Lévy.

Derlien, H.-U. 1988. "Reprecussions of Government Change on the Career Civil Service in West Germany: The Cases of 1969 and 1982." *Governance* 1: 50–78.

Di Palma, Giuseppe. 1977. *Surviving without Governing: The Italian Parties in Parliament*. Berkeley: University of California Press.

Diermeier, Daniel, and Timothy Feddersen. 1998. "Cohesion in Legislatures and the Vote of Confidence Procedure." *American Political Science Review* 92(3): 611–622.

Dixit, Avinash K. 1996. *The Making of Economic Policy: A Transaction-Cost Politics Perspective*. Cambridge, MA: MIT Press.

1997. "Power of Incentives in Private versus Public Organizations." *American Economic Review, Papers and Proceedings* 87(2): 378–382.

Dodd, Lawrence C., and Richard L. Schott. 1986. *Congress and the Administrative State*. New York: Macmillan.

Dogan, Mattei. 1975. "The Political Power of the Western Mandarins: Introduction." In Mattei Dogan (ed.), *The Mandarins of Western Europe: The Political Role of Top Civil Servants*. New York: Wiley (pp. 3–24).

1989. "Irremovable Leaders and Ministerial Instability in European Democracies." In Mattei Dogan (ed.), *Pathways to Power: Selecting Rulers in Pluralist Democracies*. Boulder, CO: Westview Press (pp. 239–275).

Dowding, Keith. 1995. *The Civil Service*. London: Routledge.

Drotning, Lucy. 1993. "An Alternative Approach to Congressional Control: The Case of the 1990 Clean Air Act Amendments." Ph.D. dissertation, University of Rochester.

Drotning, Lucy, and Lawrence S. Rothenberg. 1999. "Predicting Bureaucratic Control: Evidence from the 1990 Clean Air Act Amendments." *Law and Policy* 21(1): 1–20.

Dunleavy, Patrick. 1991. *Democracy, Bureaucracy and Public Choice*. New York: Prentice Hall.

Efficiency Unit. 1988. *Improving Management in Government: The Next Steps*. London: HMSO.

Eisenstadt, Samuel N. 1965. *Essays on Comparative Institutions*. New York: Wiley.

Elazar, Daniel J. 1984. *American Federalism: A View from the States*, 3d ed. New York: Harper & Row.

Epstein, David, and Sharyn O'Halloran. 1994. "Administrative Procedures, Information, and Agency Discretion." *American Journal of Political Science* 38: 697–722.

1996. "Divided Government and the Design of Administrative Procedures: A Formal Model and Empirical Test." *Journal of Politics* 58: 373–397.

1999. *Delegating Powers: A Transaction Cost Politics Approach to Policymaking Under Separate Powers*. Cambridge: Cambridge University Press.

Epstein, Leon D. 1980. *Political Parties in Western Democracies*. New Brunswick, NJ: Transaction Books.

Erikson, Robert S., Gerald C. Wright, and John P. McIver. 1993. *Statehouse Democracy: Public Opinion and Policy in the American States*. Cambridge: Cambridge University Press.

References

Ethridge, Marcus E. 1981. "Legislative–Administrative Interaction as 'Intrusive Access': An Empirical Analysis." *Journal of Politics* 43: 473–492.

1984. "Consequences of Legislative Review of Agency Regulations in Three U.S. States." Legislative Studies Quarterly 9(1): 161–178.

Etzioni-Halevy, Eva. 1983. *Bureaucracy and Democracy: A Political Dilemma*. London: Routledge & Kegan Paul.

Fairgieve, Bill. 1995. "Fiscal Focus. Medicaid: An Overview." Michigan House Fiscal Agency, April 1995.

Ferejohn, John A. 1974. *Pork Barrel Politics*. Stanford, CA: Stanford University Press.

1987. "The Structure of Agency Decision Processes." In Mathew D. McCubbins and Terry Sullivan (eds.), *Congress: Structure and Policy*. Cambridge: Cambridge University Press (pp. 441–461).

Ferejohn, John, and Charles R. Shipan. 1989a. "Congress and Telecommunications Policymaking." In Paula R. Newberg (ed.), *New Directions in Telecommunications Policy*, vol. 1. Durham, NC: Duke University Press (pp. 301–314).

1989b. "Congressional Influence on Administrative Agencies: A Case Study of Telecommunications Policy." In Lawrence C. Dodd and Bruce I. Oppenheimer (eds.), *Congress Reconsidered*, 4th ed. Washington, DC: CQ Press (pp. 393–410).

1990. "Congressional Influence on Bureaucracy." *Journal of Law, Economics, and Organization* 6: 1–20.

Fiorina, Morris P. 1981. "Congressional Control of the Bureaucracy: A Mismatch of Incentives and Capabilities." In Lawrence Dodd and Bruce Oppenheimer (eds.), *Congress Reconsidered*, 2d ed. Washington, DC: CQ Press (pp. 332–348).

1982. "Legislative Choice of Regulatory Forms: Legal Process of Administrative Process?" *Public Choice* 39: 33–66.

Franchino, Fabio. 2000a. "Commission's Executive Discretion, Information and Comitology." *Journal of Theoretical Politics* 12(2): 155–181.

2000b. "Control of the Commission's Executive Functions: Uncertainty, Conflict and Decision Rules." *European Union Politics* 1(1): 63–92.

Friedrich, Robert J. 1982. "In Defense of Multiplicative Terms in Multiple Regression Equations." *American Journal of Political Science* 26(4): 797–833.

Fry, Geoffrey K. 1997. "The Conservatives and the Civil Service: 'One Step Forward, Two Steps Back?'" *Public Administration* 75(Winter): 695–710.

Garrett, Geoffrey. 1998. *Partisan Politics in the Global Economy*. New York: Cambridge University Press.

Gerlach, Peter. 1992. "A Farewell to Corporatism." In Kurt Richard Luther and Wolfgang Müller (eds.), *Politics in Austria*. London: Frank Cass (pp. 132–146).

Gill, Jeff. 1995. "Formal Models of Legislative/Administrative Interaction: A Survey of the Subfield." *Public Administration Review* 55(1): 99–106.

Golden, Miriam A. 2000. "Political Patronage, Bureaucracy, and Corruption in Postwar Italy." Russell Sage Foundation: Working Paper #162.

Goodhart, Lucy. 2001. "Complex Coalitions or Clever Voters? The Mediating Effect of Coalition Government on Economic Voting." Typescript. Columbia University.

Goodnow, Frank J. 1900. *Politics and Administration: A Study in Government*. New York: Russell and Russell.

Gruber, Judith E. 1987. *Controlling Bureaucracies: Dilemmas in Democratic Governance*. Berkeley: University of California Press.

Gulick, Luther, and Lyndall Urwick. 1937. *Papers on the Science of Administration*. New York: Institute of Public Administration.

Hall, Peter. 1983. "Policy Innovation and the Structure of the State: The Politics–Administration Nexus in Britain and France." *Annals* 466: 43–59.

1986. *Governing the Economy*. New York: Oxford University Press.

Hamilton, James T., and Christopher H. Schroeder. 1994. "Strategic Regulators and the Choice of Rulemaking Procedures: The Selection of Formal vs. Informal Rules in Regulating Hazardous Waste." *Law and Contemporary Problems* 57: 111–160.

Hamm, Keith, and Roby D. Robertson. 1981. "Factors Influencing the Adoption of New Methods of Legislative Oversight in the U.S. States." *Legislative Studies Quarterly* 6: 133–150.

Hammond, Thomas H., and Jack H. Knott. 1996. "Who Controls the Bureaucracy?: Presidential Power, Congressional Dominance, Legal Constraints, and Bureaucratic Autonomy in a Model of Multi-Institutional Policy-Making." *Journal of Law, Economics, and Organization* 12: 119–166.

Hanf, K., and C. Hull. 1982. "The Implementation of Regulatory Policy: Enforcement as Bargaining." *European Journal of Political Research* 10: 159–172.

Hanf, K., and T. A. J. Toonen. 1985. *Policy Implementation in Federal and Unitary Systems*. Dodrecht: Martinus Nijhoff.

Headey, Bruce. 1974. *British Cabinet Ministers*. London: Allen and Unwin.

Health Care Financing Administration. 2000. A Profile of Medicaid: Chartbook 2000. Available at http://www.hcfa.gov/stats/2Tchartbk.pdf.

Heclo, H. 1974. *Modern Social Politics in Britain and Sweden*. New Haven, CT: Yale University Press.

Hennessy, Peter. 1989. *Whitehall*. London: Secker and Warburg.

Hibbs, Douglas. 1977. "Political Parties and Macroeconomic Policy." *American Political Science Review* 71: 1467–1487.

Hicks, Alexander M., and Duane H. Swank. 1992. "Politics, Institutions, and Welfare Spending in Industrialized Democracies, 1960–82." *American Political Science Review* 86(3): 658–674.

Hill, Jeffrey S., and James E. Brazier. 1991. "Constraining Administrative Decisions: A Critical Examination of the Structure and Process Hypothesis." *Journal of Law, Economics, and Organization* 7: 373–400.

Hoggett, Paul. 1996. "New Modes of Control on Public Service." *Public Administration* 74 (Spring): 9–32.

Hood, M. V., III, Quentin Kidd, and Irwin L. Morris. 1999. "Of Byrd[s] and Bumpers: Using Democratic Senators to Analyze Political Change in the South, 1960–1995." *American Journal of Political Science* 43: 465–487.

Horn, Murray J. 1995. *The Political Economy of Public Administration*. New York: Cambridge University Press.

References

Horn, Murray J., and Kenneth A. Shepsle. 1989. "Commentary on 'Administrative Arrangements and the Political Control of Agencies': Administrative Process and Organizational Form as Legislative Responses to Agency Costs." *Virginia Law Review* 75: 499–508.

Huber, John. D. 1996. *Rationalizing Parliament: Legislative Institutions and Party Politics in France*. New York: Cambridge University Press.

1998. "How Does Cabinet Instability Affect Political Performance?: Credible Commitment, Information, and Health Care Cost Containment in Parliamentary Politics." *American Political Science Review* 92(3): 577–592.

Huber, John. D., and Ronald Inglehart. 1995. "Expert Interpretations of Party Space and Party Locations in 42 Societies." *Party Politics* 1(1): 73–111.

Huber, John. D., and Arthur Lupia. 2001. "Cabinet Instability and Delegation in Parliamentary Democracies." *American Journal of Political Science* 45(1): 18–33.

Huber, John D., and Nolan McCarty. 2001. "Legislative Organization, Bureaucratic Capacity and Delegation in Latin American Democracies." Manuscript. Columbia University.

Huber, John D., and Charles R. Shipan. 2000. "The Costs of Control: Legislators, Agencies, and Transaction Costs." *Legislative Studies Quarterly* 25(1): 25–52.

Huber, John D., Charles R. Shipan, and Madelaine Pfahler. 2001. "Legislatures and Statutory Control of Bureaucracy." *American Journal of Political Science* 45(2): 330–345.

Iversen, Torben. 1999. *Contested Economic Institutions*. New York: Cambridge University Press.

Jackman, Robert. 1980. "Socialist Parties and Income Inequality in Western Democracies." *Journal of Politics* 42: 135–149.

Janoski, Thomas. 1994. "Direct State Intervention in the Labor Market: The Explanation of Active Labor Market Policy from 1950 to 1988 in Social Democratic, Conservative, and Liberal Regimes." In Thomas Janoski and Alexander M. Hicks (eds.), *The Comparative Political Economy of the Welfare State*. New York: Cambridge University Press (pp. 54–92).

Johnson, Chalmers A. 1995. *Japan, Who Governs?: The Rise of the Developmental State*. New York: W. W. Norton.

Katzmann, Robert A. 1980. *Regulatory Bureaucracy: The Federal Trade Commission and Antitrust Policy*. Cambridge, MA: MIT Press.

Kaufman, Herbert. 1956. "Emerging Conflicts in the Doctrines of Public Administration." *American Political Science Review* 50: 1057–1073.

Kellner, P., and Lord Crowther-Hunt. 1980. *The Civil Servants: An Inquiry into Britain's Ruling Class*. London: MacDonald.

Kerwin, Cornelius M. 1999. *Rulemaking: How Government Agencies Write Law and Make Policy*, 2nd ed. Washington, DC: CQ Press.

Kessler, M.-C. 1978. *La Politique de la Haut Fonction Publique*. Paris: Presses de la Fondation Nationale des Sciences Politiques.

Kiewiet, D. Roderick, and Mathew D. McCubbins. 1988. "Presidential Influence on Congressional Appropriations Decisions." *American Journal of Political Science* 32: 713–736.

1991. *The Logic of Delegation*. Chicago: University of Chicago Press.

King, Anthony. 1975. "Overload: The Problem of Governing in the 1970s." *Political Studies* 23: 284–296.

1994. "Ministerial Autonomy in Britain." In Michael Laver and Kenneth Shepsle (eds.), *Cabinet Ministers and Parliamentary Government*. New York: Cambridge University Press (pp. 203–235).

Kitschelt, Herbert, Peter Lange, Gary Marks, and John Stephens. 1999. *Continuity and Change in Contemporary Capitalism*. New York: Cambridge University Press.

Knott, Jack, and Gary Miller. 1987. *Reforming Bureaucracy: The Politics of Institutional Choice*. Englewood Cliffs, NJ: Prentice-Hall.

Krause, George A. 1999. *A Two-Way Street: The Institutional Dynamics of the Modern Administrative State*. Pittsburgh: University of Pittsburgh Press.

Kubota, Akira. 1969. *Higher Civil Servants in Post-War Japan*. Princeton, NJ: Princeton University Press.

Lapalombara, Joseph. 1958. "Political Party Systems and Crisis Government: French and Italian Comparisons." *Midwest Journal of Political Science* 2(2): 117–142.

Laver, Michael, and W. Ben Hunt. 1992. *Policy and Party Competition*. New York: Routledge.

Laver, Michael, and Norman Schofield. 1990. *Multiparty Government: The Politics of Coalition in Europe*. Oxford: Oxford University Press.

Laver, Michael, and Kenneth Shepsle. 1990. "Coalitions and Cabinet Government." *American Political Science Review* 84: 873–890.

(eds). 1994. *Cabinet Ministers and Parliamentary Government*. New York: Cambridge University Press.

1996. *Making and Breaking Governments: Cabinets and Legislatures in Parliamentary Democracies*. New York: Cambridge University Press.

Leichter, Howard M. 1996. "State Governments and Their Capacity for Health Care Reform." In Robert F. Rich and William D. White (eds.), *Health Policy, Federalism, and the American State*. Washington, DC: Urban Institute.

Lewis-Beck, Michael S. 1977. "Influence Equality and Organizational Innovation in a Third World Nation: An Additive-Nonadditive Model." *American Journal of Political Science* 21(1): 1–11.

Lijphart, Arend. 1999. *Patterns of Democracy: Government Forms and Performance in Thirty-Six Countries*. New Haven, CT: Yale University Press.

Linder, S. H., and B. G. Peters. 1987. "A Design Perspective on Implementation Research: The Fallacy of Misplaced Precision." *Journal of Public Policy* 4: 237–259.

Lipsky, M. 1980. *Street-Level Bureaucracy: Dilemmas of the Individual in Public Services*. New York: Russell Sage Foundation.

Lowi, Theodore J. 1969. *The End of Liberalism: Ideology, Policy, and the Crisis of Public Authority*. New York: W. W. Norton.

1979. *The End of Liberalism: The Second Republic of the United States*, 2nd ed. New York: W. W. Norton.

References

Lupia, Arthur, and Mathew D. McCubbins. 1994. "Learning from Oversight: Fire Alarms and Police Patrols Reconstructed." *Journal of Law, Economics, and Organization* 10: 96–125.

1998. *The Democratic Dilemma: Can Citizens Learn What They Need to Know?* New York: Cambridge University Press.

Lutz, Donald S. 1994. "Toward a Theory of Constitutional Amendment." *American Political Science Review* 88(2): 355–370.

Lynn, Jonathan, and Antony Jay (eds.). 1984. *The Complete Yes Minister: Diaries of a Cabinet Minister by the Right Hon. James Hacker, MP.* Topsfield, MA: Salem House.

Macey, Jonathan R. 1992a. "Organizational Design and Political Control of Administrative Agencies." *Journal of Law, Economics, and Organization* 8: 93–110.

1992b. "Separated Powers and Positive Political Theory: The Tug of War over Administrative Agencies." *Georgetown Law Journal* 80(3): 671–703.

Martin, Elizabeth M. 1997. "An Informational Theory of the Legislative Veto." *Journal of Law, Economics, and Organization* 13: 319–343.

Martin, Lanny W., and Randolph T. Stevenson. 2001. "Government Formation in Parliamentary Democracies." *American Journal of Political Science* 45(1): 33–50.

Marx, F. M. 1957. *The Administrative State: An Introduction to Bureaucracy.* Chicago: Rand McNally.

Mashaw, Jerry L. 1985. "Prodelegation: Why Adminstrators Should Make Political Decisions." *Journal of Law, Economics, and Organization* 1: 81–100.

1997. *Greed, Chaos, and Governance.* New Haven, CT: Yale University Press.

Mayntz, R., and H. U. Derlien. 1989. "Party Patronage and Politicization of the West German Administrative Elite 1970–87 – Toward Hybridization?" *Governance* 2(4): 384–404.

McCarty, Nolan, and Rose Razaghian. 1999. "Advice and Consent: Senate Responses to Executive Branch Nominations, 1885–1996." *American Journal of Political Science* 43(4): 1122–1193.

McConnell, Grant. 1966. *Private Power and American Democracy.* New York: Alfred A. Knopf.

McCubbins, Mathew D. 1985. "Legislative Design of Regulatory Structure." *American Journal of Political Science* 29: 721–748.

McCubbins, Mathew D., Roger G. Noll, and Barry R. Weingast. 1987. "Administrative Procedures as Instruments of Political Control." *Journal of Law, Economics, and Organization* 3(2): 243–277.

1989. "Structure and Process, Politics and Policy: Administrative Arrangements and the Political Control of Agencies." *Virginia Law Review* 75: 431–482.

McCubbins, Mathew D., and Talbot Page. 1987. "A Theory of Congressional Delegation." In Mathew D. McCubbins and Terry Sullivan (eds.), *Congress: Structure and Policy.* Cambridge: Cambridge University Press (pp. 409–425).

McCubbins, Mathew D., and Thomas Schwartz. 1984. "Congressional Oversight Overlooked: Policy Patrols v. Fire Alarms." *American Journal of Political Science* 28: 165–179.

Merryman, John Henry. 1985. *The Civil Law Tradition*, 2nd ed. Stanford, CA: Stanford University Press.

Meynaud, Jean. 1969. *Technocracy*, Paul Barnes, translator. New York: Free Press.

Milgrom, Paul R., and John Roberts. 1992. *Economics, Organization and Management*. Englewood Cliffs, NJ: Prentice-Hall.

Miliband, R. 1973. *Marxism and Politics*. New York: Oxford University Press.

Moe, Terry M. 1982. "Regulatory Performance and Presidential Administration." *American Journal of Political Science* 26: 197–224.

1984. "The New Economics of Organization." *American Journal of Political Science* 28: 739–777.

1985. "Control and Feedback in Economic Regulation." *American Political Science Review* 79: 1094–1116.

1987. "An Assessment of the Positive Theory of Congressional Dominance." *Legislative Studies Quarterly* 12: 475–520.

1989. "The Politics of Bureaucratic Structure." In John Chubb and Paul Peterson (eds.), *Can the Government Govern?* Washington, DC: Brookings Institution (pp. 267–329).

1990a. "Political Institution: The Neglected Side of the Story." *Journal of Law, Economics, and Organization* 6: 213–253.

1990b. "The Politics of Structural Choice: Toward a Theory of Public Bureaucracy." In Oliver E. Williamson (ed.), *Organization Theory: From Chester Barnard to the Present and Beyond*. New York: Oxford University Press (pp. 116–153).

Moe, Terry M., and Michael Caldwell. 1994. "The Institutional Foundations of Democratic Government: A Comparison of Presidential and Parliamentary Systems." *Journal of Institutional and Theoretical Economics* 150: 171–195.

Moe, Terry M., and Scott A. Wilson. 1994. "Presidents and Political Structure." *Law and Contemporary Problems* 57(1): 1–44.

Moncrief, Gary F. 1999. "Recruitment and Retention in U.S. Legislatures." *Legislative Studies Quarterly* 24(2): 173–208.

Mosher, F. C. 1968. *Democracy and the Public Service*. New York: Oxford University Press.

Moulin, Léo. 1975. "The Politicization of the Administration in Belgium." In Mattei Dogan (ed.), *The Mandarins of Western Europe*. New York: Sage Publications. (pp. 163–186).

Müller, Wolfgang C., and Kaare Strøm. 2000. "Conclusion: Coalition Governance in Western Europe." In Wolfgang C. Muller and Kaare Strom (eds.), *Coalition Governments in Western Europe*. New York: Oxford University Press (pp. 559–592).

Niskanen, William. 1971. *Bureaucracy and Representative Government*. Chicago: Aldine-Atherton.

O'Connell, Philip J. 1994. "National Variation in Fortunes of Labor: A Pooled and Cross-Sectional Analysis of the Impact of Economic Crisis in the Advanced

Capitalist Nations." In Thomas Janoski and Alexander M. Hicks (eds.), *The Comparative Political Economy of the Welfare State*. New York: Cambridge University Press (pp. 218–244).

O'Connor, J. 1978. "The Democratic Movement in the United States." *Kapitalistate* 7: 15–26.

O'Halloran, Sharyn. 1994. *Politics, Process, and American Trade Policy*. Ann Arbor: University of Michigan Press.

Offe, C. 1972. "Political Authority and Class Structures: An Analysis of Late Capitalist Societies." *International Journal of Sociology* 2: 73–108.

Ogul, Morris S. 1976. *Congress Oversees the Bureaucracy*. Pittsburgh: University of Pittsburgh Press.

1981. "Congressional Oversight: Structures and Incentives." In Lawrence Dodd and Bruce Oppenheimer (eds.), *Congress Reconsidered*, 2nd ed. Washington, DC: CQ Press (pp. 317–331).

Okimoto, Daniel I. 1989. *Between MITI and the Market: Japanese Industrial Policy for High Technology*. Stanford, CA: Stanford University Press.

Olson, Mary K. 1995. "Regulatory Agency Discretion among Competing Industries: Inside the FDA." *Journal of Law, Economics, and Organization* 11: 379–405.

1996. "Explaining Regulatory Behavior in the FDA: Political Control vs. Agency Discretion." *Advances in the Study of Entrepreneurship, Innovation, and Growth* 7: 71–108.

Orzechowski, W. 1977. "Economic Models of Bureaucracy: Survey, Extensions and Evidence." In T. E. Borcherding (ed.), *Budgets and Bureaucrats: The Sources of Governmental Growth*. Durham, NC: Duke University Press (pp. 229–259).

O'Toole, L. J. 1986. "Policy Recommendations for Multi-Actor Implementation: An Assessment of the Field." *Journal of Public Policy* 6: 181–210.

Page, Edward C. 1992. *Political Authority and Bureaucratic Power: A Comparative Analysis*, 2nd ed. New York: Harverster Wheatsheaf.

Pampel, Fred C., and John B. Williamson. 1989. *Age, Class, Politics and the Welfare State*. New York: Cambridge University Press.

Paul-Shaheen, Pamela A. 1998. "The States and Health Care Reform: The Road Traveled and Lessons Learned from Seven That Took the Lead." *Journal of Health Politics, Policy, and Law* 23: 319–361.

Peters, B. Guy. 1981. "The Problem of Bureaucratic Government." *Journal of Politics* 43: 56–82.

1988. *The Comparative Study of Public Bureaucracy*. Tuscaloosa: University of Alabama Press.

1989. *Politics of Bureaucracy*. New York: Longman.

1992. "Public Policy and Public Bureaucracy." In Douglas E. Ashford (ed.), *History and Context in Comparative Public Policy*. Pittsburgh: University of Pittsburgh Press (pp. 283–315).

1997. "Bureaucrats and Political Appointees in European Democracies: Who's Who and Does it Make any Difference?" In Ali Farazmand (ed.), *Modern Systems of Government: Exploring the Role of Bureaucrats and Politicians*. Thousand Oaks, CA: Sage (pp. 232–254).

Petry, François. 1994. "The Role of Cabinet Ministers in the French Fourth Republic." In Michael Laver and Kenneth Shepsle (eds.), *Cabinet Ministers and Parliamentary Government*. New York: Cambridge University Press (pp. 125–138).

Plowden, W. 1994. *Ministers and Mandarins*. London: Institute for Public Policy Research.

Polenberg, Richard. 1966. *Reorganizing Roosevelt's Government: The Controversy Over Executive Reorganization, 1936–1939*. Cambridge, MA: Harvard University Press.

Potoski, Mathew. 1999. "Managing Uncertainty Through Bureaucratic Design: Administrative Procedures and State Air Pollution Control Agencies." *Journal of Public Administration Research and Theory* 9(4): 623–639.

2000. "Designing Bureaucratic Responsiveness: Administrative Procedures and the Political Control–Expertise Tradeoff." Manuscript, Iowa State University.

Poulantzas, H. 1978. *State, Power, Socialism*, P. Camiller, translator. London: New Left Books.

Powell, G. Bingham, Jr. 2000. *Elections as Instruments of Democracy: Majoritarian and Proportional Visions*. New Haven, CT: Yale University Press.

Powell, G. Bingham, Jr., and Guy D. Whitten. 1993. "A Cross-National Analysis of Economic Voting: Taking Account of the Political Context." *American Journal of Political Science* 37(2): 391–414.

Putnam, Robert D. 1973. "The Political Attitudes of Senior Civil Servants in Western Europe: A Preliminary Report." *British Journal of Political Science* 3(4): 257–290.

1975. "The Political Attitudes of Senior Civil Servants in Britain, Germany, and Italy." In Mattei Dogan (ed.), *The Mandarins of Western Europe*. New York: Sage Publications (pp. 87–127).

Ramseyer, J. Mark, and Frances McCall Rosenbluth. 1993. *Japan's Political Marketplace*. Cambridge, MA: Harvard University Press.

Ranney, Austin. 1976. "Parties in State Politics." In Herbert Jacob and Kenneth Vines (eds.), *Politics in the American States*, 3d ed. Boston: Little, Brown (pp. 51–92).

Ranney, Austin, and Wiollmoe Kendall. 1954. "The American Party System." *American Political Science Review* 48: 477–485.

Redford, E. S. 1969. *Democracy and the Administrative State*. New York: Oxford University Press.

Ridley, F. 1983. "Career Service: A Comparative Perspective on Civil Service Promotion." *Public Administration* 61: 179–196.

Robinson, Glen O. 1989. "Commentary on 'Administrative Arrangements and the Political Control of Agencies': Political Uses of Structure and Process." *Virginia Law Review* 75: 483–498.

Rom, Mark Carl. 1999. "Transforming State Health and Welfare Programs." In Virginia Gray, Russell L. Hanson, and Herbert Jacob (eds.), *Politics in the American States: A Comparative Analysis*, 7th ed. Washington DC: CQ Press (pp. 349–392).

Rose, Richard. 1974. *The Problem of Party Government*. London: Macmillan.

Roseverare, H. 1969. *The Treasury*. New York: Columbia University Press.
Rothstein, Bo. 1995. *The Social Democratic State: The Swedish Model and the Bureaucratic Problem.* Pittsburgh: Pittsburgh University Press.
Rouban, Luc. 1995. "Public Administration at the Crossroads: The End of French Specificity?" In John Pierre (ed.), *Bureaucracy in the Modern State: An Introduction to Comparative Public Administration*. Brookfield, VT: Edgar Elgar (pp. 39–63).
Rourke, Francis E. 1984. *Bureaucracy, Politics, and Public Policy*, 3d ed. Boston: Little, Brown.
Russell, Bertrand. 1967. *The Impact of Science on Society*. London: Allen & Unwin.
Sabatier, P. 1986. "Top-Down and Bottom-Up Approaches to Implementation Research." *Journal of Public Policy* 6: 21–48.
Sachs, Jeffrey D., and Nouriel Roubini. 1989. "Political and Economic Determinants of Budget Deficits in the Industrial Democracies," *European Economic Review* 33: 903–933.
Sacks, P. M. 1980. "State Structure and the Asymmetrical Society." *Comparative Politics* 12: 349–376.
Sappington, David E. M. 1991. "Incentives in Principal–Agent Relationships." *Journal of Economic Perspectives* 5: 45–66.
Sauveplanne, J. G. 1981. *Codified and Judge Made Law: The Role of Courts and Legislators in Civil and Common Law Systems*. Amsterdam: North-Holland.
Scheinman, Lawrence. 1965. *Atomic Energy Policy in France Under the Fourth Republic*. Princeton, NJ: Princeton University Press.
Scher, Seymour. 1963. "Conditions for Legislative Control." *Journal of Politics* 25: 526–551.
Schneider, Saundra K. 1997. "Medicaid 1115 Waivers: Shifting Health Care Reform to the States." *Publius* 27(2): 89–109.
Seidman, Harold, and Robert Gilmour. 1986. *Politics, Position, and Power: From the Positive to the Regulatory State*, 4th ed. New York: Oxford University Press.
Selznick, Philip. 1949. *TVA and the Grass Roots: A Study in the Sociology of Formal Organization*. Berkeley: University of California Press.
Shipan, Charles R. 1997. *Designing Judicial Review: Interest Groups, Congress, and Communications Policy*. Ann Arbor: University of Michigan Press.
1998. "Keeping Competitors Out: Broadcast Regulation from the Federal Radio Act of 1927 to the Telecommunications Act of 1996." In Monroe Price and Roger Noll (eds.), *A Communications Cornucopia: Markle Foundation Essays on Information Policy*. Washington, DC: Brookings Institution Press (pp. 473–498).
2000. "The Legislative Design of Judicial Review: A Formal Analysis." *Journal of Theoretical Politics* 12: 269–304.
Siaroff, Alan. 1999. "Corporatism in 24 Industrial Countries: Meaning and Measurement." *European Journal of Political Research* 36: 175–205.
Sparer, Michael D. 1996. "Medicaid Managed Care and the Health Reform Debate: Lessons from New York and California." *Journal of Health Politics, Policy and Law* 21(3): 433–460.

Spence, David B. 1997. "Administrative Law and Agency Policymaking: Rethinking the Positive Theory of Political Control." *Yale Journal on Regulation* 14(2): 407–450.

1999a. "Agency Discretion and the Dynamics of Procedural Reform." *Public Administration Review*. 59: 425–442.

1999b. "Managing Delegation Ex Ante: Using Law to Steer Administrative Agencies," *Journal of Legal Studies* 28: 413–459.

Squire, Peverill. 1988. "Member Career Opportunities and the Internal Organization of Legislatures." *Journal of Politics* 50: 726–744.

1992. "Legislative Professionalization and Membership Diversity in State Legislatures." *Legislative Studies Quarterly* 17: 69–79.

Steiner, Kurt. 1972. *Politics in Austria*. Boston: Little, Brown.

Stevens, A. 1985. "*L'Alternance* and the Higher Civil Service." In P. G. Cerny and M. A. Schain (eds.), *Socialism, the State, and Public Policy in France*. London: Frances Pinter.

Stevenson, Randolph. 2001. "Economic Voting and the Media Model of Public Opinion." Typescript, Rice University.

Stonecash, Jeffrey M., and Anna M. Agathangelou. 1997. "Trends in the Partisan Composition of State Legislatures: A Response to Fiorina." *American Political Science Review* 91(1): 148–155.

Strauss, E. 1961. *The Ruling Servants*. London: Allen & Unwin.

Strøm, Kaare. 1984. "Minority Governments in Parliamentary Democracies: The Rationality of Non-winning Solutions." *Comparative Political Studies* 17: 199–227.

1990. *Minority Government and Majority Rule*. Cambridge: Cambridge University Press.

2000. "Delegation and Accountability in Parliamentary Democracies." *European Journal of Political Research* 37(3): 261–289.

Suleiman, Ezra N. 1974. *Politics, Power, and Bureaucracy in France*. Princeton, NJ: Princeton University Press.

1978. *Elites in French Society: The Politics of Survival*. Princeton, NJ: Princeton University Press.

(ed.). 1984. *Bureaucrats and Policy Making: A Comparative Overview*. New York: Holmes & Meier.

Taylor, Frederick. 1911. *The Principles of Scientific Management*. New York: W. W. Norton.

Teske, Paul E. 1990. *After Divestiture: The Political Economy of State Telecommunications Regulation*. Albany: State University of New York Press.

Teske, Paul. 2001. "The Institutional Role in State Regulatory Policy." Presented at the meeting of the American Political Science Association, September, San Francisco.

Thiébault, Jean-Louis. 1994. "The Political Autonomy of Cabinet Ministers in the Fifth French Republic." In Michael Laver and Kenneth Shepsle (eds.), *Cabinet Ministers and Parliamentary Government*. New York: Cambridge University Press (pp. 139–149).

References

Thies, Michael F. 2001. "Keeping Tabs on Partners: The Logic of Delegation in Coalition Governments." *American Journal of Political Science* 45(3): 580–598.

Thomas, Clive S., and Ronald J. Hrebenar. 1999. "Interest Groups in the States." In Virginia Gray, Russell L. Hanson, and Herbert Jacob (eds.), *Politics in the American States: A Comparative Analysis*, 7th ed. Washington, DC: CQ Press (pp. 113–143).

Thomas, H. 1968. *Crisis in the Civil Service*. London: Anthony Blond.

Tirole, Jean. 1986. "Hierarchies and Bureaucracies: On the Role of Coercion in Organizations." *Journal of Law, Economics, and Organization* 2: 181–214.

1994. "The Internal Organization of Governments." *Oxford Economic Papers* 46(1): 1–29.

Tsebelis, George. 1999. "Veto Players and Law Production in Parliamentary Democracies: An Empirical Analysis." *American Political Science Review* 93(3): 591–608.

2002. *Veto Players: How Political Institutions Work*. Princeton, NJ: Princeton University Press, and New York: Russell Sage Foundation.

Tucker, Joshua A. 2001. "All Incumbents Are Not Created Equal: Economic Conditions and the Vote for Incumbent Parties in Russia, Poland, Hungary, Slovakia, and the Czech Republic from 1990–1996." *Post Soviet Affairs* 17(4): 309–331.

Van Hassell, Hugo. 1975. "Belgian Civil Servants and Political Decision Making." In Mattei Dogan (ed.), *The Mandarins of Western Europe*. New York: Sage Publications (pp. 187–195).

Volden, Craig. 2002a. "A Formal Model of the Politics of Delegation in a Separation of Powers System." *American Journal of Political Science* 46(1): 111–133.

2002b. "Delegating Power to Bureaucracies: Evidence from the States." *Journal of Law, Economics, and Organization* 18(1): 187–220.

Waldo, D. 1948. *The Administrative State*. New York: Ronald Press.

Warwick, Paul. 1994. *Government Survival in Parliamentary Democracies*. New York: Cambridge University Press.

Watson, Alan. 1981. *The Making of Civil Law*. Cambridge, MA: Harvard University Press.

Weber, Max. 1946. "Bureaucracy," in *Max Weber: Essays in Sociology*. Hans Heinrich Gerth (ed.) and C. Wright Mills (translator). New York: Oxford University Press (pp. 196–228).

Weingast, Barry R. 1984. "The Congressional-Bureaucratic System: A Principal–Agent Perspective (with Applications to the SEC)." *Public Choice* 44: 147–191.

Weingast, Barry R., and Mark J. Moran. 1983. "Bureaucratic Discretion or Congressional Control: Regulatory Policymaking by the FTC." *Journal of Political Economy* 91: 765–800.

Weir, Stuart, and David Beetham. 1999. *Political Power and Democratic Control in Britain*. London: Routledge.

West, William F., and Joseph Cooper. 1989–1990. "Legislative Influence v. Presidential Dominance: Competing Models of Bureaucratic Control." *Political Science Quarterly* 104(4): 581–606.

Williams, Philip M. 1964. *Crisis and Compromise: Politics in the Fourth Republic*. Hamden, CT: Archon Press.

Williamson, Oliver E. 1996. *The Mechanisms of Governance*. New York: Oxford University Press.

Wilson, James Q. 1980. *The Politics of Regulation*. New York: Basic Books.

1989. *Bureaucracy*. New York: Basic Books.

Wilson, V. S., and O. P. Dwivedi. 1982. *The Administrative State in Canada*. Toronto: McGraw-Hill Ryerson.

Wilson, Woodrow. 1887. "The Study of Administration." *Political Science Quarterly* 2: 197–222.

Wood, B. Dan. 1988. "Principals, Bureaucrats, and Responsiveness in Clean Air Enforcement." *American Political Science Review* 82: 213–234.

1990. "Does Politics Make a Difference at the EEOC?" *American Journal of Political Science* 34: 503–530.

Wood, B. Dan, and Richard Waterman. 1991. "The Dynamics of Political Control of the Bureaucracy." *American Political Science Review* 85(3): 801–828.

1994. *Bureaucratic Dynamics: The Role of a Bureaucracy in a Democracy*. Boulder, CO: Westview Press.

Wright, Vincent. 1978. *The Government and Politics of France*. London: Hutchinson of London.

Yates, Douglas. 1982. *Bureaucratic Democracy*. Cambridge, MA: Harvard University Press.

Zweigert, Konrad, and Hein Kötz. 1998. *Introduction of Comparative Law*, 3rd rev. ed., translated by Tony Weir. Oxford: Clarendon Press.

Author Index

Subject Index

Continuation of list of books in series

Gerald Easter, *Reconstructing the State: Personal Networks and Elite Identity*
Robert F. Franzese, *Macroeconomic Policies of Developed Democracies*
Roberto Franzosi, *The Puzzle of Strikes: Class and State Strategies in Postwar Italy*
Geoffrey Garrett, *Partisan Politics in the Global Economy*
Miriam Golden, *Heroic Defeats: The Politics of Job Loss*
Jeff Goodwin, *No Other Way Out: States and Revolutionary Movements, 1945–1991*
Merilee Serrill Grindle, *Changing the State*
Anna Gryzmala-Busse, *Redeeming the Communist Past: The Regeneration of Communist Parties in East Central Europe*
Frances Hagopian, *Traditional Politics and Regime Change in Brazil*
J. Rogers Hollingsworth and Robert Boyer, eds., *Contemporary Capitalism: The Embeddedness of Institutions*
Ellen Immergut, *Health Politics: Interests and Institutions in Western Europe*
Torben Iversen, *Contested Economic Institutions*
Torben Iversen, Jonas Pontusson, and David Soskice, eds., *Unions, Employers, and Central Banks: Macroeconomic Coordination and Institutional Change in Social Market Economies*
Thomas Janoski and Alexander M. Hicks, eds., *The Comparative Political Economy of the Welfare State*
David C. Kang, *Crony Capitalism: Corruption and Capitalism in South Korea and Philippines*
Robert O. Keohane and Helen B. Milner, eds., *Internationalization and Domestic Politics*
Herbert Kitschelt, *The Transformation of European Social Democracy*
Herbert Kitschelt, Peter Lange, Gary Marks, and John D. Stephens, eds., *Continuity and Change in Contemporary Capitalism*
Herbert Kitschelt, Zdenka Mansfeldova, Radek Markowski, and Gabor Toka, *Post-Communist Party Systems*
David Knoke, Franz Urban Pappi, Jeffrey Broadbent, and Yutaka Tsujinaka, eds., *Comparing Policy Networks*
Allan Kornberg and Harold D. Clarke, *Citizens and Community: Political Support in a Representative Democracy*
Amie Kreppel, *The European Parliament and the Supranational Party System*
David D. Laitin, *Language Repertories and State Construction in Africa*
Fabrice E. Lehoucq and Iván Molina, *Stuffing the Ballot Box: Fraud,*

Electoral Reform, and Democratization in Costa Rica

Mark Irving Lichbach and Alan S. Zuckerman, eds., *Comparative Politics: Rationality, Culture, and Structure*

Pauline Jones Luong, *Institutional Change and Political Continuity in Post-Soviet Central Asia*

Doug McAdam, John McCarthy, and Mayer Zald, eds., *Comparative Perspectives on Social Movements*

Scott Mainwaring and Matthew Soberg Shugart, eds., *Presidentialism and Democracy in Latin America*

Anthony W. Marx, *Making Race, Making Nations: A Comparison of South Africa, the United States, and Brazil*

Joel S. Migdal, *State in Society: Studying How States and Societies Constitute One Another*

Joel S. Migdal, Atul Kohli, and Vivienne Shue, eds., *State Power and Social Forces: Domination and Transformation in the Third World*

Scott Morgenstern and Benito Nacif, eds., *Legislative Politics in Latin America*

Wolfgang C. Muller and Kaare Strom, *Policy, Office, or Votes?*

Maria Victoria Murillo, *Labor Unions, Partisan Coalitions, and Market Reforms in Latin America*

Ton Notermans, *Money, Markets, and the State: Social Democratic Economic Policies since 1918*

Simona Piattoni, ed., *Clientelism, Interests, and Democratic Representation*

Paul Pierson, *Dismantling the Welfare State? Reagan, Thatcher, and the Politics of Retrenchment*

Marino Regini, *Uncertain Boundaries: The Social and Political Construction of European Economies*

Jeffrey M. Sellers, *Governing from Below: Urban Regions and the Global Economy*

Yossi Shain and Juan Linz, eds., *Interim Governments and Democratic Transitions*

Theda Skocpol, *Social Revolutions in the Modern World*

Richard Snyder, *Politics after Neoliberalism: Reregulation in Mexico*

David Stark and László Bruszt, *Postsocialist Pathways: Transforming Politics and Property in East Central Europe*

Sven Steinmo, Kathleen Thelan, and Frank Longstreth, eds., *Structuring Politics: Historical Institutionalism in Comparative Analysis*

Susan C. Stokes, *Mandates and Democracy: Neoliberalism by Surprise in Latin America*

Susan C. Stokes, ed., *Public Support for Market Reforms in New Democracies*
Duane Swank, *Global Capital, Political Institutions, and Policy Change in Developed Welfare States*
Sidney Tarrow, *Power in Movement: Social Movements and Contentious Politics*
Ashutosh Varshney, *Democracy, Development, and the Countryside*
Elisabeth Jean Wood, *Forging Democracy from Below: Insurgent Transitions in South Africa and El Salvador*